Paul's Non-Violent Gospel

Paul's Non-Violent Gospel

*The Theological Politics of Peace
in Paul's Life and Letters*

JEREMY GABRIELSON

PICKWICK *Publications* · Eugene, Oregon

PAUL'S NON-VIOLENT GOSPEL
The Theological Politics of Peace in Paul's Life and Letters

Pickwick Publications
An Imprint of Wipf and Stock Publishers
199 W. 8th Ave., Suite 3
Eugene, OR 97401

www.wipfandstock.com

ISBN 13: 978-1-62032-945-0

Cataloging-in-Publication data:

Gabrielson, Jeremy

Paul's non-violent gospel : the theological politics of peace in Paul's life and letters / Jeremy Gabrielson.

xiv + 204 pp. ; 23 cm—Includes bibliographical references and indexes.

ISBN 13: 978-1-62032-945-0

1. Bible. Epistles of Paul—Criticism, interpretation, etc. 2. Paul, the Apostle, Saint—Political and social views. 3. Peace—Religious aspects—Christianity-History of doctrines—Early church, ca. 30–600. I. Title.

BS2655 P64 G17 2013

Manufactured in the USA

For Sarah Joy

Contents

Illustrations

Acknowledgments

Words can scarcely repay what is owed to those who have contributed to the writing of this work. Still, the desire to register my gratitude to friends and colleagues overrides the suspicion that no words will measure up.

I must first say thank you to my supervisor through most of this process, Bruce Longenecker. Bruce's unswerving commitment to seeing my project come to a fruitful end hardly begins to name the lengths to which he went to assist me. For his frank critique, unreserved belief in the merits of the project, and stellar supervision in every way, I can only say a humble thank you.

Kelly Iverson supervised the project through its completion, and I am grateful for his careful and appreciative reading of my work and his wise counsel and encouragement through the final stages in the process.

My external examiners, Grant Macaskill and Kathy Ehrensperger provided helpful critiques that I trust have led to a better argument. Any failings that remain are obviously not the responsibility of those, examiners and supervisors alike, who only wanted to see the thesis strengthened.

Several others offered helpful comments or supervision at various stages in the process. I thank Joel Green and Mark Elliott for their role as interim supervisors, and for comments and suggestions regarding the project. Richard Bauckham provided some advice at an early stage, when the thesis was beginning to take a recognizable shape. Michael Gorman generously provided a pre-publication copy of a chapter from his book which proved helpful in articulating my view of Paul's conversion vis-à-vis violence.

Kristin De Troyer's mentoring was a happy accident occasioned by our sons' friendship. Her guidance and support have been immeasurable during our time in St. Andrews and beyond. Any who know her will not be surprised to hear of her tireless support of students and their families.

John Wright and Robert Smith of Point Loma Nazarene University set me loose in the discipline, and I have them to thank for awakening my interest and supporting me long after I left their care as a student. I will always remember a walk with John in Edinburgh during which an early outline for the thesis was discussed. Rob Fringer contributed much to my formation at Point Loma, and his friendship is still one I cherish. I cannot stress enough the impact these men have had in my life, and I hope their efforts and prayers are repaid with something of more lasting value than a thesis which will one day be only a heap of dust and ashes.

My time in St. Andrews would have been very different had it not been for a number of friends, not only my own, but those whose lives enriched those of my wife and children, too. Although I am sure to omit someone, I'll thank especially the Tallons, McCoys, Drivers, Kueckers, Dillers, Liebengoods, Chandlers, Schmidts, Matavas, Tony Lang and Nicki Wilkins and their children, Mariam Kamell, Drew Lewis, John Edwards, and Stephen Presley. My experience would have been impoverished without such faithful friends.

The congregation of Westfield Presbyterian Church provided financial assistance at various stages of our time here, and I will always be grateful for the support they offered. The people of St. Andrews Church, St. Andrews, have been our fellow-pilgrims during nearly five years of study and worship, and I am beginning to grieve leaving our church even now, weeks before the fact.

Family has been instrumental in making our time in St. Andrews possible, whether it was through offering prayers, financial support, or making timely visits. My parents, Rudy and Pam Macias, Jeff and Stacy Gabrielson, and my wife's parents, Robert and Joyce Bardeen, all made our time in St. Andrews more comfortable, even when the support offered kept young grandchildren thousands of miles away. Of course, their support didn't begin five years ago—can one even begin to say thanks for a lifetime of love and support?

My children, Caleb, Joshua, Abigail, and Elisabeth (the last three born in Scotland), provided the best possible disruptions to the daily grind of producing the thesis. They will be more than thrilled to see their prayers finally answered "for Daddy to be done with his work." I thank them for their unfailing trust that I could indeed one day finish. I hope this thesis makes a small contribution to making the world they inherit a more peaceable place.

Finally, to my wife, Sarah Joy: We did it! Although she would be the first to dismiss her contribution to the achievement, my wife's support was crucial (and I choose the term carefully) from beginning to end. She sacrificed much to provide time for me to study and write, but never failed to pursue her own ministry of supporting and teaching others in our community. I've often believed her impact here in St. Andrews has been of far greater consequence than the argument I have produced, and I am confident that there are many women who have left St. Andrews who would agree wholeheartedly with that belief. Words cannot express how thankful I am for her support and, more importantly, belief in me, and for these reasons and many more, I dedicate this work to her.

Jeremy Gabrielson
The Roundel
St. Andrews, Scotland
Ash Wednesday 2010

I considered rewriting the acknowledgments for brevity's sake, but I couldn't bring myself to cut anyone out. Mercifully, dear reader, I will add only one more person who contributed to bringing this from thesis to publication: my daughter Havilah, who like her older siblings brought much joy to our family life, even when her daddy was preoccupied with tardy revisions.

J. G.
Scotts Valley, California
Easter 2013

Abbreviations

ABD	*The Anchor Bible Dictionary.* 6 vols. Edited by David Noel Friedman. New York: Doubleday, 1992.
BDF	Friedrich Blass and Alfred Debrunner. *A Greek Grammar of the New Testament and Other Early Christian Literature.* Translated and revised by Robert W. Funk. Chicago: University of Chicago Press, 1961.
BDAG	Walter Bauer, Frederick W. Danker, W. F. Arndt, and F. W. Gingrich. *Greek-English Lexicon of the New Testament and Other Early Christian Literature.* 3rd ed. Chicago: University of Chicago Press, 2000.
BMC	*Coins of the Roman Empire in the British Museum.* London: Trustees of the British Museum, 1923–.
CIL	*Corpus inscriptionum latinarium.* Berlin: de Gruyter, 1968–.
EJ	Victor Ehrenberg and A. H. M. Jones, eds. *Documents Illustrating the Reigns of Augustus and Tiberius.* 2nd ed. Oxford: Clarendon, 1955.
ILS	*Inscriptiones latinae selectee.* Edited by H. Dessau. 3 vols. Berlin: Weidmann, 1892–1916.
LCL	*Loeb Classical Library.*
OED	*The Oxford English Dictionary.* 2nd. edition.
OGIS	*Orientis graeci inscriptiones selectae.* Edited by W. Dittenberger. 2 vols. Leipzig: S. Hirzel, 1903–1905.

RPC *Roman Provincial Coinage I.1–2, From the Death of Caesar to the Death of Vitellius (44 BC–AD 69).* Edited by A. M. Burnett, M. Amandry, and P. P. Ripollès, 1992.

SEG *Supplementum Epigraphicum Graecum.* Edited by J. Hondius. Alphen: 1923–.

TDNT *Theological Dictionary of the New Testament.* 10 vols. Edited by Gerhard Kittel and Gerhard Friedrich. Translated by Geoffrey W. Bromiley. Grand Rapids: Eerdmans, 1964–1976.

All ancient author abbreviations and biblical references conform to the guidelines set forth in:

Alexander, Patrick, et al., editors. *The SBL Handbook of Style: For Ancient Near Eastern, Biblical, and Early Christian Studies.* Peabody, MA: Hendrickson, 1999.

1

Introduction

When Jesus exhorts us to love our enemies, he does not expect us
to stop annihilating them. If they are enemies of God, they must be
dispatched to the safekeeping of hell, and as rapidly as possible.[1]

Accounting for the genesis of one's interest in a particular topic can be a
difficult thing, especially when the origins of that interest are clouded
by several years spent pouring over monographs and pecking at keys on
a keyboard. Quotations like the one above, however, have a way of jog-
ging one's memory. Recent interest in the political setting of Paul and his
letters has irrupted within the field of New Testament studies. Rhetorical
and Jewish "backgrounds" have had and continue to have their turn in the
limelight, but it seems that Roman imperial politics has now arrived to take
its turn as the grounding for a growing number of Pauline studies. Neil
Elliot wrote, "We have not yet seen a full-length exploration of Paul's
rhetoric in the wider contexts of imperial or colonial *rhetorics*, that is, the
discourses shaped by the social dynamics of imperialism and colonialism,
what James C. Scott has called the 'great' and 'little traditions,' or 'public' and
'hidden transcripts.'"[2] Having read dozens of fresh studies of Paul's engagement with Roman imperial themes, I was struck by the repetitive portrayal
of violence in Roman literature. With the violence of antiquity fresh in my
mind, a warning in Elliot's essay piqued my interest: "To continue seeking

1. Singer, *Nature of Love*, 1:262.
2. Elliot, "Paul and the Politics of Empire," 27.

analogues to Paul's letters in the classical rhetorical handbooks, without giving sustained attention to the publicly acknowledged relationship between rhetorical patterns of persuasion and the coercive force inhering in slavery and empire, would be profoundly inattentive to the sources themselves."[3] What struck me at the time was not so much that interpreters of the New Testament had failed to pay sufficient attention to the violence which was the counterpart of rhetoric, but that Paul himself had previously engaged in violent action and evidently had left that part of his life behind him after his Damascus-road[4] experience.

As briefly and pointedly as can be stated, my argument is this: adoption of a politics of non-violence was, for Paul and the communities he established, a constitutive part of the gospel of Jesus Christ. Rather than viewing Paul's references to peace and non-retaliation as generalized ethical principles drawn from his Jewish background (though this no doubt contributes to Paul's understanding of these concepts), these terms and their corresponding practices are linked to Paul's experience of being a violent persecutor of Jesus' followers whose violent life was shattered on the road to Damascus. Enlivened by the risen Jesus from this point on, Paul's task of announcing the gospel to the nations involved calling and equipping assemblies of people whose common life was ordered by a politics (by which I mean, chiefly, a mode of corporate conduct) characterized by peaceableness.

In this introduction I will set some parameters for the following study by defining *violence* and *politics* as they are used in this work before outlining the direction of the remainder of the present study.

Defining Violence

It is perhaps best to begin by recognizing the challenge of offering a simple definition of violence. What at first seems so straightforward a task quickly becomes a conundrum. In the words of one introductory text, "Violence itself . . . defies easy categorization. It can be everything and nothing;

---

3. Ibid., 29.

4. I use "Damascus-road" as a shorthand here, fully aware that Paul never reveals the location (or exact nature) of his experience. Though this particular detail is derived from Acts, I do not intend to base my construction of Paul's so-called pre-conversion life on the account in Acts. I will make my own constructive case from Paul's letters. See chapter 4.

legitimate or illegitimate; visible or invisible; necessary or useless; sense-less and gratuitous or utterly rational and strategic."[5] In the light of such a slippery subject, it may be useful to offer a fixed point, and adjust the scope of the definition from there. The most convenient point of departure for a working definition of *violence* for this study is to be found in the *Oxford English Dictionary*: "The exercise of physical force so as to inflict injury on, or cause damage to, persons or property; action or conduct characterized by this; treatment or usage tending to cause bodily injury or forcibly inter-fering with personal freedom."[6]

The importance of beginning with this particular definition is to focus our attention quite specifically on physical force. The aim in doing so is not to discount the possibility that non-physical action can be defined as violent, but to limit (*not eliminate*) our focus on that possibility in the field of inquiry for the present study. Despite focusing on concrete forms of vio-lence, I will pay attention to the "boundary" between physical expressions of violence and their non-physical counterpart, that is, for instance, where verbal "violence" begins to carry over into forms of violence that are en-acted in clearly physical ways. The presentation of Jesus at various points in the gospels, as well as certain points in the Pauline letters, are regarded by many interpreters as language which occupies the border between physical violence and verbal violence. So, although I will focus principally on physi-cal expressions of violence, verbal attacks will call for my attention too, as indeed they should.

Another aspect of violence which is not captured by the definition offered, but that we wish to address throughout is that form of violence which is systemic (and sometimes indirect) rather than acute (and direct). This systemic violence will be traced in Paul's context(s) by seeking to identify the sometimes "subtle forms of coercion that sustain relations of domination and exploitation, including the threat of violence."[7] I am more

---

5. Scheper-Hughes and Bourgois, "Making Sense of Violence," 2. Cf. Brubaker and Laitin, "Ethnic and Nationalist Violence," 427: "Despite its seemingly palpable core, vio-lence is itself an ambiguous and elastic concept . . . shading over from the direct use of force to cause bodily harm through the compelling or inducing of actions by direct threat of such force to partly or fully metaphorical notions of cultural or symbolic violence."

6. *OED*, s.v. "violence," 1.a.

7. Žižek, *Violence*, 8. Although I employ Žižek's terms here, my attention throughout is concerned with subjective forms of violence which he claims is a distraction (10): "One should resist the fascination of subjective violence . . . subjective violence is just the most visible of the three" forms of subjective, objective, and symbolic violence.

interested in the systemic violence perpetuated by those in positions of power in the cities in which Paul lived and worked, but Paul and the communities he established too have been scrutinized for the ways in which they inevitably create and sustain relationships characterized by coercion.[8] I do not wish to dismiss such approaches to Paul and his communities, however, I want to focus instead on the way in which Paul's (minority) assemblies lived and related in societies where "outsiders" maintained social control in part through structural/systemic violence.[9]

In short, the present study includes in its assessment of violence those actions and systemic/structural features that employ physically coercive behavior or the threat of using it to construct and maintain a particular political or social arrangement. Put differently, we will examine those practices and communal habits that orientate life in the Roman world around the concept of peace created and sustained through physical coercion.

DEFINING POLITICS

Politics too has a wide range of meaning. Rather than viewing politics or the political as only "the effort to sustain a hegemonic, territorial, sovereign entity, embodied in a physical collective of human beings and articulated to action for its own self-preservation,"[10] I include aspects of human ways

8. Cf. Marchal, *Hierarchy, Unity, and Imitation*; Hack Polaski, *Paul and the Discourse of Power*; Briggs Kittredge, *Community and Authority*; Castelli, *Imitating Paul*.

9. Scheper-Hughes and Bourgois, "Making Sense of Violence," 4, claim that most studied approaches to violence "fail to address the totality and range of violent acts, including those which are part of the normative fabric of social and political life. Structural violence is generally invisible because it is part of the routine grounds of everyday life and transformed into expressions of moral worth." I hope to show how Paul's gospel sought to create communities that were able to live under different (i.e., less violent) norms than those living around them in the Roman empire. Certainly Paul (and Jesus) could be said to have failed to challenge *all* forms of structural violence (e.g., beliefs about divorce and the resulting conditions that perpetuate systemic violence against women), but my goal is to address where they have directed their followers towards less violent (subjective and systemic) modes of living. Though I will not address every instance of their failures, I will try to identify prominent ways in which Jesus (as Matthew presents him) and Paul failed to recognize forms of violence that are re-inscribed by particular teachings or writings.

10. Heilke, "On Being Ethical," 513. Heilke points out that the Anabaptist ethic of peaceableness is not political when politics is thus defined, but he goes on to challenge this position when he claims that their pacifism "simply rejects a fundamental premise on which [political] life and [ethical] debate is often based." Pacifism does not, in other words, necessarily entail quietism.

of relating to one another (i.e., practices/behaviors that create and sustain human community) which might normally be thought of as falling outside of the political realm. For instance, I will concentrate on multiple instances in which community admonition figures in Paul's "political" order. The practices of mutual correction and forgiveness fall outside the political concerns of civic authorities in antiquity, but I show how these practices are part of Paul's instructions to his communities that are meant to address the peculiar challenges of living peaceably in a world which too often settles disputes by violent means.

The sense of politics just outlined at any rate may better capture all that was thought to be included in politics in antiquity. A summary of Aristotle's view of politics is worth repeating:

> Aristotle's use of the term political (*politikos*) is much broader than most modern definitions. . . . For Aristotle, the political includes all aspects of living together in a community . . . [which] includes marriage, family, and household relationships (*oikos*), friendships, economic relationships, and what we now call political relationships, such as being members of or leading the assembly. Aristotle considers the *polis* the highest form of community (*koinonia*) because it exists not for the sake of merely living together, but for the sake of living well. . . . In other words, Aristotle understands the political (*politikos*) to include other kinds of communities or relationships now labeled "social" rather than "political."[11]

It is in this spirit that I will write of the politics of an assembly of people called together to engage in common practices which support them in living as a community of Christ's followers.[12] It is hardly surprising, given Aristotle's parameters, that Paul's assemblies were politically significant in their time.[13] What is worth restating and exploring in depth is my further claim that Paul's politics, in marked contrast to the politics of Rome (and played out in communities great and small all over the empire), were

11. Sokolon, *Political Emotions*, 29.

12. Cf. Horrell, *Solidarity and Difference*, 2, who formulates his approach in this way: "A study of Paul's ethics as social or political ethics, by which I mean ethics concerned with the formation and maintenance of human community, and with reflection on the ways in which this human sociality should rightly be sustained."

13. Cf. Judge, "Did the Churches Compete," 501–24, on the one hand dismisses any "provocative" political sense of the term *churches* (ἐκκλησία) (514), and on the other identifies the (late) moniker *Christians* (Χριστιανοί) as one which "classifies people as partisans of a political leader" and "appears to have arisen in the questions posed for Romans over the political loyalty of the followers of Christ" (515).

necessarily non-violent, built as they were on the shoulders of the politics of Jesus.

POLITICS, RELIGION, AND ETHICS IN ANTIQUITY

One aspect of politics that is not addressed by the lengthy quotation from Marlene Sokolon above is that, in marked contrast to prevailing (contemporary) popular assumptions, politics and religion did not operate in separate spheres in antiquity. Classical scholars for more than half the twentieth century largely discounted the religious significance of the imperial cult(s), and biblical scholars faired only marginally better in ascertaining the political significance of the Jesus movement. The publication of S. R. F. Price's seminal monograph[14] seems to mark the turning of the tide, when the political *and* religious significance of the imperial cult in Asia Minor necessarily had to be viewed together once again. Subsequent to the publication of his work, biblical studies also has seen a revitalized interest in the political aspects of the Jesus movement.[15]

The prevailing attitude, that politics and religion operate in different spheres, is a relatively modern invention.[16] Of the modern separation of "politics" and "religion" ancient authors are innocently unaware.[17] So-called "statesmen" regularly served as priests in civic cults, and so-called "religious" leaders, in the course of their priestly duties, commonly performed functions we might slate as civic—providing for the building of roads or public gymnasiums, aqueducts, and similar "public" works. There was no division of interests because this fusion of politics and religion existed all

14. Price, *Rituals and Power*.

15. For a commanding reassessment of the political importance of Acts, see Rowe, *World Upside Down*, 4: "In its attempt to form communities that witness to God's apocalypse, Luke's second volume is a highly charged and theologically sophisticated *political document* that aims at nothing less than the construction of an alternative total way of life—a comprehensive pattern of being—one that runs counter to the life patterns of the Graeco-Roman world" (emphasis added).

16. See Cavanaugh, "Rise of the State," 397–420, and *Torture and Eucharist*, 5.

17. Rowe, *World Upside Down*, 8–9, observes: "In contrast to the cultural encyclopedia relevant to modern democracies, Luke has no idea of a basic bifurcation that many people now claim is necessary, namely, the separation of religion from politics; this distinction is simply not part of the conceptual configurations or political practices current in the first century (or anywhere in antiquity for that matter). To access the cultural encyclopedia of the text of Acts is immediately to become aware of the unity of religion and politics in one form of life."

the way up to the emperor, who was *pontifex maximus*, high priest of the entire empire. For this reason, at various points in the present work I will refer to theological politics, and by using this expression I have tried to capture how these allegedly separate spheres were conjoined in the cities and provinces in which Paul worked.

Although it is increasingly common to see scholars highlight the political import of early Christian (or Jewish) theological commitments, it is still rare to encounter studies that take seriously the political significance of the ethical or moral dimension of Christian discourse.[18] But if we take a more culturally conditioned[19] approach to the theme *politics* (identified succinctly by Sokolon's summary), we will immediately see that just as there was no division in antiquity between a thing called "politics" and a thing called "religion," so too we should not so neatly divide politics from (theologically grounded) ethics. So when Paul (or Matthew) advocate a particular ethical virtue, we should view it not only as an effect of a particular theological idea, but also as the fruition of belonging to that particular political community which is so shaped by its politic-generating narrative(s).

VIOLENCE IN THE ROMAN WORLD

Violence permeated the ancient world. One need not read far into the histories of Tacitus or Polybius, or Apuleius's *Metamorphoses*, before encountering the brutal conflicts that characterized life in antiquity. Life under Roman rule was certainly not unique in this regard, though it is the empire with which I am concerned since Paul wrote during Rome's sway over a vast empire. It was not only literature, but coins, too, that left a considerable deposit of violent images, though they may appear on the face of it to be more benign than threatening. Images of peace and victory, war and

18. The seminal treatment of Meeks, *Origins of Christian Morality*, is a benchmark in showing how the ethical dimension of Pauline theology is meant to reinforce the "political" position of early Christians in the Roman empire. That is, if there is a political dimension to Paul's ethics, it is a dimension that is meant to allow Roman outsiders to assent to Christian norms that are not terribly different.

19. Again referring to the work of Rowe, *World Upside Down*, 8–9, who provides a brief defense of employing MacIntyre's "historically situated rationality" for his own study. To attempt to take seriously the historically situated rationality of any given (New Testament) author's work is to endeavor to read the texts with greater sensitivity to the vast cultural (read in the broadest possible terms, i.e., political, social, economic, and religious) gulf between ancient authors and modern interpreters.

defeated barbarians saturate the imperial ideology that was transmitted on coins, emblazoned in statues, and incorporated into the very fabric of public space during the first century of the common era. Evidence is found in every corner of the empire.

To claim that violence was ubiquitous is no exaggeration, even once one tempers such a claim by admitting the real benefits, and the extraordinarily complex cultural negotiation,[20] which accompanied the spread of Roman imperial peace. Whatever benefits were had under the Romans, there is no denying that Roman violence is legendary. The most obvious place to look for Rome's reputation is its military, made up of roughly twenty-five legions "with unfettered readiness for violence" who, once deployed, imposed their so-called peace "without restraint."[21] Although the "gruesome orgies of violence were . . . a fundamental and unquestioned element of Roman warfare," the strategy was hardly novel.[22] Shock and awe have long played a role in military campaigns, and the terror and fear generated by the spread of such reports was a pragmatic political tool for an empire too large for its legions to manage.[23]

It would be a mistake, however, to limit our consideration of violence in Roman antiquity to military incidents, for violence between private individuals peppers literature from the age too. Banditry on the roads and piracy on the seas were common enough experiences that the eventual suppression of them by Augustus became a cliché. Banditry (*latrocinium*), an all-encompassing term for violence perpetrated by persons who were not a recognized authority, was such a common danger that a formulaic expression can be found on tombstones—"killed by bandits."[24] Violence needn't

20. Shaw, "Rebels and Outsiders," 361, points out: "The empire was a militarily created hegemony of immense land mass that harboured hundreds, if not thousands, of different societies." Massive unity and massive diversity problematize any attempts to reduce Romanization to a unidirectional project. Cf. Woolf, "Beyond Romans and Natives," 341, who suggests: "Rather than conflict, competition, or interaction between two cultures, we have to do with the creation of a new imperial culture that supplanted earlier Roman cultures just as much as it did the earlier cultures of indigenous peoples."

21. Zimmermann, "Violence in Late Antiquity," 346. On the number of legions, which was fairly stable across time, see Keppie, "Army and the Navy," 387–89, who identifies twenty-five at the death of Augustus (14 CE) and twenty-eight or twenthy-nine in 70 CE.

22. Zimmermann, "Violence in Late Antiquity," 346.

23. Ibid. So too Lendon, *Empire of Honour*, 3–4. Levick, *Government of the Roman Empire*, 40, notes that the mobility of the legions was making a virtue of necessity: "Rome could not afford to support more" legions.

24. See Shaw, "Bandits in the Roman Empire," 10–11: *interfectus a latronibus.*

originate with the empire's most unsavory characters either. Senators were in as much danger from their fellow senators as they were traveling beyond city walls. And in an ironic twist, later jurisprudence protected the individual who used force, *even lethal force*, to quell the activities of bandits.[25]

It will not do, however, to create or perpetuate an assumption that ancient societies had a greater tolerance of or inclination toward violence.[26] The bloodiest century in human history (I'm thinking of the twentieth, though the twenty-first has not started promisingly) should disabuse us of holding such views. Instead, what I wish to assume is that the violence depicted in the literary and material remains of the first centuries is just the tip of the proverbial iceberg and that the shared experience of violence was much more immediate than it might be for many who read and write academic monographs today.[27] This immediacy of violence is the light by which I want to consider Paul's letters. That is, if Paul's letters were written in and to contexts where violence was an ever-present threat, how do Paul's teaching and indeed even his personal biography vis-à-vis violence intersect with this particular political reality of his day?

This question is all the more important when one considers that Paul once himself participated in a violent, community boundary-policing action, and did so notoriously;[28] only *after* his encounter with the risen Christ did he cease to participate in violent opposition to this assembly of God. Paul's "conversion" (i.e., his "joining" of the "Christian" group)[29] most cer-

25. The laws in question, *CJ* 3.27.1–2 and 9.16.3 are admittedly quite late (the former is late fourth century CE, the latter from the third century) and highly uncharacteristic. However, they demonstrate the importance placed on maintenance of the "common peace," even at the expense of normal avenues of justice. See Shaw, "Bandits in the Roman Empire," 19. The Greek equivalent of *latrones/latrocinium*, of course, was λῃστής (the culprit) or λῃστεία (the activity).

26. Zimmermann, "Violence in Late Antiquity," 351.

27. Although demonstrating what I assume in these few paragraphs might be helpful, I hardly think it necessary. It is uncontroversial to suppose that violence was experienced *and wielded* by people from every social or economic status, by individuals and groups (official or unofficial), and by people of any variety of ethnic, tribal, or cultural difference. The use and experience of violence discriminated against none.

28. Lopez, *Apostle to the Conquered*, 223n8, points out this curiosity: "In many of the most famous pictures [representing Paul's conversion], he is represented as a Roman warrior." Cf. ibid., 230–31n54. Paul himself hints at the notoriety he gained through his activity in Gal 1:13 and 23.

29. Since this is not the place to address the complicated issues surrounding my choice of terms, I put the three in scare quotes to flag my awareness that each term is charged with meaning and requires greater definition if more is to be made of Paul's experience.

tainly explains Paul's turn from violence, but only partially. Few have ever considered what contribution a non-violent Jesus made to Paul's disavowal of his once violent ways. I want to consider the point.

THE ARGUMENT AND STRUCTURE OF THIS STUDY

As briefly as it can be stated, my thesis is this: After his transformational encounter with the risen Jesus, Paul became a herald of the gospel of Jesus, a message that included at its core a commitment to eschewing the inherently violent politics of the present evil age. This dramatic transformation cannot be reduced to a new commitment to non-violence on Paul's part, but this aspect of the story and effect of Jesus' life and teaching is fundamental; indeed, I would submit that non-violence (of Jesus, and subsequently his followers) is one of the most enduring features of the gospel, and its presence, indeed centrality, in Paul's gospel has been overlooked in studies of Paul's theology. The history of the reception of this aspect of the gospel may throw up hard questions for my thesis, but I feel that it is entirely suitable to put my thesis for the significance of non-violence in early Christianity in such strong terms since the evidence in favor of viewing non-violence as a core teaching *and way of life* of Jesus and his followers is overwhelming.

In order to build a case for the weight I wish to give to non-violence in early Christian circles, I must begin by demonstrating that Jesus was remembered by his followers as a person who eschewed violence. In order to maintain a small measure of control on a topic that could be greatly expanded, I will trace the construction of a non-violent Jesus through Matthew's gospel, referring to the other gospels only where it is particularly illuminating. At the beginning of chapter 2, I will present a brief methodological justification for choosing Matthew and for my strategy of focusing primarily on the narratively presented Jesus rather than trying to reconstruct the so-called historical Jesus. One reason among others for why I chose Matthew is because a similar effort has been made already for Luke's gospel,[30] and even though Matthew possesses the most famous of all passages that presses in the direction of non-violence (i.e., the Sermon on the Mount), it also includes some of the most challenging material to a "pacifist" position.[31] In chapter 2, I will demonstrate that Matthew preserves the memory of Jesus as a teacher of non-violence who also embodies

---

30. Yoder's seminal *Politics of Jesus* argued primarily from Luke's gospel.

31. E.g., Matt 10:34–39; we will look at more in the next chapter.

his teaching all the way to his violent death on the cross. I will also show how those passages that have commonly challenged this picture of a non-violent Jesus instead provide the context for Jesus (and later, his followers) to eschew violent politics by trusting in the justly-judging God. The core of this second chapter illustrates that Jesus' non-violence is far from apolitical quiescence; he remains unreservedly political while refusing to become a mirror image of the politics of Rome, i.e., a violent revolutionary. In short, I trace the non-violent teaching and behavior of Jesus through Matthew's gospel, but demur from making Jesus into a passive isolationist on the one hand or a violent revolutionary on the other.

In chapter 3, I will focus on one of the most vexing problems of Pauline studies—how much Jesus Tradition Paul knew. By narrowing the focus of my study to the issue of non-violence in Paul and Jesus, I hope to bypass some of the more entrenched debates among exegetes, and demonstrate that the continuity between Jesus and Paul on the issue of non-violence is critical to understanding the importance of a non-violent praxis in early Christianity. My aim in this chapter is to demonstrate that the traditions preserved in the gospels which point to the memory of a non-violent Jesus are found in *nuce* in Paul's letters, and that this results not from a shared cultural heritage of the two,[32] but instead springs from Paul's encounter with Jesus and his subsequent receipt of "authorized" testimony about Jesus that confirmed what Paul may have already known on reflection—Jesus, though the option of (messianic) violence was open to him, chose instead the way of the cross, of self-emptying, non-violent engagement with those who rejected him. Establishing this link is critical to demonstrating that the early Christian commitment to the centrality of non-violence is quite early and geographically widespread. In other words, non-violence was such a central feature of the gospel that there is concrete evidence for it (in terms of teaching and praxis) as early as 50 CE (when 1 Thessalonians was written), and the evidence taken in aggregate points to the reliability of the gospels on this point such that we can be confident (the historical) Jesus eschewed the use of violence to further his own ends.

Having established the non-violent teaching and praxis of Jesus, and the subsequent continuity of Paul in this regard, chapter 4 of this book traces the trajectory of violence in the biography of Paul, attending to his letter to the Galatians. The two main reasons for selecting Galatians as the primary text for tracing a trajectory of violence (and peace) in Paul's biography are

---

32. *Pace* Zerbe, *Non-Retaliation*, 23. Paul and Jesus still shared the same cultural heritage when Paul was operating in the mode of violent persecutor.

these: first, Galatians contains the longest single autobiographical narrative among all his letters, and second, among those biographical details is Paul's self-description of persecuting the church with the goal of destroying it. It also stands to reason that if a trajectory towards peace can be established for this, what some interpreters might call his most angry letter, then we have argued for the non-violence of Paul from perhaps the most difficult of positions. In addition to sketching the arc from violence to peace in Paul's story, chapter 4 also follows the inverse arc of Paul's Galatian audience. Whereas Paul's biographic trajectory turned on his encounter with the risen Jesus, the Galatians' "biography" turned on the influence of the agitators. That is, one transformation turned a violent zealot into a peacemaking Apostle; the other transformation turned a group once influenced by the spirit of Jesus into an assembly realigning itself with relations governed by violence.

In the penultimate chapter, I use 1 Thessalonians as a test case, attempting to tie the strands of my argument together. I demonstrate in this chapter that there are competing theo-political paradigms at work in Paul's mission to the nations. The gospel of Jesus, which we will have shown to be political, which we will have argued Paul is in continuity with, is orientated toward non-violent conflict with the politics of the present evil age. The gospel of Caesar, which is clearly political, which Paul once mirrored through his own violent persecution, is orientated around the use or threat of violence.[33] In short, what I hope to show in chapter 5 is that the new assemblies Paul formed in Thessalonica (and across the empire) shared both an assumption that they would encounter violent opposition for their theo-political activity and beliefs, and that the proper response to such opposition unequivocally ruled out violent measures. Paul's non-violence was not merely pragmatic, but tells instead of the alternative politics to which the churches were committed.

In the final chapter, I summarize the argument(s) that are advanced in this book, which *together* fill an important gap in scholarly treatments of Paul. It is my hope that the argument presented here will call greater attention to the centrality of peacemaking and non-violent confrontation of friends and enemies alike which suffused early Christian discourse and discipleship.

33. Although it is not in the context of announcing the gospel of Caesar, Velleius Paterculus' (*Roman History* 2:126 [Thayer, LCL]) pithy expression of the effects of Augustus' theo-political success demonstrates with clarity the acceptable response to Caesar's gospel: "All citizens have either been impressed with the wish to do right, or have been forced to do so by necessity."

2

The End of Violence
in the Gospel of Matthew

Given the violent context in which the gospels were fashioned, it comes as no surprise that they repeatedly feature episodes that bear witness to the ubiquity of violence in the first century. Anecdotes can easily be marshaled to show that violence infected society at every level: "politicians" and military commanders exercised brutal force against "popular" resistance movements; old inter-ethnic feuds continued to be sustained in successive generations; small groups of bandits inflicted terror on local populations; religious-political leaders were assassinated by rivals; enslaved prisoners of war fought to the death before the masses. If one searches long enough, violence seemingly can be found under every rock in antiquity. Readers (or auditors) of the gospels were familiar enough with the corrosive infection of violence through all parts of society, and from within this violent milieu Jesus' words and deeds were first heard.

In the present chapter, Matthew's gospel will serve as the focal point for illustrating Jesus' engagement,[1] through both his teachings and lived ex-

---

1. A word about methodology is important. I read Matthew from a narrative-critical approach, and consequently do not primarily aim at offering a reconstruction of the so-called historical Jesus. The difficulty is that my argument turns on the non-violent practices of the man Jesus of Nazareth. That is, it could be argued that if Jesus of Nazareth was not, historically speaking, non-violent, Paul's "conversion" from violent opponent to non-violent advocate is not dependent on the Jesus of history. Furthermore, Paul's letters predate the (final) composition/redaction of the gospels. How do I circle this square? Although I am not *primarily* interested in proving the non-violence of the historical Jesus, I do think the preponderance of evidence, from the gospels and Paul's letters, points to

ample, with the violence of the Roman world. In addition, we will attempt to describe the goals and aims of certain types of violence in first-century Roman Palestine, especially as the motives and goals may shed light on the contrast Jesus posed to many of his contemporaries—both Jewish and Roman.[2] In short, we will illustrate how Matthew's gospel is typical of early Christian gospels in that it preserves the collective memory of Jesus as a teacher and practitioner of non-violence. By demonstrating Jesus' challenge to contemporaries on the use of violence, we hope this chapter sets the stage for comparing Paul's "pre-conversion" use of violent means of conflict (attested to in his own letters) with his turn away from such tactics subsequent to his encounter with Jesus.

ON "USING" MATTHEW'S GOSPEL: METHODOLOGICAL REFLECTIONS ON THE HISTORICAL JESUS, MATTHEW, AND PAUL

Beginning the present study in the Gospel of Matthew inevitably raises questions about the justification of using this (later) text to support a subsequent reading of Paul, whose letters are earlier textually when compared to Matthew's gospel. I want to address a few points at the beginning of this chapter in order to identify clearly my own methodological presuppositions and aims in this chapter. It may be instructive, then, to identify reasons why one might consider *not* beginning with Matthew, and face those challenges head-on.

(the historical) Jesus' non-violent engagement with enemies. Although Paul's letters are textually earlier, gospel traditions, whether oral or written, demonstrably antedate Paul's letters. Not every reader will be convinced of Paul's knowledge of Jesus Tradition, but it is certainly plausible to argue (as I will in Chapter Three) that those instances where Paul echoes or alludes to Jesus Tradition are just that—Paul alluding to traditions preserved *about* the *historical* Jesus, not, as some may argue (plausibly too), traditions Paul (or other earlier followers of Jesus) created *ex nihilo* to turn Jesus into the exemplar *par excellence* for a politics of non-violence. For further methodological reflection, see below.

2. Recognizing the danger of starting with a simple caricature of "Jewish" or "Roman" attitudes toward or participation in violence is possible even when one finally identifies the generally overwhelming acceptance of violent action in the first century in particular and the ancient world more generally. Richard Horsley's warnings (e.g., "By the Finger of God," 75) are important, but should miss the mark of any careful reconstruction of Jesus' place in Roman Palestine.

First, since Matthew's gospel is by all accounts later than Paul's letters, how can one dismiss the possibility that Paul's letters contributed to the shape of Jesus Traditions in Matthew's gospel? In short, I think the honest answer is that one cannot eliminate this possibility entirely. It is certainly possible that Paul influenced the synoptic presentation of Jesus rather than the other way around. Indeed, this has been argued by Jürgen Sauer and later, Michael Goulder.[3] The problem, however, is that though all agree that Matthew was composed later than Paul's letters (indeed, most scholars would date *all* the canonical gospels to a post-Pauline period), much of Matthew's source material[4] comes from a significantly earlier period than when it received its final redaction by "Matthew,"[5] and some traditions clearly originated from a period before Paul wrote. The most significant portion of my attention within Matthew's gospel is directed to parts of the Sermon on the Mount and the passion, two blocks of material that show strong indications of existing (in oral or written form) before Paul composed his letters.[6]

---

3. Sauer, "Traditionsgeschichtliche," and Goulder, *Midrash and Lection*, esp. 144–48, 154–55, 170.

4. I assume throughout the two-source theory, though I am less than an enthusiastic supporter of those who assume Q was necessarily a written document. See my brief discussion of an oral paradigm for transmission of Jesus Tradition in the next chapter.

5. I put "Matthew" in quotation marks merely to note the doubt cast on the identity of the author of the first gospel. I do not feel compelled to rehearse the arguments here, but see, e.g., Davies and Allison, *Matthew*, 1:7–58, for an extensive summary of views.

6. Luz, *Matthew*, 3:301 opines that it is "hardly controversial" to see the Markan passion narrative as the sole written source for Matthew's passion. Bauckham, *Jesus and the Eyewitnesses*, 243, stresses the early (40s CE) "connected narrative" of Mark's passion; Theissen, *Gospels in Context*, 166–99, recognizes the limits of our knowledge of the *scope* of a pre-Markan Passion story (169), but proposes Jerusalem as its origin (due to the use of protective anonymity, 188–89) and "critical shaping" of the narrative sometime between 30 and 60, "probably" between 41–44 CE (198–99). Koester, *Ancient Christian Gospels*, 136–37, writes that the Q section that provides the basis for the Sermon on the Mount "has not only preserved many sayings which circulated widely at a very early date, it was most likely a cluster of sayings that existed independently in a number of variants in oral or written form before it was used by the author of Q." Robinson, "Real Jesus," writes that the logia preserved in Matt 5:38–44 are "sayings most characteristic of the *real* Jesus" (emphasis added). Robinson proposes that the Sermon on the Mount contains a "very old" independently composed unit of the historical Jesus' teaching. Betz, *Sermon on the Mount*, 8, is somewhat circumspect in his comments on the dating of the source material for the Sermon on the Mount. He writes: "Written collection of the kind we have in the SM and the SP did in fact exist by the end of the first century CE; these collections were based on older sources *going back to Jesus* and even to Jewish wisdom literature" (emphasis added).

Relatedly, it can be queried whether or in what way Matthew's Jesus corresponds to the so-called historical Jesus. This objection might take the following form. If Matthew's Jesus is (a step) removed from the Jesus of history, how can we be sure that any one aspect of his teaching or lifestyle was indeed a feature of the ministry of the historical Jesus? And if we cannot presuppose the historicity of Jesus' commitment to non-violence, then Paul's move from violence to non-violence cannot be identified with his being conformed to this practice of Jesus. I consider this a serious challenge to my thesis, but not an insuperable one. Every source about Jesus faces the challenge of what, if anything, it tells us about the historical Jesus. Mark's gospel may be, *to a degree*, less suspect, but no one assumes his early gospel is "untainted" by the subjectivity of its author.

If we look at the issue under review in this particular study, I submit that the evidence that the historical Jesus taught and lived a politics of peaceableness is robust. The (in)famous criteria[7] applied to much historical Jesus research *can* be seen (not *must* be seen) to speak with a steady voice: there is (arguably) *multiple attestation* to his teachings on non-violence;[8] Jesus' non-violent message is *coherent* within both first-century Judaism (in all its diversity) and the movement that found its genesis in him;[9] his non-violent politics is also *dissimilar* to the politics espoused by some of his near-contemporaries in Judaism, and by Christians only a few generations removed from Jesus' closest followers;[10] there would appear to be good reason to tick the box *embarrassing* too, since Jesus' teaching to love enemies

7. Meier, *Marginal Jew*, offers clear reflections on the much-discussed criteria.

8. Matt 5:38–42; Luke 6:27–35; Rom 12:17, 21; 1 Pet 3:9. Cf. 1 Thess 5:15; James 5:6; Rom 13:10; Gal 6:10; 1 Thess 3:12.

9. Non-violent resistance is not completely novel in Judaism; cf. Josephus *Ant.*, 18:55–59; *T. Benj* 4:3; the evidence for early Christian attitudes towards participation in the imperial army is presented by Cadoux, *Christian Attitude to War*, 49–243; see also the extreme example in *Opus imperfectum*, 12:699: "For if you hit back, you have . . . denied that you are a disciple of Christ, not with words but with deeds."

10. Jesus' politics of non-violence were clearly dissimilar to those violent rebels who arise in the decades after Jesus to liberate Jerusalem from Roman control; followers of the "Prince of Peace" begin to entertain the possibility of military careers by the end of the second century (see note above). Koester, *Ancient Christian Gospels*, 89–90, points out that synoptic parallels with the Gospel of Thomas "are especially frequent in sections of Q which became the basis of the Lukan Sermon on the Plain . . . and the Matthean Sermon on the Mount." However, Koester fails to recognize that the Q logia on enemy love is conspicuously absent. This is one prospect for future research, as it highlights the possibility that we can begin to see a drift away from the strenuous enemy-love ethic of Jesus as early as Thomas' gospel, however we choose to date it.

was (and still is) not considered to be a very practical political position to espouse; and though his death is more challenging to explain, it can be explained on grounds other than his commitment to non-violence (e.g., his strained relationship with religious and political authorities, a point underscored by Matthew, but present in other sources as well).

Unpacking the evidence for each of these criteria would represent too large a diversion from the point of the present chapter, but the value is not in any case placed on any one criterion. The weight of the evidence together suggests that (the historical) Jesus and his immediate followers practiced non-violent peacemaking, and this thread is picked up in Matthew's sources and included in Matthew's narrative. Particular sayings or events are rightly to be debated, but dismissing the probability that Jesus was non-violent seems ill-advised.[11] The rest of this chapter is an attempt to make the case, from Matthew's text, that Jesus was indeed non-violent. Whether Matthew's gospel "faithfully" reproduces the history of Jesus at other points is not for me to say in this particular study. What I do say is that, *in relation to Jesus' theological politics of peace*, Matthew gives us a reliable picture.

Another objection might be "Why not Mark?" One natural reason to appeal to Mark, of course, is the presupposition that his text is earlier. This claim is firmly established, but the payoff is not as strong as one might suppose. As I note above, dating the individual gospels is somewhat more straightforward than is dating of particular strands of tradition. Matthew may indeed preserve material (Q) which is earlier (in terms of tradition history) that Mark did not include or did not know for reasons that we will surely never know. For that reason, Mark's gospel, unless it offers a picture which disconfirms the picture composed by Matthew, is not

---

11. Although I offer (only) a rough sketch here for why I think it advisable to consider the historical Jesus was non-violent, in the present chapter I will more often than not treat Jesus *as Matthew presents him*. This narratival approach is not meant to dismiss the relevance of Jesus' historicity, but I agree with Hays, *Moral Vision*, 159, that focusing on the narrative logic of individual gospels is a better way to constrain our own hermeneutical presuppositions when studying the life of Jesus. Meier, *Marginal Jew*, 1:167–68, provides a sober reality check to any who might be tempted to suppose we can get back to the "real" Jesus through the science of critical research: "The criteria of historicity will usually produce judgments that are only more or less probable; certainty is rarely to be had. Indeed, since in the quest for the historical Jesus almost anything is possible, the function of the criteria is to pass from the merely possible to the really probable, to inspect various probabilities, and to decide which candidate is most probable. Ordinarily, the criteria cannot hope to do more."

necessarily a "better" or more reliable source for the activity or teaching of the historical Jesus.[12]

In one sense, appealing to Matthew (rather than Mark) clearly works to my advantage. The most obvious advantage is that Matthew includes more material, and part of that material is the Sermon on the Mount. However, many elements of Matthew's gospel present a challenge too. For example, Matthew paints a picture of a violent eschatological judgment, a picture that puts a serious question mark beside the motive for non-violence for Jesus' disciples. Similarly, Matthew's Jesus tells parables that portray God as violent. Since these tensions exist within Matthew's text, I will be forced to deal with some significant theological tensions, and the reader is directed to see the relevant sections toward the end of the present chapter.

There is yet another reason to deal with Matthew rather than Mark (or Luke)—it is widely acknowledged that Matthew's gospel has certain features that present difficulties for those who wish to see agreement between Matthew and Paul. David Sim's work is the most relentless on the discontinuity of the two,[13] although Ulrich Luz quips that these two "would certainly not have struck up a strong friendship."[14] Michael Goulder claims it is self-evident that Matthew's "theological sympathies are far apart from the apostle's."[15] We could adduce witnesses who hold the opposite view, but it is perfectly appropriate to see *at least* tension between these two early Christian authors. Although I will not come to Paul's defense vis-à-vis Sim's argument (my view is that Sim has overstated his case for Matthew as an anti-Pauline gospel), it would be all the more impressive, would it not, if these two thinkers, between whom we are to see a great abyss,[16] exhibit

12. Sim, "Matthew and Jesus," 155–72, argues for a historical preference for Matthew in two ways. Sim argues that Matthew's portrait of Jesus' attitude towards Gentile mission and Torah observance are closer to that of the historical Jesus than the corresponding portrait provided by Mark. For Sim, *historical continuity* is decisive here. I simply want to extend the argument of historical continuity on my own theme from the historical Jesus, through the Jerusalem church, to Paul and finally to Matthew. Sim may think Matthew and Paul are at odds in many ways, but on the issue of non-retaliation and peace, the two will be shown to be in lockstep.

13. Sim, *Apocalyptic Eschatology in Matthew*; Sim, *Matthew and Christian Judaism*; Sim, "Matthew's Anti-Paulinism," 767–83; Sim, "Milieu of Matthew,"; Sim, "Gentile Mission," 377–92.

14. Luz, *Theology*, 146–53.

15. Goulder, *Midrash and Lection*, 170. So too Harrington, "Matthew and Paul," 11: ". . . two very different theological voices."

16. Luz, *Theology*, 149.

a unified or complementary picture of Jesus' commitment to a politics of peace? Of the three Synoptics, Matthew, we are urged to believe, would hold out the greatest possibility of containing a picture which disconfirms the one presented in Paul's letters. If Sim's argument has merit, then he has indirectly made the case for me that non-violence was a core feature of Matthean and Pauline Christianity since it is one place where Matthew has chosen not to "correct" Paul's theological politics.[17]

Although I begin by identifying a politics of peace for Matthew's Jesus before moving on to describe a similar politics in the life and letters of Paul, I do not want this "directionality" to give the impression that I treat Matthew's gospel as a document relevant to the "background" of Paul's letters. In fact, we are probably safer to speak of "backgrounds," if we want to do so, the other way around.[18] Although I think many individual traditions preserved in Matthew may indeed antedate the composition of Paul's letters, it is perhaps better to treat the traditions preserved in Matthew (on a case-by-case basis) as *one* context, among many which influence Paul, for the occasion of his individual writings.

Indeed, if we wish to look for an appropriate "background" to Paul (or Matthew, for that matter), it would be better to begin by identifying the scriptures of Israel as the context *par excellence*, from which Paul (and Matthew) make sense of the meaning and importance of the story of Jesus of Nazareth for the life of communities that gather in his name.[19] To say

17. Indeed, ironically, Sim's argument would seem to suggest that the strong evidence for disagreement vis-à-vis Torah observance between Matthean and Pauline strands of early Christianity should relativize the emphasis we place on the issue of a law-observant versus law-free mission, while their agreement on the issue of a non-violent politics should make us reconsider the centrality of this issue in diverse (or competing) strands of early Christianity.

18. So Goulder, *Midrash and Lection*, 154–55: "One of the most widespread, and, if I may say so, one of the most idiosyncratic presuppositions of this century in NT scholarship has been the watertight compartment view of churches. The picture given us in Acts and the Pauline Epistles is of the Hellenist apostles and their lieutenants in continual movement, linking the churches together in a constantly renewed network of visits and letters. . . . [They] post o'er land and ocean without rest, from the late 40s to the early 60s. The Pastorals, if we allow their evidence, extend the period and the area. Yet orthodoxy would have us believe that in the 70s and 80s the Church of God was like the battleship *Bismarck*, subdivided by watertight bulkheads, so that those who would pass from one to the next cannot, with the treasure of Pauline theology, or the L, M, and Q *logia*. How should this be? . . . *Nothing is more natural than that Matthew should have read the whole Pauline corpus*" (emphasis added).

19. See Ehrensperger, *Paul and Power*, 6–9, who states that Israel's Scriptures "constitute the world in which [Paul] lived and thought."

that Israel's Scriptures are the context *par excellence* does not mean that no other contexts are important for making sense of early Christian discourse, Pauline or otherwise. We must of course also consider the shape of Roman imperial discourse, the heterogeneous praxis of local authorities in their reliance on violent means of governance, and the traditions about Jesus that were known by Paul before they were codified in the (canonical) gospels.

In short, though I do not wish to appear to be "using" Matthew's gospel to serve as a "background" for Paul's letters, I have decided to place the treatment of Matthew first because his gospel points us in the direction of Jesus, and the logic of my argument necessitates arguing that Jesus (as Matthew "remembers" him, and to some degree as he "really was," historically speaking,) was a teacher and practitioner of non-violence before I move on to demonstrate that Paul became so committed after the apocalypse of Jesus in him. Although Matthew's gospel follows Paul's letters compositionally speaking, there are many factors (identified above) that allow us to consider Matthew rather than one of the other Synoptics, and to do so before examining this theme in Paul's life and letters.

THE SOCIAL SETTING AND LITERARY REMAINS OF VIOLENCE IN FIRST-CENTURY ROMAN PALESTINE AND MATTHEW'S GOSPEL

Violence by Elite Jews and Gentiles in Matthew's Gospel

The Gospel of Matthew evinces a particularly sharp conflict between church and synagogue, resulting in the general impression that Matthew exonerates Pilate (and Rome by extension) in Jesus' death and places the blame squarely on "the Jews." Although it is true that Matthew's portrait of Jesus' Jewish opponents is unflattering when compared with, for example, Mark's, it is hardly monochromatic.[20] Attending to Matthew's construction of violence and identity reveals that those who initiate violence in Matthew's gospel are frequently distinguished by socio-economic categories rather than ethnic ones.[21] So, for example, rather than portraying Jewish violence

---

20. Longenecker, "Evil at Odds with Itself," 512–13, notes that Matthew consistently excises positive portraits of Pharisees which he received from Mark.

21. Carter, "Constructions of Violence," 96: "The dominant (though not exclusive) association of violence with the ruling elite, both Jewish and Roman, indicates that *social*

against Jesus and his followers, Matthew consistently constructs a picture of elite violence—Jewish *and* Gentile—against Jesus and his disciples.

Beginning with the vicious "Slaughter of the Innocents" by Herod (2:13–20), and culminating in the alliance of the elite Roman governor and the elite Jewish authorities (Caiaphas, the scribes, elders, chief priests, the whole council) to bring about Jesus' crucifixion (26:57–66), Matthew's gospel tends to portray the ordinariness of elite violence against the masses of non-elites who had no realistic recourse to resist in first-century Roman Palestine.[22] Matthew's narrative is punctuated from beginning to end with real, predicted, or fictional violence. Not only does Herod kill all the children in and around Bethlehem under the age of two (2:16–18), his son Antipas imprisoned and decapitated John the Baptist (4:12; 14:3–12). Running contrary to the narrative's value-system, Jesus warned his disciples that they would be flogged by councils, led before kings and governors, betrayed to death by brothers, fathers or children, hated and persecuted by all, each scenario being a consequence of the message they announced—"the Kingdom of heaven has come near"—and the activities in which they

---

status plays a more important role than ethnicity" (emphasis added). The notable exception to the consistent portrayal of violence in Matthew's gospel as stemming from elites is the way Matthew constructs cosmic and eschatological violence—that is, violence carried out by God or God's agent on the Day of Judgment (eschatological) or violence perpetrated by (or against) the cosmic adversary of God, the satan (cosmic). We will return to the issue of divine/eschatological violence towards the end of the present chapter. See Matt 13:19, 28, 38–39; 8:28–34 for examples of violence perpetrated by the satan or the satan's agents.

22. Carter, "Constructions of Violence," 93, states: "Societal leaders use their leadership positions and societal institutions (such as judicial processes, military personnel, and slavery), along with their wealth, power, and alliances, to protect a vertical social structure that is of enormous benefit to themselves and of great harm to others. Consistent with a basic principle of Roman justice, namely, that punishment fits the societal (non)status of the person, Jesus' crucifixion serves to protect elite interests against a provincial who challenges his assigned place in society, the elite's right to assign it, and the order of the society that the elite shapes." That Matthew repeatedly signals elite-sponsored violent activity does not necessarily mean that non-elites fail to participate. Matt 27:15–26 clearly portrays non-elite (Matthew's favored designation, the "crowd/s") interest in a violent end for Jesus, not least in the infamous phrase which would seem to indicate their commitment to Jesus' violent death: "His blood be upon us and upon our children" (27:25). Although Matthew's narrative interest in 27:11–26 is the assignment of blame, the center of gravity for Matthew rests with the chief priest and elders who thrust Jesus before Pilate and persuaded the crowds to condemn Jesus rather than Barabbas (27:20). Cf. Davies and Allison, *Matthew*, 3:593. Thus nuancing Carter's treatment of non-elite participation in violence in Matthew's gospel would only serve to strengthen his otherwise fair assessment.

were to engage (10:5–25). Elites are frequently portrayed in Jesus' parables in such a way as to betray their reliance on "ordinary" violence to maintain social position and control. Elites engage in economic sabotage of one another (13:24–30), use torture to punish debtors (18:23–34), kill rebellious (and themselves murderous) vineyard tenants (21:33–41), and destroy the people who killed the slaves of a king, who himself crowned his own retaliation by burning their city (22:1–7).

Violence by Non-Elites in Matthew's Gospel

It is hardly surprising that violence is also characteristic of non-elite relationships. One slave is portrayed as physically beating other slaves (24:48–49), one assaults and imprisons another slave who owed a debt (18:28–30). One of Jesus' own disciples, or at least one person who was with him, violently defended Jesus on the Mount of Olives (26:51) before Jesus put a stop to his counter-attack. Those who scourged and crucified Jesus were not elite in an economic sense, but were themselves the tip of the elite sword, non-elites doing the gruesome work of maintaining "peace" at the fringes of the Roman Empire. The examples could be multiplied, but the point can be made with confidence: violence was common in interpersonal relations at every socio-economic level, and Matthew's gospel reflects the grim reality of first-century conflict.

Although social-scientific or ideological methods could be marshaled to demonstrate the point, it is not controversial to suggest that such violence or the threat of it was used primarily by elites to maintain the status quo of social position and economic stability—at least stability for those with money or the resources of high social rank. This observation is hardly unique to Roman Palestine; examples can be found throughout the Roman Empire. Jesus' lifestyle and teaching challenged elite interests, resulting in the constant specter of violence against him and those who lent him support. Of course, eventually his life ended in the most extreme form of punishment, reserved for slaves, the poor, or treasonous criminals,[23] which was available to those maintaining "peace" in Jerusalem. While economic factors play a critical role in relation to violence in Matthew's gospel, they are not the only factors. Matthew's gospel also evinces the pan-economic prevalence of recourse to violence in the first century.

---

23. See Hengel, *Crucifixion*, 46–63, for numerous primary texts.

THE SERMON ON THE MOUNT

Jesus as Paradigmatic Teacher

Into this culture of violence, Matthew broadcasts Jesus' strategy for engagement. One of the characteristic features of the portrait of Jesus that Matthew paints is Jesus' clear role as an authoritative teacher. The first gospel contains five units of Jesus' discourses, thought by many to signal Jesus' correspondence with Moses as one upholding the Torah, or alternatively, as instituting a new fivefold Torah after the fashion of Moses.[24] There are also at least twelve "fulfillment" quotations trailing throughout the gospel, further indicating Jesus' relationship to the Torah as one of continuity rather than contestation.[25] In addition to fulfillment formulae, Matthew 5:17 puts the issue on the lips of Jesus: "Do not think that I have come to abolish the law or the prophets; I have come not to abolish but to fulfill." Matthew's portrait of Jesus indicates consistently that, despite his many heated exchanges with scribes and Pharisees, Jesus shared much in common with them, including the desire to remain faithful to the Torah.

Jesus' instructions, most notably the antitheses of the Sermon on the Mount, frequently center on the interpretation of the Torah. Traditions about Jesus preserve memories of him as a witty teacher, skilled in the craft of storytelling and able to deploy a pithy phrase to vex or delight his audience. Matthew juxtaposes Jesus' teaching authority with that of the scribes, signaled by the crowds' amazement at his most famous discourse (7:28–29) and by his own claim to be their sole teacher and instructor (23:8, 10). Matthew's placement of the Sermon on the Mount at the beginning of his gospel serves as a launching point for his "career" and fixes the perception of Jesus as a great teacher in the first gospel and, in light of its placement in

24. Most famously advanced by Bacon, *Studies in Matthew*. The five discourses in Matthew's gospel are widely accepted, found from (1) chapters 5–7; (2) 10; (3) 13; (4) 18; (5) 24–25. Davies and Allison, *Matthew*, 1:61–72, advance the additional argument that the five discourses are all organised into triads, as is narrative material in the first twelve chapters.

25. The number very much depends upon what counts as part of a formulaic expression. In the following list, the twelve most clear quotation formulae are unmarked; a further four possibilities are set in brackets. Matt 1:22; [2:5–6]; 2:15, 17, 23; [3:3]; 4:14; [5:17]; 8:17; 12:17; [13:14–15]; 13:35; 21:4; 26:54, 56; 27:9. The exact figure is less important than the relative importance Matthew gives to the significance of fulfillment of scripture. Matthew uses *fullfill* (*plēroō*) twelve times in reference to scripture whereas Mark and Luke use the term once and twice, respectively. See Mark 14:49; Luke 4:21; 24:44.

the (Christian) canon, in Christian tradition more generally. By highlighting Jesus' role as authoritative teacher, Matthew calls his readers' attention to the content of Jesus' teaching, especially as Jesus' teaching demonstrates his fulfillment or even intensification of Torah (5:17–20).

Early in his narrative, Matthew portrays Jesus teaching his disciples the way in which they ought to deal with the most banal forms of violence faced in Greco-Roman Galilee. The Sermon on the Mount is indisputably one of the most important blocks of teaching in the Gospel of Matthew and part of Jesus' teaching within the Sermon, the first of Matthew's five great discourses by Jesus, is focused on the fulfillment of the law and the prophets through greater righteousness (Matt 5:17, 20). In this fundamental unit of Jesus' teaching, he instructs his disciples to eschew recourse to violence, replacing seemingly legitimate retaliatory violence with active non-violent responses. With Jesus' attitude toward retaliation as our focal point, we will examine Matthew 5:38–39, highlighting the various linguistic and historical issues that address the proposal that Matthew's gospel is representative of early Christian memories of Jesus as a teacher and practitioner of non-violence.

The Literary Setting of the Sermon

Matthew's Sermon on the Mount follows closely on the story of the call of Jesus' disciples (4:18–22) and the gathering of great crowds to listen to his teaching (4:23–25). As the inaugural teaching of Jesus in Matthew's gospel, the sermon serves as Jesus' "programmatic disclosure of the kingdom of God and of the life to which the community of disciples is called."[26] In Hans Dieter Betz's view, the Sermon on the Mount functions much in the same way as a philosophical *epitome*:[27] the sermon summarizes the most important teachings of Jesus for providing "the disciple of Jesus with the necessary tool for becoming a Jesus theologian."[28] The goal of this collection of Jesus' instructions is not to inform Matthew's audience about some important things Jesus said, but to enable Jesus' disciples to hear the words

26. Hays, *Moral Vision*, 321.

27. Betz, *Sermon on the Mount*, 77.

28. Betz, "Sermon on the Mount," 296. Betz's proposal that the Sermon on the Mount is a type of *epitome* is not widely followed, but it is hardly controversial to suggest that the sermon preserves *some* of the most important or characteristic teachings ascribed to Jesus of Nazareth. See Allison, review of *Sermon on the Mount*.

of Jesus and act on them like the wise man who built his house upon rock (Matt 7:24). If Jesus' authoritative teaching (7:28–29) at the beginning of his ministry serves as the "definitive charter for the life of the new covenant community,"[29] one of the community's principle obligations involves actively breaking the cycle of violence perpetuated by retaliation.

Matthew 5:38–39

> You have heard that it was said, "An eye for an eye and a tooth for a tooth." But I say to you, Do not resist an evildoer. But if anyone strikes you on the right cheek, turn the other also. (NRSV)

Matthew 5:38–39 may be the *locus classicus* of all non-violent claims about Jesus. The verses that follow (vv. 40–42) illustrate further Jesus' command not to resist, but perhaps no other example (save Jesus' death on a cross) has the same influence upon discussions of the issue of Christian non-violence. In light of its importance, four main issues will guide our investigation of the fifth "antithesis": Jesus' citation of the *lex talionis*, the translation of *resist/retaliate* (ἀντιστῆναι), the translation of *the evil one* (τῷ πονηρῷ), and the action received by the victim—being struck on the right cheek. In each case, other significant interrelated issues will be raised and addressed as necessary.

The Lex Talionis

Continuing his pattern from the four previous "antitheses" of citing authoritative texts from his tradition, Jesus begins his fifth with the *lex talionis*—the eye for eye, tooth for tooth punishment common in antiquity. The phrase is found in similar form in three places in the Septuagint (hereafter, LXX): Exodus 21:24; Leviticus 24:20; and Deuteronomny 19:21. W. D. Davies and Dale Allison suspect the third of these was in mind, given the forensic setting of each (cf. Matt 5:40) and the presence of *evil* (πονηρός, Deut 19:19) and *resist* (στήσομαι, Deut 19:17).[30] Rather than attempt to identify the *one* text to which Matthew refers, it is better to suggest that he had the *concept*

---

29. Hays, *Moral Vision*, 321.

30. Davies and Allison, *Matthew*, 1:540. However, they also note (1:504) that Matthew may have structured the antitheses so that 5:21–32 drew from laws in Deuteronomy and 5:33–48 drew from laws in Leviticus.

of the law in mind. This would align with each of the previous "antitheses," which all (save 5:31) have multiple points of reference in the LXX.[31]

A common thread throughout the LXX *lex talionis* texts is that the law is applied *at least* within the community; that is, the punishment of fellow Israelites is in view. Leviticus 24:16, however, also addresses the alien in Israel's midst. Thus, although the context is given as Moses' words to all Israel, the application is to *anyone* (cf. Lev 24:15, 17, 18, 21) among them, alien and citizen alike (προσήλυτος and αὐτόχθων 24:16; προσηλύτῳ καὶ τῷ ἐγχωρίῳ 24:22), who kills or maims another person or blasphemes the name of the Lord. Similarly, the Deuteronomy passage (19:21) immediately precedes a discussion about going to war against Israel's enemies. The *talionic* laws are not applied in warfare, but what this illustrates is that if the passage from Deuteronomy influenced Matthew's portrayal of Jesus' reflections on the *lex talionis*, his connection with teaching on proper behavior towards enemies (Matt 5:44) is a natural one.

The *lex talionis* principle is usually thought to involve simply the limitation of retributive justice. That is, when something unjust occurs, the punishment should fit, but not exceed, the crime. For instance, if a goring ox kills someone, the ox should be killed; if a notoriously mean-spirited ox is not restrained by its owner and it kills, both the ox and the owner are to be put to death (Exod 21:28–32). But this interpretation of the *lex talionis* falters in cases when it is difficult to apply equivalent retributive justice or in situations regarded as offensive in the extreme. For instance, a pregnant woman's miscarriage caused by a brawl (Exod 21:22–23) results in a monetary fine (unless the woman dies or is injured, in which case we are back to the *lex talionis*); an equivalent punishment would be difficult to exact in this case, so an alternate monetary punishment is sanctioned. Or a child striking or cursing a parent is a capital offense (Exod 21:15, 17); the strict application of the *lex talionis* would seemingly call for cursing the child or striking the child, but this particular transgression merits a more serious punishment. Or again, a non-fatal blow to an opponent results in what amounts to covering medical expenses and lost wages (Exod 21:18–19); a return "shot" is not granted the victim, only financial restitution is demanded. It would seem, then, that in *some* cases the punishment

---

31. E.g., Matt 5:21 on murder = Exod 20:13; Deut 5:17; Matt 5:27 on adultery = Exod 20:14; Deut 5:18; Matt 5:31 on divorce = Deut 24:1–4; Matt 5:33 on swearing oaths = Exod 20:7; Lev 19:12; Num 30:3–15; Deut 23:21–23; Ps 50:14; Zech 8:17; Wis 14:28; Matt 5:43 on loving neighbors = Lev 19:18.

equals or stops short of equivalence, in which case the principle of *limiting* retribution holds true.

The problem with the limitation interpretation (whether fitting or falling short) is that, in some special cases, the punishment appears to exceed the offense. The rebellious child (Exod 21:15, 17) noted above is one such instance where the punishment seems to exceed the crime.[32] Another tricky scenario is when someone is kidnapped (Exod 21:16). Instead of an equivalent punishment (which is hard to envisage) or monetary compensation, death is the kidnapper's punishment. Things also become complicated when the status of the offender differs from the victim. If a slave owner, for example, blinds one of his slaves, or knocks out one tooth, the slave does not get to exact vengeance (Exod 21:26–27). However, the slave owner, to compensate for the offense, was required to free the slave. Common to these cases, however, is the presupposition that there is a fitting retribution for any particular offense and the "universal" applicability of the laws to aliens and citizens alike.

Rather than quibbling over whether the *lex talionis* restrained vengeance or legitimated it, Jesus interrupts the trajectory of the debate before it reached retribution. In other words, the *lex talionis* may give an answer to what is legally permissible to do in response to being struck on the right cheek, *but it provides an answer to the wrong question.* If we take Jesus' examples as representative of his "retaliation" for particular offenses, we may identify the question at the heart of his teaching. If the slap to the right cheek is meant to be a dishonorable insult, the "proper" response would be an equally if not more insulting slap. It is not difficult to envisage the scenario as it plays out. A man is shamed in his society by a backhanded slap. Those who witness the shaming slap wait with anticipation to see whether the conflict will escalate into more violence. That is the expectation. But rather than escalate the conflict by returning the slap or attempting to injure the offending party, Jesus' disciple stands firm, offering the other cheek rather than his (or her) own fist. Jesus' proposed alternative is a deliberate refusal to participate in the spiral of violence.

---

32. One might suppose this simply betrays my own modern sensibilities and that for people in antiquity this may well not be a punishment which "exceeds" the crime.

Resist, Retaliate, Rebel? Translating a Tricky Word (ἀντιστῆναι)

Another disputed point is how to translate ἀντιστῆναι: Jesus forbids legal retaliation; Jesus forbids *stasis* (i.e., violent rebellion); Jesus forbids testifying in court against an evildoer.[33] Much is at stake in the interpretation of ἀντιστῆναι. If Jesus forbade "legal resistance," his instructions had a very specific context, applying only to individual conduct in a law-court setting. If he forbade violent rebellion, the implications applied more broadly to corporate, public conduct. The difficulty of translating the term is well illustrated by tensions expressed by Davies and Allison, who (to name only two modern interpreters) maintain that Matthew 5:38–42 speaks only to interpersonal relationships and should not be used to guide "state institutions."[34] In other words, Jesus' instructions forbid personal self-defense but offer no instructions applicable to larger corporate, "political" bodies.

The evidence, however, is not so univocal. The term ἀντιστῆναι often has corporate, political and violent overtones. In the LXX, it is most often used to refer to armed resistance in military encounters.[35] Davies and Allison themselves allow that even if these verses apply strictly to inter-personal conflict, they cannot be fully emptied of their political consequences due to the "Jewish situation of the first century," and, in fact, "on the lips of Jesus, 5.38–42 *could not but have had pacifistic implications.*"[36] Rather than choosing between personal and corporate implications of these verses, it may be better to see Jesus' exhortation as one that makes demands on individual disciples as well as collective groups seeking to heed Jesus' teaching. So while the Sermon on the Mount does refer to self-defense (i.e., an individual's response to violence), when Jesus' teaching is taken together

---

33. See Weaver, "Transforming Nonresistance," 33.

34. Davies and Allison, *Matthew*, 1:542. Horsley, *Spiral of Violence*; and Horsley, "Ethics and Exegesis," 72–101, offers a similar alternative—the setting of the historical Jesus makes his demands highly specific; they are directed towards Galilean village life. Cf., however, the differing views of Hays, *Moral Vision*, 324–29; and Wink, "Counter-response," 133–36.

35. Wink, "Neither Passivity nor Violence," 114. See, e.g., Lev 26:37; Deut 7:24; 25:18; 28:7. According to Wink, forty-four out of seventy-one occurrences in the LXX refer to armed conflict, while Josephus uses it fifteen out of seventeen times in this same way. Whatever the actual number (cf. Davis, *Lex Talionis in Early Judaism*, 108, claims twenty-one occurrences), it is not surprising that it usually describes armed conflict given the subject of Josephus' writing.

36. Davies and Allison, *Matthew*, 1:542, emphasis added. Davies and Allison refer to "pacifistic implications" in the context of potential political revolt against Rome.

with his conduct throughout Matthew's gospel as a whole, the "larger para-digm . . . indicates a deliberate renunciation of violence as an instrument of God's will."[37] Individuals *and* groups who read Matthew's gospel were equally addressed and constrained by Jesus' words. Jesus' teaching on non-violence cannot but be political (i.e., have *corporate* consequences) when he is viewed (as he was by some) as the figurehead of a movement who announced the coming or present Kingdom of Heaven and yet refused to use violent means to bring about that reign.

One way to translate ἀντιστῆναι, then, considering its corporate and individual character, is "do not retaliate."[38] With this, we try to avoid sug-gesting that Jesus calls his disciples to acquiesce in the face of violence; instead, their "aggressive nonviolent actions" unveil evil without mimick-ing it.[39] The spirit of the *lex talionis* is preserved ("you shall purge the evil from your midst," Deut 19:19), but it is done without recourse to mimetic violence. Jesus arms his disciples with "nonretaliation as a weapon to com-bat evil and to help justice prevail."[40] It is, in fact, the "weapon" deployed by Jesus in his passion, where Matthew repeatedly records Jesus' peace-able, non-retaliatory behavior when he is arrested (Matt 26:47–56), beaten (26:67–68; 27:30), and finally crucified (27:32–54).[41]

Against Whom Is One Not to Retaliate? Translating τῷ πονηρῷ.

Three possibilities are generally identified as the object against which Jesus' disciples are not to "retaliate": an evil person; the evil one (i.e., the devil); or Evil (as an impersonal force). Considering the immediate context, the first option makes the most sense. The "evil person" is the one who strikes Jesus' disciple on the cheek, seizes clothing in pledge for debts incurred, and forces one to carry a burden for a mile.[42] τῷ πονηρῷ represents the one

37. Hays, *Moral Vision*, 323.

38. See Betz, *Sermon on the Mount*, 280.

39. Wink, "Neither Passivity nor Violence," 113.

40. Betz, *Sermon on the Mount*, 284.

41. Note that in Jesus' passion, Simon of Cyrene was *compelled* (ἠγγάρευσαν) to carry Jesus' cross by the Roman soldiers (27:32; cp. 5:41); Jesus' *garments* (ἱμάτια) were divided among the soldiers (27:35; cp. 5:40); those passing by *derided* him (ἐβλασφήμουν, 27:39); and even the bandits crucified with him *taunted* him (ὠνείδιζον, 27:44; cp. 5:11); all save *deride* (ἐβλασφήμουν) are mentioned in the context of the Sermon on the Mount—but even here see the equivalent expression of 5:11.

42. So Betz, *Sermon on the Mount*, 281; Davies and Allison, *Matthew*, 1:543.

who treats Jesus' disciples unjustly just as τὸν πονηρόν represents the person who falsely testifies against a neighbor (Deut 19:19).

Richard Horsley maintains that the "evil person" here envisaged is a fellow Galilean villager, that is, only *local* enemies could be in view when Jesus begins to address the question of how to respond to enemies (5:43–44). It seems, however, that Horsley can only maintain such a narrow view of "enemies" by discarding Matthew 5:41 as irrelevant to the "enemies" who should be loved in the very next breath. Horsley distances himself from the standard explanation of 5:41 without giving an alternative explanation: it is "supposedly in response to the imperial requisition of labor" and falls within the "section dealing with interpersonal relations . . . and not in the section on love of enemies."[43] If 5:41 does not refer to requisitioned transport by imperial agents, Horsley should offer an alternative to the virtually unanimous understanding of this verse. In addition, his position verges on self-contradiction. Insistent on the importance of Q for identifying speech that is "characteristic" of Jesus, Horsley excludes 5:41 from the discussion of the enemies of 5:43–4 because of its location in Matthew (it is "not in the section on love of enemies"), but in Q, the example of requisitioned transport *follows* the command to love enemies. In other words, in Q the example *is* in the section on enemy-love.[44] It is far better to maintain that the examples used in 5:39–42 include both local and foreign aggressors.

The Right Cheek

Matthew's detail about being struck on the right cheek inspires almost unanimous agreement that it represents an insulting backhanded slap of a superior to an inferior. Care must be taken, however, not to allow emphasis to fall on the mechanics of the action at the expense of obscuring the fact that it is an act of aggressive violence. The display of violent aggression may indeed contain varying levels of humiliation[45] depending on what scenario

43. Horsley, "Ethics and Exegesis," 82. It should be noted that understanding the statement as referring to requisitioned transport does not require one to understand Galilee as occupied territory; transport is not required of garrisoned troops, but of troops and imperial representatives *on the move.*

44. Horsley, "Ethics and Exegesis," 80–82; See Q 6:27–30 in Robinson et al., *Critical Edition of Q*, 56–62. Matthew 5:41 is marked as probable but uncertain, and Davies and Allison, *Matthew*, 1:547, offer that Luke's omission of the verse makes sense "because of his general tendency to exonerate the Romans."

45. E.g., Why does no one take seriously that the slap came from the left hand? This

is envisaged, but in *any* scenario, this is still a violent incident. Rather than returning violence in kind, the one struck appears to invite more violence (perhaps with an implicit demand for human dignity, but not necessarily so). The point is that Jesus demands his disciples[46] forswear their rite to exact vengeance in kind—in the case of receiving (humiliating) violence, one must not strike back; but neither should one shrink back. Instead, Jesus instructs them to "turn to him the other cheek also," a defiant, but non-violent response. This pattern is rehearsed again in the examples that follow. To put Jesus' strategy into practice would demonstrate to the perpetrator that the power appealed to in violence is undone and ineffective when directed against people of God's kingdom.

Horsley argues, however, that the slap is no more than an insult; the fifth "antithesis" never has the issue of violence or non-violence in view. [47] Appealing to Robert Tannehill's "focal instance," he argues that the slap is "an extreme example . . . used to cover similar actions up to and including the literal case," but it does not apply to anything more serious than a formal insult.[48] What Horsley fails to consider is that if Jesus' disciples followed the *lex talionis*, the potential for greater violence would only increase. Abiding by Jesus' instructions, his disciples would halt the cycle of violence before it advances beyond the formal insult. Even granting Horsley's claim that the slap is not a violent incident (which is by no means clear, unless, as Horsley does, you simply define violence in such a way that aggression that does not result in *permanent* physical harm does not qualify),[49] violence is not "addressed" precisely because at the point where violent retaliation is expected, (i.e., where the conflict would escalate into greater violence with the expected response), Jesus commands an alternative to retaliation.

---

would seem to be even more insulting than a backhanded slap with the right hand in a culture where the left hand is reserved for unclean tasks. Cf. 1 Esdr 4:29–30.

46. Note in Matthew, the Sermon begins with the disciples *and* crowds in view (5:1–2), and ends with the crowds marveling at his authority (7:28–29); Luke directs the Sermon on the Plain at his disciples specifically (6:20), but there is a larger crowd present there, as well (6:17, 19).

47. Horsley, "Ethics and Exegesis," 82, 86.

48. Ibid., 86. Cf. Tannehill, "'Focal Instance,'" 380: the focal instance is "the point of clarity within a larger field of reference of which the instance is a part, a field which appears because of the tension in this extreme instance."

49. Horsley, "Ethics and Exegesis," 86–87, asserts that since its chief significance was insult and resulted in no physical damage to the person, a slap is not violent.

That non-retaliation is *commanded* is important, not least when it is inevitably seen as part of the teaching Matthew expected Jesus' disciples to teach the nations (28:20). The transmission of Jesus' teaching was not meant to be a depot of knowledge about Jesus; the disciples where to teach the nations "*to obey* everything I have commanded you." Matthew's deliberate organization of the five teaching discourses signals that it is especially these discourses (and Matthew 5–7 as the first, programmatic, discourse) Matthew would have had in mind when composing 28:20.

Love Your Enemies—Matthew 5:43–48

> You have heard that it was said, "You shall love your neighbor and hate your enemy." But I say to you, "Love your enemies and pray for those who persecute you." (Matthew 5:43–44)

Arguably one of the most memorable "antitheses" uttered by Jesus,[50] the core of 5:44 became one of the most cited dominical logia of the early church.[51] This "characteristic" teaching of Jesus' is perhaps the least ambiguous of the six antitheses in Matthew 5, and its importance is underscored by its final position among those antitheses. If Matthew 5:43–48 (especially verse 44) is less ambiguous than the rest, it is certainly not free from interpretive decisions. I will focus briefly on two issues: the scope of *enemies* and the warrant given in Matthew for loving enemies rather than hating them.

50. We could say "Matthew's Jesus" here, but when even Bultmann, *History of the Synoptic Tradition*, 105, treats Matt 5:43–48 as containing something "characteristic of the preaching of Jesus," it seems fair to proceed without further ado on the assumption that Jesus did point his disciples toward the counterintuitive praxis of loving their enemies by uttering some version of the love command, and that it was a regular feature of Jesus' ethical teaching.

51. Klassen, "Love Your Enemies," 8, claims it was the "most frequently cited saying of Jesus in the second century." See, e.g., Did 1:3; 2 Clem 13:4; Pol *Phil* 12:3; Justin 1 *Apol* 15.9: "'But I say unto you, pray for your enemies and love them that hate you, and bless them that curse you, and pray for them that despitefully use you.'" Cf. Justin *Dial.* 96:3; Athenagoras *Leg* 11:1: "What then are those teachings in which we are brought up? 'I say unto you Love your enemies; bless them that curse you; pray for them that persecute you; that ye may be the sons of your Father who is in heaven.'" Tertullian *Scap* 1: "For our religion commands us to love even our enemies, and to pray for those who persecute us, aiming at a perfection all its own . . . it is peculiar to Christians alone to love those that hate them." And Tertullian *Pat* 6, "Christ says 'Love your personal enemies, and bless your cursers, and pray for your persecutors, that ye may be sons of your heavenly Father.'"

Which Enemies?

I already briefly mentioned Richard Horsley's attempt to restrict the definition of enemies in Matthew 5:43–44 to personal enemies of Palestinian villagers.[52] Horsley's principle complaint seems to be that interpreters tend to move too quickly to overly-generalized ethical constructs that are the *product* of Jesus' self-evident command. He wants to see rather more engagement with the "social context" of the saying than is usually evident in order to provide a more concrete understanding of the identity of enemies in Matthew 5:43–44 and its Lukan parallel (Luke 6:27–28, 35).

Attending to the literary and social context of *enemies* does not, however, ultimately lead to the limiting interpretation that Horsley proposes. The first problem is that *enemy* (ἐχθρός) is a general term which in the LXX is used of both personal and national enemies.[53] Tellingly, it is used in Deuteronomy 20:1 of military enemies: "When you go out to war against your *enemies*," a passage immediately preceded by the *lex talionis* formula (Deut 19:21). Since personal and national enemies are both legitimate philological possibilities, the context must be decisive if there is any possibility of specifying further whom Matthew considers to be the enemies Jesus instructs his disciples to love.[54]

The only clue to the identity of the enemies is Matthew's parallel command to "pray for those who persecute you." No restrictive clauses are provided by Matthew (nor, for that matter, by Luke or Q). In the absence of further particulars, we are left to infer that the context permits a wide understanding of enemies, including religious, political, and personal enemies.[55] An open view of the identity of enemies is further supported if the immediately preceding context is permitted to influence our definition. If the one who slaps (5:39) or takes away the undergarment and tunic (5:40) of the disciple is envisaged to be a local adversary, the most likely possibility of one who presses a person to walk a mile (5:41) is a foreign (military or political) official.[56]

---

52. Horsley, "Ethics and Exegesis," 79–80.

53. This dual usage is true for the Hebrew root (אֹיֵב) too.

54. Horsley's effort is sometimes hindered by his attempt to weave together his assessments of the Matthean, Lukan, and Q recensions of the tradition in an attempt to arrive at the socio-historical situation Jesus himself addressed. Better is Hays's focus on Matthew's interest alone; see Hays, *Moral Vision*, 328.

55. Kuhn, "Das Liebesgebot Jesus," 194–230.

56. Cf. Mitchell, "Requisitioned Transport," 128, who notes that "there is ample

The Warrant for Loving Enemies

The second issue to address is the warrant given in Matthew's gospel for loving one's enemies. The discipline of loving enemies is introduced by a purpose conjunction: "*so that* you might become sons of your father in heaven." No move is made by Matthew to make out of enemy love a missional purpose. Ulrich Luz insists that the purpose of enemy-love "was not a chance for the enemy to become something better or even a test he must pass in order to do so."[57] Jesus' command was not the utterance of a naïve teacher of peace, but was delivered in full awareness (and anticipation) of meeting the "enemy in all of his harshness and brutality."[58] Instead of finding warrant in a hoped-for transformation of enemies, Matthew grounds the discipline of enemy-love in the character of the God who demonstrates, in utterly common, pragmatic ways, his love for the righteous and unrighteous alike. To become (or show oneself to be) children of the heavenly father (cf. Matt 5:9), one must necessarily imitate something of God's own discipline of loving enemies, even in their "total maliciousness."[59] The warrant for such an unnatural engagement with one's enemies is not pragmatic; instead, Matthew roots the warrant for enemy-love in the activity of God[60] and the costly discipleship of imitating him in imitating the life of his son.

---

evidence to show that abusive requisitioning on a minor scale by soldiers was almost universal." The verb used is also the technical term for pressing into service; see Price, "Response," 179n12.

57. Luz, *Matthew*, 1:293.

58. Ibid. So also Davies and Allison, *Matthew*, 1:556.

59. Luz, *Matthew*, 1:286. Davies and Allison, *Matthew*, 1:554, point out that the three thematic elements of love, imitation of God, and divine sonship are joined (*inter alia*) in Eph 5:1–2 in a similar way: "Therefore be imitators of God, as beloved children, and live in love as Christ loved us and gave himself up for us, a fragrant offering and sacrifice to God" (NRSV).

60. Matthew also presents images of God that would seem to be at variance with the one preserved here. I do address Matthew's alternative picture of a violent God later in the present chapter.

The Garden of Gethsemane and the Arrest of Jesus (Matthew 26:36–56)

Jesus teaching role in the first gospel is both paramount in Matthew's portrait of Jesus and bindingly normative for Jesus' disciples.[61] But in addition to the very basic observation that Matthew seems to portray Jesus as a new Moses, it is important to observe also that Matthew narrates Jesus' story in such a way that establishes Jesus' own actions as a model to be followed; Jesus is the definitive exemplar of living as a child of God. Matthew's narrative constructs "*a world stabilized and given meaning by the authoritative presence of Jesus Christ*."[62] The impact this has on Matthew's community is that "right and wrong are defined with clarity, and full-hearted obedience is to be expected as the norm within the church."[63] Jesus' teaching and example in Matthew's gospel are far from an "impossible ideal" to imitate; obedience is seen, rather, as "*a simple possibility* for those who hear the word of Jesus."[64] One of Jesus' most challenging demands of his disciples was put to the test during Jesus' final moments on the Mount of Olives. Only the perfect correspondence between Jesus' demanding saying at 5:38–39 and his total commitment to embodying that peaceableness in the Garden of Gethsemane would confirm that Matthew's impression of Jesus,

---

61. Again, Matt 28:20 reveals the fundamental role of teaching for Jesus' own disciples.

62. Hays, *Moral Vision*, 109.

63. Ibid.

64. Hays, *Moral Vision*, 110. Luz, *Matthew*, 1:277–80, divides interpreters into two broad camps, "rigoristic" and "moderating." See also Burridge, *Imitating Jesus*, 222, whose central contention is that "ancient biographical narratives were written to encourage the imitation of their central subject." Cf. Burridge, *Imitating Jesus*, 73. The "impossible ideal" hinted at above is part of the hoary tradition of finding ways to dispense with the normative force of a simpler interpretation of the sermon. Hays, *Moral Vision*, 320, identifies six common strategies used to slip free from Jesus' costly demands. I cannot summarize each position here, nor can I show their fatal weaknesses, but it is possible to attain a sense of the strategies by giving them shorthand titles: impossible ideal (i.e., a vision of life in the *fulfilled* kingdom); interim ethic (i.e., for Jesus' immediate disciples); the innocent third party exception (i.e., Jesus forbids self-defense but not violence in defense of others); "council of perfection" (i.e., only for those of a special gifting or vocation); impossible demands which produce a recognition of sin and need for grace (i.e., another version of "impossible ideal"); contingent commands (i.e., Jesus forbade very specific actions, such as taking an enemy to court). Hays, *Moral Vision*, 320, remarks that careful exegesis shows "none of these proposals renders a satisfactory account of Matthew's theological vision."

from beginning to end, was shaped by Jesus' unreserved commitment to a non-violent encounter with evil.

The Mount of Olives in the Old Testament

While it is undoubtedly the case that the Mount of Olives, on which the Garden of Gethsemane lies, was a logical place for Jesus to spend his last time of prayer before his arrest—since it is situated between Bethany (where he and his disciples spent the evening, 26:6) and Jerusalem (where he spent his last days teaching in the Temple precincts)—there is also a minor, albeit significant, symbolic resonance to this location. The prophet Zechariah undeniably informs Matthew's account of Jesus' last days in and near Jerusalem, and although the "day of the Lord" announced by Zechariah is the only clear instance where the Mount of Olives serves as a landmark for an impending judgment, its geographical significance is worth exploring before examining Matthew's use of the mountain and Jesus' final moments spent there.

For its proximity to the temple mount and its equally imposing presence east of Jerusalem, the Mount of Olives plays a surprisingly minor role in the Old Testament, with only two clear references.[65] Second Samuel 15:30 reports of the time King David fled Jerusalem and ascended the Mount of Olives in distress in response to Absalom's rebellion. The only other time the mountain is mentioned explicitly is Zechariah 14:4–5, when YHWH's "feet shall stand on the Mount of Olives" on "that day"—i.e., the Day of YHWH.[66] Zechariah is important not least because a number of themes reappear in Matthew's gospel: that YHWH/the Lord will become king over all the earth (Zech 14:9) matches, *mutatis mutandis*, the *titulus* affixed to Jesus' cross (Matt 27:29, 37);[67] the absence of traders in the Temple (Zech 14:21) is echoed by Jesus' driving out those who sold and bought, changed money, and sold pigeons (Matt 21:12–13); the 30 shekels of silver (Zech

---

65. Heard, "Mount of Olives," 5:13.

66. The expression *that day* ("ἐκεῖνος ἡμέρα") appears in Matthew at least six times in the sense of a day of judgment—not necessarily the last judgment. See 7:22; 24:19, 22, 22, 29, 36. It also features positively in 26:29 as the day of the messianic feast. Somewhat surprisingly, ἡμέρα (*day*) is never modified by the genitives κυρίου (*lord*), θεοῦ (*God*), or Χριστοῦ (*Christ*) in the gospels.

67. If the eschatological King of the Jews was to be seen as the rightful king of all the nations as well.

11:12–13) which are thrown into the temple treasury find their mirror in the money Judas received to betray Jesus (Matt 26:15; 27:9); and of course the prediction of the king's entry on a donkey (Zech 9:9) is quoted to demonstrate Jesus' entry into Jerusalem as fulfillment of prophecy (Matt 21:5). Since Matthew repeatedly alludes to Zechariah, it is worth querying what sorts of characteristics the "day of YHWH" might have for a devout reader of Zechariah who likewise recognized Jesus' connections to the Zecharian strand of tradition in Matthew's presentation.

The theme of "that day" or "day of the Lord" appears 17 times in the final three chapters of Zechariah, saturating the climax of Zechariah's prophecy with images of divine judgment at YHWH's return to Jerusalem. The judgment is primarily reserved for the nations that have banded together against Jerusalem and whom the Lord will seek to destroy (Zech 12:9). At Zechariah 14:12, the gruesome judgment of those who wage war against Jerusalem is revealed: "Their flesh shall rot while they are still on their feet; their eyes shall rot in their sockets, and their tongues shall rot in their mouths." In contrast, on "that day" a cleansing fountain is made available to Jerusalem's inhabitants (Zech 13:1). The Day of the Lord will see Judah become "like a flaming torch among sheaves," devouring all the surrounding peoples who had previously "come together against" Jerusalem (Zech. 12:6, 12:3). The result of YHWH's coming will be his enthronement as king over all the earth (14:9) and the divine establishment of the security of Jerusalem (14:11). In short, disaster will befall Jerusalem's enemies and the Lord will return the fortunes of Zion. And the strategic geographic marker where the Lord will plant his feet on that day; the Mount of Olives.

Although the evidence is merely suggestive, another "messianic" figure of the first century seems to have capitalized on the role of the Mount in Zechariah. The figure whose possible appropriation of the same tradition has come down to us through Josephus (and probably Acts 21:38) is the Egyptian "false-prophet" who led a band of followers to the Mount of Olives before his planned advance on the city "to force (βιάζεσθαι) an entrance into Jerusalem" and attempt to overpower the Roman garrison there (*War* 2:261–63). He led his 30,000 "dupes" "by a circuitous route from the desert" to the Mount of Olives.[68] Predictably, his plan was anticipated by

---

68. 30,000 could be, of course, another exaggeration by Josephus. Whether Luke is closer to the real number in Acts 21:38 (4,000) is immaterial to the present argument—however many he duped, it was a large group assembled on the Mount of Olives waiting for a divinely assisted collapse of Roman military power. What is curious is that the narrative in *Ant.* 20:167–72 implies he gathered people *in* Jerusalem, before leading them

the Roman procurator Felix, who went with his heavy infantry to "meet" them. The Egyptian escaped; many of his followers did not. The account in Josephus' writings is so compact that it provides little to connect this Egyptian false-prophet to the Zecharian image of YHWH standing on the Mount of Olives, but the considerable lack of references to the mountain in both the Old Testament and Josephus at least raises the question of whether other first-century Jews anticipated a coming, eschatological judgment (*especially of foreign occupiers*) as relating in some fashion to the strategically important Mount of Olives.

One Final Temptation—The Cup of Suffering or the Sword of Insurrection

Bearing in mind the Egyptian false-prophet and the imagery of Zechariah, the setting of Jesus' arrest as a *bandit* (λῃστής) on the Mount of Olives (26:55; cf. 27:38, 44) adds a final degree of tension that is resolved only when Jesus' disciples abandon him (26:56). If revolutionary activity is sustained as a real possibility for Jesus and his disciples, at least two aspects of the arrest scene are clarified. The sword wielding actions of "one who was with Jesus" (26:51) demonstrate his incomprehension of Jesus' thoroughgoing commitment to non-violence while simultaneously proving that disciple's grasp of what is necessary to enthrone a king announcing a new kingdom. Holding out the possibility for revolution also explains the disciples' delay in abandoning Jesus—it is not until *after* he has disarmed his follower(s) that they abandon him. Knowing no other options for how to defend him except through the force of weapons, his disciples flee.[69] Rare is the commentator, however, who seriously considers what the passing of the cup would have entailed. Davies and Allison, for example, allow that Jesus considers the possibility that the cup could be removed, but "his prayer reveals that he has set aside his own will." At most, Jesus' prayer for "a route around suffering" elevates the pathos of Matthew's audience for Jesus; it does not indicate a real possibility.[70] The alternative that Jesus

---

through the desert to the Mount of Olives. Why lead a rebel group *out* of the city if it is the same city the group wishes to take unless the Egyptian leader put greater significance on the Mount of Olives than Josephus' narrative seems to indicate?

69. Hauerwas, *Matthew*, 225.

70. Davies and Allison, *Matthew*, 3:496, 502. Luz, *Matthew*, 3:396, asks what the prayer means, but focuses entirely on the meaning of the cup rather than on its potential to be set aside.

considers is not taken seriously; what would it mean for the cup to pass by Jesus? Are we to envisage Jesus returning quietly to Galilee to live out the rest of his days in acquiescent peace?[71]

Although he focuses on Luke's account, John Howard Yoder draws on the other evangelists as well to show that Jesus was tempted, one last time, by the option of "messianic violence."[72] In Matthew 26:52–54, Jesus rejects the disciples' immediate response to a threat against him; after admonishing the sword-wielding disciple[73] to put his weapon away, Jesus warns "all who take the sword will perish by the sword. Do you think that I cannot appeal to my Father, and he will at once send me more than twelve legions of angels? But how then would the scriptures be fulfilled, which say it must happen in this way?"[74] If Matthew's audience is meant to envisage the scale of twelve legions of angels, Jesus reprimands his disciples for not realizing he could have more than seventy thousand celestial "troops" at his command for a violent revolution. This show of force easily could have removed the cup from Jesus' hands, but he finally chose not to employ such force against his adversaries.[75] Instead, the gnome of 26:52b is employed by Jesus to eschew violence, even in defense of his own innocence. Luz concludes:

71. Although dated, Trocmé, *Jesus and the Nonviolent Revolution*, 103, noted that "Jesus seemingly had only two alternatives: violent resistance or flight into the desert— the Zealot temptation of force or the Essene option of withdrawal. But Jesus chose to do neither."

72. Yoder, *Politics of Jesus*, 46. An almost identical argument could be mounted for the temptation to disavow any offensive remarks or behavior and return to a quiet life, as mentioned above. However, earlier in Matthew's narrative (4:1–11) he had already tabled the temptation to exercise global rule, which Jesus rejected not in principle but because the means to rule was idolatrous (4:8–10). Jesus also rejected Peter's way of assessing the value of a suffering (rather than conquering) Messiah (16:23). Here Matthew provides a glimpse into what other route around suffering he might have taken (26:53). This narrative thread in Matthew speaks in favor of seeing his temptation in the garden as being a temptation to use force.

73. Only the Gospel of John identifies the sword bearer as Peter (John 18:10).

74. It could be that Matthew is concerned only with the necessity of Jesus' death, and not with the non-violent praxis of his disciples. However, given the programmatic nature of Matthew's Sermon on the Mount and the Jesus' command to teach the nations "to obey everything I have commanded you" (28:20), it seems fair to recognize more than one referent in 26:54. True, it plainly refers to Jesus' death, but it equally may also refer to coming of God's kingdom without duplicating the world's violence.

75. Luz, *Matthew*, 3:420n80, notes: "According to 2 Kgs 19:35 and 2 Macc 15:22 a single angel killed 185,000 men in the Assyrian army." N.B., the *entire* Roman imperial army consisted of approximately twenty-five legions. By these standards, one angel (much less twelve legions of them) could annihilate the *entire* Roman army. For other

For Jesus the consequence derived from this maxim is *absolute defenselessness and absolute rejection of violence.* He himself offers no resistance at his arrest, and he also forbids the same to his disciples. With the gnome of v. 52b that he offers as a justification, *his behavior becomes a general rule for Christians.* Verse 52 reminds the reader of the fifth antithesis of the Sermon on the Mount: "Do not resist the evildoer" (5:39). With his own behavior Jesus illustrates what that means—*radical, uncompromising pacifism that has no room even for self-defense.*[76]

Poignantly, Jesus' last instructions to his disciples before his death in Matthew's gospel recapitulate one of the first lessons he gave them: "Do not resist an evildoer . . . love your enemies . . . so that you may be children of your father in heaven" (Matt 5:39, 44–45). With his familiar words to them ringing in their ears, Jesus' faithfulness to his own teaching would be tested before his disciples in the final hours of his life.

The Misunderstanding of the Crowds— Bearing Swords and Clubs

It is an ironic or perhaps tragic twist that the crowd that comes to seize Jesus bears swords and clubs, in spite of his teaching prohibiting violent retaliation (Matt 26:47; Mark 14:43; cf. John 18:3 "weapons"). Yet it must be seen as confirmation that the possibility for revolutionary activity on Jesus' part had not been ruled out by the chief priests and elders who sent the crowd to arrest Jesus. When the crowd arrives, the evangelists attribute to Jesus a question he addresses to the crowd: "Have you come out with swords and clubs to arrest me as though I were a revolutionary?"[77] Jesus' question identifies the tragic irony of the situation. The one who taught openly by day and publicly drove out of the temple the real *bandits* or *robbers* (λῃστῶν) (Matt 21:13; cf. Mark 11:17; Luke 19:46) is now being seized under the cover of darkness as if *he* was the revolutionary/bandit (λῃστής). Although the gospels would remain cryptic or dismissive of this charge in the context of Jesus' trial, they each record the mocking title nailed to Jesus'

texts describing angelic armies, see 2 Macc 5:2–3; 10:29–31; 1QM 12.4–5, 8–9.

76. Luz, *Matthew*, 3:419 (emphasis added).

77. Translation is the NRSV with one change—my *revolutionary* for NRSV's *bandit*. See *BDAG*, 594, #2. The wording in the Synoptic Gospels is identical save Luke's omission of "to capture/arrest me" at the end of the question.

cross, which indicated the degree of suspicion that the Roman authorities had regarding Jesus' intentions—the "King of the Jews" crucified alongside of two other bandits (λῃσταί).[78]

CHALLENGES TO A PORTRAIT OF A NON-VIOLENT JESUS IN MATTHEW'S GOSPEL

Despite the evidence for the picture of Jesus we have traced thus far, there are several passages from Matthew's gospel that have the effect of attenuating this view of Jesus. Objections to a non-violent Jesus have ranged from the fantastic (S. G. F. Brandon's now widely discredited thesis, that Jesus and the earliest disciples were failed violent revolutionaries whose violence the early church excised from the tradition) to the more credible (Richard Horsley).[79] Where previous challenges to the picture of a non-violent Jesus focused on problematical sayings [e.g., "I have not come to bring peace but a sword" (Matt 10:34b)] or the incident at the temple (Matt 21:12–13),[80] recent objections have focused on the violence of the eschatological judgment envisaged by Jesus or (similarly) the violent endings of his parables, or again on his vituperative language directed against the "scribes and Pharisees" in contrast to his command to love enemies. We will first focus attention upon these latter objections that seem to offer more difficulties than those former passages which have traditionally been seen as problematical.

Jesus' Conflict with the Pharisees and His "Violent" Language

Matthew 23 is the prime example of Jesus' use of "violent" language against the scribes and Pharisees he so often finds himself in conflict with in the

---

78. For the title, cf. Matt 27:37; Mark 15:26; Luke 23:38; John 19:19. Matthew and Mark alone call the others crucified with Jesus bandits (λῃσταί), cf. Matt 27:38, 44; Mark 15:27. John (18:40) calls Barabbas a bandit (λῃστής).

79. Horsley limits the scope of Jesus' command to love enemies (and not to retaliate against them) to the local Galilean village setting, so that Jesus' teaching contains no general ethical principle. For a succinct critique of Horsley's position, see Hays, *Moral Vision*, 327–28, and my own treatment above.

80. I do not mean to suggest that these are pericopes that no longer continue to foster debate. On the contrary, they continue to be scrutinized from every possible angle. Indeed, I address both later in the chapter.

first gospel.[81] In this chapter alone, Jesus calls them hypocrites (23:3, 13, 15, 23, 25, 27, 28, 29); vain and prideful (23:5–7); blind and ignorant or deceived and deceiving guides (23:15–22); unjust, unmerciful, unfaithful (23:23); greedy and self-indulgent (23:25); lawless (23:28); self-deceived (23:30–31), snakes/a brood of vipers (23:33); and murderers (23:34, 35). Although the laundry list of names Jesus calls these opponents is quite acerbic (and arguably belongs to that hard-to-define category of violent speech), the real violence of this chapter is found in the "woes" he pronounced.[82] It is not only Jesus' pronouncement of woes, but the deplorable practice of some subsequent Christian interpreters taking up these warn-

81. It is worth noting that Matthew's redactional interest is quite evident here. Luz (*Matthew*, 3:170–71; 1:49–56) proposes that the painful, recent parting of the ways accounts best for the "severity of the polemic" in Matthew 23, and that the best way forward in dealing with the tragic *Wirkungsgeschichte* is to engage in "explicit and public *theological criticism of its contents* [Sachkritik]" (Luz, *Matthew*, 3:175). In what might be a most important interpretive step of stalling agreement with Matthew's text is Luz's recognition that "a text that had been written for a shaken and suffering Jewish Christian community became the theological possession of other people who were neither Jews nor suffering" (*Matthew*, 3:177). Such a shift calls for great care when approaching the text today.

82. I do not dismiss the challenge that Jesus' language in Matthew 23 presents difficulties for claiming Jesus was non-violent, especially when such invective seems to evince Jesus' own hypocrisy regarding the way one speaks to or treats enemies. Cf. Matt 5:22, 44–48. However, I find it crucially important to emphasize Jesus' own choice not to elevate his violent discourse into the key of violent action. The *potential* effects of Matthew's text *must be distinguished from* the actions of Jesus. Jacobs, afterword to *Must Christianity Be Violent?*, 234, insists a distinction between violence and persuasion obtains at just this point: "Persuasion simply is *not* force, and this can be clearly illustrated by the frequency with which people resist it. That is, after all, what makes force force, violence violence: irresistibility. We do not increase our understanding of the world by doing away with the distinction between irresistible acts of force and eminently resistible acts of suasion." Much more deserves to be written here, but I would insist that Matthew's gospel and the historical Jesus (or even Jesus as he was remembered) should be carefully distinguished here. I agree with Amy-Jill Levine ("Anti-Judaism," 19n26) that anti-Jewish polemic, whatever the mitigating circumstances, is deplorable "if that polemic leads to violence or hatred." Despite being convinced by her essay that there are indeed anti-Jewish *elements* in the Gospel of Matthew, I am finally more readily able to endorse Warren Carter's careful response to Levine ("Response," 47–62). Carter, "Response," 62, writes: "*My fear is that parts of Matthew can be construed as anti-some-forms-of-Judaism by some readers at some times. My great joy is not all parts, not all Judaisms, and not by all readers.*" Carter's revision of Levine's thesis allows one to accept that (Christian) appropriation of certain Matthean texts has led to violence in the past, while maintaining that Matthew's own narrative and theological program contains within itself the means to deconstruct or critique the validity of such readings. Levine, "Anti-Judaism," 11, fairly upbraids interpreters who domesticate Matthew's text by placing the blame for anti-Jewish effects of the gospel on readers rather than on the author of the first gospel.

ings as a guide to the eschatological destination of Jews *qua* Jews which comes to have a violent effect.[83] In Matthew 23, Jesus fixes his critique on the "scribes and Pharisees, *hypocrites!*" The leaders of Israel, and more specifically the leaders who "do not practice what they teach" (23:3), are the ones whom Jesus skewers. In fact, Jesus tells the disciples and the crowd to indeed "do whatever they teach you and follow it" since they sit on Moses' seat (23:2–3). What is deplorable (from the perspective of Matthew 23) is the duplicity of upholding the Torah from Moses' seat and yet failing miserably to live according to it, ignoring the "weightier matters of justice, mercy, and faith," or indeed the failure to recognize the presence among them of the author of Torah who laments: "How often have I desired to gather your children together as a hen gathers her brood under her wings, and you were not willing" (23:37).

The woes that Jesus announces do not seem to be final, to leave no room for repentance, but the course does seem already to have been determined—the camel has already been swallowed (23:24), turning back now would be more than distasteful, it would be nothing less than dangerous to one's socio-economic position in society. However, appropriating Matthew 23 to justify a violent "reading" of Jesus (or indeed, to justify violent treatment of Jesus' "enemies" by Christians) would be to make the error of reading the present chapter in light of Jesus' later rejection and crucifixion.[84] In other words, one should not read Matthew 23 with an a priori view that "the Jews" will reject Jesus and kill him; Jesus' severe comments don't come during his resurrection appearances, but before his passion commences. More important still is the recognition that "Jesus condemns the scribes and Pharisees from a position of weakness. . . . Christians betray Jesus when they make judgments—like those that Jesus makes against the scribes and Pharisees—from positions of power that transform those judgments into violent and murderous actions rather than attempts to call our brothers and sisters to a better life."[85] While it is true that Jesus' words in

---

83. Luz, *Matthew* 3:174–75, 177, asserts that Matthew 23 historically played "a relatively small role" in Christian anti-Jewish polemic. However, the text as a whole "*is a betrayal of Jesus' commandment to love one's enemies*" and should remain important theologically today not "because it reveals God's truth but because *it exposes human reality—yes, human sin.*"

84. Luz, *Matthew*, 3:169, offers a different caution: violent actions justified on the basis of Matthew 23 would also make the mistake of confusing genres, for Matt 23:15–22, 27–39 has "no direct parenetic significance."

85. Hauerwas, *Matthew*, 197.

Matthew 23 cause concern in the post-Holocaust era, it would be a mistake to assume that Jesus' hostile language exceeds the scope of other Hebrew prophets before him who likewise warned Israel's leaders, political and religious, of the march towards destruction they were upon.[86] Notwithstanding his hostile language, it is equally clear that Matthew maintains that Jesus deliberately chose to confront his contemporaries *without taking action which physically threatened or violated them.* But this brings us to the other major challenge to viewing Jesus as a "peaceable" messiah in Matthew's gospel.

Violent Eschatological Judgment in the Parables of Jesus (Matthew 24–25)

Matthew's gospel contains another theme that is potentially challenging or deconstructive to the view of Jesus as the inaugurator of a peaceable kingdom. The violence of Matthew's eschatology creates a tension that threatens the enduring priority of peace and non-violence in Matthew's narrative. The problem arises chiefly in the way God is portrayed in the parables of chapters 24–25 [22:1–14 is worth discussing too]. An objection may be that though I have depicted Matthew's consistent portrait of *Jesus* as a practitioner of non-violence, does the image of *God* that Matthew attributes to Jesus cause intractable theological tension? If God is ultimately (in eschatological judgment) violent, what warrant is there for Jesus' disciples to be non-violent when they are meant to imitate their heavenly father (cf. Matt 5:48)? Does the "proleptic moral suasion" of eschatological judgment ultimately topple the call to imitate Jesus in his own non-violent action?[87]

I think the most honest way to proceed through this difficulty is to 1) identify those images which lead to the tension; 2) and address why these admittedly violent images are a) not problematical for Matthew's audience[88] and b) not normative for the conduct of Jesus' disciples. The fact

---

86. Levine, "Anti-Judaism," 26, significantly summarizes: "I cannot support the view that the First Gospel represents prophetic polemic or reveals the hermeneutics of prophetic criticism. *Even if these terms are appropriate for a study of the historical Jesus—and I believe they are*—they are not appropriate for the interpretation of the Gospel of Matthew" (emphasis added).

87. Neville, "Toward a Teleology of Peace," 135.

88. This is different, of course, from addressing whether the apparent inconsistency is problematical for modern interpreters.

that eschatological judgment looks violent in an overwhelming amount of Christian and Jewish literature demands that we come to terms with the expectation of divine violence at the eschaton among virtually all early Christian authors. What remains to be seen is whether the anticipation of such violence "taints" non-violent practices. Does non-violence lose some of its ideological force when it is motivated in part by violent eschatological judgment?

What Are the Violent Images?

If we scan back a bit further than Matthew 24–25, leapfrogging over Matthew 23, we come to the so-called parable of the Wedding Banquet at 22:1–14. In this "unsettling" and inconsistent story,[89] the king whose in- vitation is refused becomes enraged (ὠργίσθη) at the personal slight and the murder of some of his slaves, so he sends troops to destroy the offend- ers and set fire to the city (Matt 22:7). At the end of the parable, the king severely punishes an invited guest for failing to attend in the proper gar- ment.[90] The king commands his servants to throw the guest into "darkness, where there will be weeping and gnashing of teeth" (22:13), phrasing that is unmistakable in its reference to final judgment in Matthew's gospel. The picture of the king is inescapably violent. Scores are slaughtered at his com- mand (whether the provocation is proportional doesn't seem to be an issue that concerned Matthew or his audience), and one guest who assumed his fitness for the wedding feast is expelled, not simply denied admission. The king is uncompromising and, if not graceless, quite severe in his dealing with those who offended him or murdered his slaves.

This violent image of the king (i.e., God) is extended in Matthew 24. Matthew alludes to the expectation of doom in 24:30, where the tribes of the earth will mourn on the day of judgment ("the Son of Man coming on the clouds of heaven")—presumably because they are cognisant of their im- pending judgment. No details are offered, however. The image is reinforced allusively too in the reference to the days of Noah, when God destroyed almost everything that inhabited the earth. Credit for drowning virtually every living creature does not mark one out as a non-violent God.

89. Luz, *Matthew*, 3:47.

90. Attempts to situate this story in an alleged common cultural practice (i.e., there was an appropriate "wedding garment") have failed. See Luz, *Matthew*, 3:55–56.

The imagery returns in the parable of the wise and wicked slave (24:45–51), when the master[91] returns only to find the slave whom he entrusted with caring for the household to be abusing his fellow slaves and eating and drinking with drunkards.[92] The master "will cut him in pieces (διχοτομήσει) and put him with the hypocrites, where there will be weeping and gnashing of teeth." Rather than translating the distressing διχοτομέω in a figurative or metaphorical sense, it is better to understand the verb in the most literal sense: an object hewn in two. The fate of the wicked slave has many grisly precedents in antiquity (though few are described with the same verb), and the image thus understood points to a violent end for the wicked slave.[93] Better to admit here that Matthew leaves us an extremely violent image, one that puts a point on the challenge to the presentation of Jesus as a non-violent messiah.

From this parable, the violent images begin to descend from the "peak" of a slave being hewn asunder. The "wicked and lazy" slave of 25:14–30 is merely thrown into outer darkness, the master's judgment being portrayed as stern and violent, at least indirectly so.[94] Those apportioned with the goats in the so-called parable of the last judgment (25:31–46) are cast into the eternal fire that was "prepared for the devil and his angels." Matthew doesn't draw attention to vivid details of judgment, but again, the judgment is *at least* indirectly violent. We must admit that in all of these passages, the actor employs violence after judging those characters deemed deficient in the narrative. Sometimes the action is direct and clear (e.g., the wicked slave sawn in two by the enraged master), other times the violence is in-

---

91. Luz, *Matthew*, 3:225, points out that the master is understood to be Jesus in his role as eschatological judge. The master's *return* is delayed. Although this imagery paints Jesus (rather than God) as violent, I include it in this section since it addresses eschatological rather than temporal judgment.

92. Why the latter charge should disturb Matthew is puzzling—Jesus himself is accused of the same scandalous behavior. See Matt 11:18–19. Although I am contending in this section with the image of a violent judge, it is at least worth pointing out that one of the key infractions of the wicked slave is that he begins to violently beat (τύπτειν) his fellow slaves (24:49).

93. See, e.g., 1 Sam 15:33; (LXX) Amos 1:3; Sus 55, 59 [= LXX Dan 13:55, 59]; 3 *Bar* 16:2; Heb 11:37; Epictetus *Diss.* 3.22.3; Suetonius, *Calig.*, 27.

94. There are a variety of issues that complicate the interpretation of this parable, and in other circumstances I would give to it more careful attention. However I have chosen to move quickly over this parable since the violent imagery is less compelling that the imagery in the surrounding parables—that is, the challenge of this parable's imagery is less pressing than the imagery of a master who saws his servants into pieces.

direct (e.g., the king sending troops to burn and destroy murderers; the son of man sending the accursed into eternal punishment 25:41), often the details are left to the imagination (e.g., eternal fire; eternal punishment; throw him into outer darkness).

Why Are These Violent Images Not Normative for Jesus' Disciples?

To claim, as I want to do, that these violent images do not pose an intractable problem for Matthew or his audience requires careful nuancing. First, I do not think it is enough merely to recognize that violent imagery was so commonplace that images of a violent God simply fit the pattern expected by Matthew or Matthew's audience. If this is the case, we could simply claim that Matthew's conflicting imagery simultaneously bears witness to Matthew's violent "inheritance" even as he preserves the memory of Jesus' non-violent teaching and praxis. Frankly, this is easiest way to deal with the tension, and several scholars have addressed the issue accordingly, even if they go about rereading Matthew in different ways.[95] Matthew's violent imagery is a relic of violent views of God which are challenged by the non-violent activity of Jesus. But I think it is necessary to parry the charge of conflicting views of God's activity in another way.

It may be true that violence ultimately colors Matthew's view of the judgment of the world, but one constant is that if violence is eventually used, it is God alone (or Jesus *as eschatological judge*) who employs violence in eschatological judgment. This is a crucial restriction placed on the use of violence by Matthew. We might appropriately call this a "theological" or even "ontological" restriction—for Matthew, violence is only appropriately employed by God or the eschatological judge; it is never condoned for humans. Humans are not God and by definition lack the proper ontological resources to make just judgments regarding the eschatological fate of the cosmos. One advantage of this restriction that is evident in Matthew (and discounting for a moment its potential for abuse) is that it allows Jesus' disciples presently to eschew violent retaliation since *God* will be the agent of any vengeance on the last day. Eschatological violence is reserved for God alone so that the "disciples of Jesus are bound by his teaching to confront evil, injustice and violence nonviolently."[96] It is this very assurance of the

95. See, e.g., Neville, "Toward a Teleology of Peace," 131–61. Reid, "Violent Endings," 237–55. See also Carter, "Constructions of Violence," esp. 98–102.

96. Neville, "Toward a Teleology of Peace," 149. Cf. Davies and Allison, *Matthew*,

eschatological judgment of God that affords to the Christian a non-violent response to enemies.[97]

Matthew, if he recognized the tension, does not seek to answer why it is justifiable for the heavenly father to employ violence while creatures are meant to refrain from doing violence. Matthew partly grounds the restriction on violence for disciples in the ontological difference between God and humanity, and disciples are provided constructive guidance by the teaching and activity of Jesus *before the day of judgment*. Still, the danger of the imagery's "proleptic moral suasion" all too easily overcomes the decisive gap that a retributive-apocalyptic worldview is meant to create between God and God's human representatives as agents of violent judgment.

This ontological restriction does not, however, mean that disciples are not meant to imitate their father in heaven (Matt 5:43–48). Rather, throughout Matthew's gospel, disciples are tasked with performing actions that are in their control: to turn the other cheek, to give their coat and lend without expecting anything in return. They will be rewarded (to move to a different parable, 25:31–46) for making pragmatic gestures of provision, for clothing the naked, feeding the hungry, visiting the infirm and prisoner, and giving a drink to one in need. Matthew's implied reader discerns that a disciple's ethical norms are to be governed by Jesus' teaching and actions *during his earthly life*, not from his (as yet only partially disclosed) role as eschatological cosmic judge.

Although David Neville approaches the problem differently than I have here (drawing especially on Matthew's Immanuel Christology), he too highlights an ontological difference (though he doesn't write using the term) that pertains at just this point. Neville suggests that "the memory of Jesus' nonviolent message and mission, which disciples are instructed to emulate, should be privileged over whatever lies beyond the capacity of any human being to know. As incarnation precedes the *eschaton* historically,

---

1:540: "So the law of reciprocity is not utterly repudiated but only taken out of human hands to be placed in divine hands."

97. Carter, "Constructions of Violence," 100; cf. Volf, *Exclusion and Embrace*, 302: "The close association between human nonviolence and the affirmation of God's vengeance in the New Testament is telling . . . Without entrusting oneself to the God who judges justly, it will hardly be possible to follow the crucified Messiah and refuse to retaliate when abused. *The certainty of God's just judgment at the end of history is the presupposition for the renunciation of violence in the middle of it.* The divine system of judgment is not the flip side of the human reign of terror, but a necessary correlate of human nonviolence" (emphasis added).

incarnation likewise takes precedence over the *eschaton* epistemologically and ethically."[98]

Matthew 28:18–20 (especially the clause "teaching them to obey all that I have commanded you") demarcates the right practice of disciples from the resurrection of Jesus until the "end of the age"; casting aspersions and violently expelling unbelievers is not commanded by Jesus, but loving enemies and turning the other cheek is. In short, Jesus' disciples should not act as if the eschatological *telos* of "opponents" is a certain or foregone conclusion, or indeed a decision that they are even capable of making.[99]

In sum, the violent images of God and/or Jesus at the end of Matthew are real, that is, they should not be explained away. There is a notable tension between a non-violent messiah and a violent world judge, but I have tried to show that for Matthew, the tension is held, significantly, at just the point no human can properly circumvent. Judgment (expressed in Matthew's gospel in part through eschatological violence) is reserved for the consummation of time. And the most crucial factor in proscribing violence for Matthew's audience(s) (and by extension, contemporary disciples of Jesus) is that consistently throughout Matthew's gospel, violence is condemned when it is employed by humans and justifiably used by God alone (or the eschatological son of man).[100] Violence is taken off the table completely for Jesus' disciples. That followers of Jesus have subsequently ignored the temporal and theological limits of violence does not mean that the limits are not there in Matthew's gospel.

A Contemporary Reassessment—Is There a Problem with Matthew's Violent God?

One final tension I wish to address is that the preceding discussion would seem to challenge the view that God, in view of Jesus' non-violent life, is

98. Neville, "Toward a Teleology of Peace," 155–56. That is, Neville identifies what humans can know, namely, the teaching and praxis of the earthly Jesus; and he identifies what humans are not privileged to participate in, namely, judgment which is eschatological in nature.

99. See Collins, "Zeal of Phinehas," 3–21, in which the author concludes that certitude is the hallmark of biblically "sanctioned" violence.

100. This is true, for example, of the violence used in the parables discussed above. So the violent treatment of the messengers in Matt 22:6 is contrasted with the violence of the king in 22:7. The violence of the wicked slave (24:49) is contrasted with the violence of the master (24:51). Cf. Carter, "Constructions of Violence," 102.

characteristically non-violent. I have in fact tried to avoid describing God in this way, but it is a fairly understandable corollary to the view that Jesus was non-violent, and characteristically so. If Jesus eschews violence, but at the end of history God and Jesus do not, then is non-violence constitutive of the character of the God Christians worship, or is non-violence better understood as a temporally restricted virtue, a (political) practice, not a character trait?

In an effort to maintain some academic integrity (and at the risk of weakening the force of my argument), I must confess that I think the Christian Scriptures, though polyphonic on many themes, seem to suggest that non-violence is a chosen politic, not something that is constitutive of (the triune) God's character.[101] If I were to restrict my treatment to Matthew's gospel, I would certainly have to say that Matthew assumes that violence (by God, in eschatological judgment) is not inherently incompatible with a view that maintains the non-violent politics of Jesus' earthly life and the life of the church before the return of the Son of Man.[102] Moreover, I don't see any reason to think that expanding the evidence to the rest of the New Testament would necessitate a change on this point—virtually every author imagined eschatological judgment, and it would be disingenuous to force those ancient Christian authors to say what I wish they had—that eschatological judgment is actualized without God's recourse to violence.

If I were to name an attribute (of God)[103] that explained the motivation for the non-violent politics of Matthew's Immanuel, surely I could do no better than to point to the patience of God for God's creation. Although vastly more could be made of this "genetic" mapping of the non-violent

101. To suggest otherwise would open the door to many "problems" with images of God in the Old Testament.

102. Let it be noted too that presenting the issue in this way also permits us to allow the possibility that the historical Jesus taught that eschatological judgment would be violent. That is, if instead of trying to maintain the dialectical tension that we find in Matthew's gospel, we deploy a judicious use of *Sachkritic* to create distance between our modern sensibilities about the effects of judgment language on the one hand, and the judgment language present in the gospel on the other hand, we would be forced to reconsider the issue if it can be demonstrated that the historical Jesus expressed similar views—that is, if it is not just Matthean redaction but the historical Jesus' actual teaching which gave rise to the problem in the first place. If so, (and I have no interest in traveling down that path in the current study), I am already in a position that does not threaten to undo the normative power of the politics of peace for the church prior to eschatological judgement.

103. Not in the classical sense of omnipotence, etc.

politics of God, I must leave further explicating to another project. What I will say though, is that in refusing to identify non-violence as a character-istic or attribute of God, I do not think we therefore surrender the ability to identify the *polity created by the gospel* as characteristically non-violent. That is, the church is not God. The church is called to imitate God not in God's being, but to imitate the one who fully discloses what it means to be humans in fellowship with God and with one another. I have tried to point to how a politics of peace is characteristic of the community gener-ated by the gospel that witnesses to the non-violent politics of Jesus' earthly ministry.

What I have attempted to do is bracket out, vis-à-vis the ethical praxis of the followers of Jesus, the violent judging activity of God in Matthew's gospel. I have identified the way in which Matthew (I suspect knowingly) motivated a non-violent politics within his community, and the two main motives are: 1) (on the positive side) the normative activity of Jesus in an-nouncing and inaugurating God's kingdom, and 2) (on the "negative" side) that violent action, if it is ever justifiable, is only appropriate to the one who is able to judge justly. Although retaining the tension may seem to some that I have not gone far enough in excising the potentially negative effects of judgment language in Matthew, I am increasingly (not *fully*) satis-fied with this solution, especially given the sober warnings of Miroslav Volf from his profound work, *Exclusion and Embrace.*

> My thesis that the practice of nonviolence requires a belief in divine vengeance will be unpopular with many Christians, espe-cially theologians in the West. To the person who is inclined to dismiss it, I suggest imagining that you are delivering a lecture in a war zone (which is where a paper that underlies this chapter was originally delivered). Among your listeners are people whose cities and villages have been first plundered, then burned and lev-eled to the ground, whose daughters and sister have been raped, whose fathers and brothers have had their throats slit. The topic of the lecture: a Christian attitude towards violence. The thesis: we should not retaliate since God is perfect noncoercive love. Soon you would discover that it takes the quiet of a suburban home for the birth of the thesis that human nonviolence corresponds to God's refusal to judge. In a scorched land, soaked in the blood of the innocent, it will invariably die. And as one watches it die, one will do well to reflect about many other pleasant captivities of the liberal mind.[104]

104. Volf, *Exclusion and Embrace,* 304.

To repudiate the view that Christian non-violence corresponds to God's refusal to judge is not to reject in principle the propriety of a politics of peace for the church. Instead, it is to reorient the church's politics of peace around the disclosure of the church's vocation to be witnesses to God's patience in a world that is too eager to settle conflict through the impatience of violent coercion.

Other Challenges to a Pacific View of Jesus (Matthew 10 and the Temple Action)

Matthew 10:34

"Do not think that I have come to bring peace to the earth; I have not come to bring peace, but a sword." Isolated from its literary context, Matthew 10:34 would seem to vitiate the claims made about Jesus' commitment to non-violence.[105] Read in light of the surrounding discourse, however, the tension dissolves. Jesus' saying comes on the heals of his instructions warning the disciples of the opposition they will face on their missionary journeys, and his pithy simile for his disciples' vulnerability ("See, I am sending you out like *sheep* into the midst of wolves; so be wise as serpents and innocent as doves") demonstrates that at 10:34, Jesus envisages the disciples at the tip of the sword, rather than being the bearers of it. Matthew 10:17–23 strikes the same note: Jesus' disciples will be handed over and flogged, betrayed and hated on account of Jesus' name. Rather than providing a foothold for an argument for Jesus' violent politics, Matthew 10:34 and its surrounding verses contribute to the non-violent picture of Jesus and his disciples by envisaging the opposition they will face without recourse to violent resistance.

The Temple Incident (Matthew 21:12–17)

Whenever the subject of Jesus' peaceableness is discussed, questions about the incident at the temple invariably arise. Does this scene not, at minimum, put a question mark by Jesus' commitment to non-violence? The secondary literature on Matthew 21:12–13 is voluminous, and we cannot hope

---

105. Not surprisingly, Matt 10:34 appears as the frontispiece on Brandon's *Jesus and the Zealots*.

to cover every issue here. But what is required here is an account of why the incident at the temple, particularly as it is crafted by Matthew, fails to raise serious objections to the portrait of Jesus that I have presented thus far.

To begin with, Matthew's characters appear to be unimpressed by the "violent" part of Jesus' actions. Jesus entered the temple, drove out traders (both sellers and buyers) and upended tables and chairs. What kindles the ire of the chief priests and scribes, however, is not this series of actions, but that Jesus heals the blind and the lame, and receives public acclamation because of it. Jesus' "violent" behavior in the temple merits no more attention in Matthew's narrative, so that Luz can claim his action "has no importance of its own in the Gospel of Matthew."[106] The account reads as though the chief priests and scribes were unaware of his "violent" actions, otherwise it is difficult to explain why they asked Jesus about the cries of children rather than about his authority to drive out the people who carried out what was, ostensibly, a legitimate service to the temple.[107]

Matthew evidently sees no (intractable) tension between the actions of Jesus in the temple and his teaching in 5:38–41. In a variety of scenarios in Matthew's gospel, the gentle Jesus (11:29; 21:5) demonstrates "forcible behaviour."[108] To evacuate Jesus of all forceful speech and action would be to denude him of his prophetic role, a role which many interpreters see to be at play in just this passage where he engages in a bit of prophetic "street theater."[109] Rather than serving as a warrant for "violent" behavior, the temple demonstration serves to highlight Jesus' alignment with the prophets who aggressively opposed the social and economic injustices that were rife even among God's people (e.g., Jer 7:1–15).[110]

In sum, the Gospel of Matthew, composed in a culture steeped in the ubiquity of violence, preserves the unmistakable fingerprints of violence in

106. Luz, *Matthew*, 3:10.

107. Ibid., 3:11, finds it historically "plausible that only a relatively obscure event would explain why neither the temple police nor the Roman garrison intervened." On the legitimate role of sellers and money changers (and agreement with Luz on the minor role of the incident), see Davies and Allison, *Matthew*, 3:136–37; and Catchpole, "'Triumphal' entry," 333.

108. Davies and Allison, *Matthew*, 3:137.

109. Cf. Jer 27:1–22 for one instance of symbolic "street theatre" by a Hebrew prophet. The term comes from Hays, *Moral Vision*, 334. See Hengel, *Was Jesus a Revolutionist?*, 16–17; Wright, *Jesus and the Victory*, 413–28; Davies and Allison, *Matthew*, 3:133–34; Catchpole, "'Triumphal' entry," 334.

110. On the economic advantages of the priestly class in Jerusalem, see Josephus *Ant.* 20:181, 205–6, and *As. Mos.* 7.6.

the stories its author recorded or composed. From beginning to end and across all levels of socio-economic relationships, Matthew's gospel reflects the acceptance of violent conflict as part of the status quo of human life. Invading our violent human history, Matthew's Immanuel, arriving as a vulnerable infant, interrupts the norms of human conflict by teaching and demonstrating that returning good for evil, loving enemies, forgiving, and welcoming strangers are the God of Israel's strategies for engaging enemies and conquering evil. God's empire comes humbly, not resisting Caesar's empire on Caesar's terms (like the zealots of the middle decades of the first century), but equally not blessing the politics of violence that uphold Caesar's rule and by which the nations "lord over" their subjects. Matthew's gospel consistently records the non-violent ethos of Jesus' teaching, and Jesus' actions cohere with his sayings. Despite the apparent difficulties created by the violent eschatological judgment recorded in Matthew's gospel, I submit that this eschatological assurance of judgment serves to preserve the non-violent witness of Jesus' first disciples. To borrow and extend James Dunn's phrase, what is clear is not just that Jesus was remembered, but that he was remembered as one who chose non-violent resistance instead of violent resistance, even when it cost him his life.

3

The Memory of a Non-Violent
Jesus in Paul's Letters

Paul's Use of the Jesus Tradition

If Matthew's gospel is representative of the early church's memory of Jesus as one who eschewed violence, Paul's letters hold the potential to push the evidence for this picture of Jesus earlier still. Surprisingly, little has been made of this particular continuity between Jesus and Paul, and the present chapter will be an attempt not just at filling this gap in the scholarly treatments already on offer, for I will also demonstrate that this particular continuity is one of the most salient features of early Christianity, Pauline or otherwise.

At the very real risk of falling into the familiar ruts of exploring the continuities (or in some cases divergences) between Jesus and Paul,[1] I want to revisit this issue by focusing on the very particular theme of non-violence. This theme offers a bypass of the traditional problems since one need not be confined to identifying allusions or quotations of Jesus Tradition alone; there is ostensibly a *corresponding pattern of non-violent behavior* that should be discernible as well. In the following pages, I want to highlight one place where Paul follows Jesus in both sayings (teaching) and actions (example) and explain why *this* particular continuity between Jesus

1. Perhaps the best recent treatment of the topic is Still (ed.), *Jesus and Paul Reconnected*.

and Paul is critically important for determining the place of non-violence in early Christianity.[2]

A Pauline Text That Advises Non-Retaliation

The most secure starting point for such an investigation is any Pauline text that exhorts his audience to refrain from retaliation when wronged by another. Although this will be our starting point, the theme of non-retaliation does not convey the full measure of Jesus' (and Paul's) non-violent ethics. Other themes that will demand our attention are reconciliation, peace, love, doing good, and Paul's own willingness to suffer abuse for the sake of his apostolic witness. We will focus initially on non-retaliation in Paul's letters and in his own example of non-retaliation in his willingness to suffer abuse for the sake of the gospel.

The proper response of Christians to mistreatment—whether from fellow Christians or outsiders—is clear in Paul's letters.[3] Before attempting to demonstrate Paul's continuity with Jesus Tradition, the texts in which Paul advocates non-retaliation should be brought into view. Only once the startling frequency of Paul's teaching is in view can one appreciate the material correspondence between Paul and Jesus on this issue.[4]

2. In view of the stated focus of this investigation, the three clearest instances of Paul's use of Jesus Tradition will be set aside. It is only in 1 Corinthians where Paul clearly quotes a saying of Jesus, and in each case the saying is unrelated to the issue of non-violence (1 Cor 7:10–11 (Mark 10:11–12; Matt 5:32); 9:14 (Luke 10:7; Matt 10:10); 11:23–25 (Luke 22:19–20; Mark 14:22–24). A similar conclusion must be drawn from the next two clearest examples—2 Cor 12:9 and 1 Thess 4:15—neither passage addresses the issue of non-violence directly. In order to investigate the continuity or divergence between Jesus and Paul on the theme of non-violence, one must examine those elements of Paul's letters which both address the theme of non-violence and arguably appear to be allusions to the teaching of or about Jesus.

3. Zerbe, *Non-Retaliation*, 211, writes that "references to proper behavior in response to injury or persecution appear in nearly all his extant letters and in a variety of genres."

4. I borrow the phrase *material correspondence* from Furnish, "The Jesus-Paul Debate," 46, though I use the term in this case to refer to one aspect of the correspondence between Jesus and Paul, whereas Furnish uses the phrase to refer to a broader range of issues.

- "Bless those who persecute you, bless and do not curse them." (Rom 12:14)

- "Do not repay anyone evil for evil, but take thought for what is noble in the sight of all. If it is possible, so far as it depends on you, live peaceably with all. Beloved, never avenge yourselves, but leave room for the wrath of God, for it is written: 'Vengeance is mine, I will repay says the Lord.' No, 'if your enemies are hungry, feed them, if they are thirsty, give them something to drink; for by doing this you will heap burning coals on their heads. Do not be overcome by evil, but overcome evil with good." (Rom 12:17–21)

- "When reviled, we bless; when persecuted, we endure; when slandered, we speak kindly." (1 Cor 4:12–13a)

- "Let your gentleness be known to everyone. The Lord is near." (Phil 4:5)

- "Be at peace among yourselves. And we urge you, beloved, to admonish the idlers, encourage the faint hearted, help the weak, be patient with all of them. See that none of you repays evil for evil, but always seek to do good to one another and to all. (1 Thess 5:13b–15)

- "As God's chosen ones, holy and beloved, clothe yourselves with compassion, kindness, humility, meekness, and patience. Bear with on another and, if anyone has a complaint against another, forgive each other, just as the Lord has forgiven you, so you also must forgive. Above all, clothe yourselves with love, which binds everything together in perfect harmony. And let the peace of Christ rule in your hearts." (Col 3:12–15a)[5]

Several more examples could be given, but these few examples bring the issue of non-retaliation to the table.[6] Clearly the issue of non-retaliation,

5. Apart from the Colossians quotation, the rest are in canonical order. I placed Colossians last only to flag that I am aware that the authorship of the letter is a disputed issue. It is not necessary to the present argument, but does show a continuation of Paul's emphasis if it was by one of his own "disciples."

6. Zerbe, *Non-Retaliation*, 214, for example, adds 2 Cor 6:3–10, where Paul's endurance through suffering is catalogued in terms of his *forbearance* (μακροθυμία) and *genuine love* (ἀγάπη ἀνυποκρίτῳ); Gal 5:16–24, where love, peace and forbearance are the fruit of the Spirit (which are at war with the works of the Flesh). On Galatians, see Chapter Four. Compare also 1 Cor 6:1–8, where the believer is exhorted to prefer being wronged to finding judicial vindication outside of the Christian assembly. Finally, 1 Corinthian 13 identifies love as forbearing, not counting evil, and enduring all things (13:4, 5, 7). The preponderance of the theme of enduring suffering in 1 Thessalonians suggests that Paul's church there was successfully resisting the urge to retaliate in the face of unjust suffering

as I have presented it here, includes far more than the prohibition of returning evil for evil. Vengeance, cursing, litigating, and tallying up evils received are all related to the theme of retaliation; all of these activities are off-limits in Paul's letters. Likewise, positive responses that Paul advises as alternatives to retaliation are doing good, blessing, conciliating, forgiving, and loving. Not only are these various actions and prohibitions part of Paul's paraenetic material, these themes appear in a variety of other genres: Paul's descriptions of his own behavior in trying circumstances (i.e., the peristasis catalogues); the hymn extolling love; and the "virtue" and "vice" lists of Galatians. The preponderance of texts advocating non-retaliation has exercized its proper influence: there is little debate about the *presence* of the theme of non-retaliation in Paul's letters. Disagreement simmers around the discussion of the *motivation* for Paul's instructions and the traditio-historical *background* of the material.[7]

Romans 12:14 and 17 are considered two of the most identifiable allusions to dominical sayings in Paul's letters. What follows is an examination of whether Paul's exhortation in Romans 12 shows signs of dependence on early (i.e., pre-synoptic) traditions about Jesus and his teaching.

Romans 12:14

COMPARING THE SAYINGS (ROM 12:14; LUKE 6:27–28; MATT 5:44)—Romans 12:14 is perhaps the most readily accepted dominical allusion in Paul's letters.[8] When Paul's language is compared to parallels in Matthew (5:44) and Luke (6:27–28), the reason for the majority view becomes clear.[9]

---

brought about by their "own compatriots" (cf. 1 Thess 1:6–7; 2:14–15; 3:1–8; 5:13b–15), see chapter 5.

7. Zerbe, *Non-Retaliation*, 216. It could be objected that including "lesser" evils (e.g., enduring verbal abuse, an unspecified admonition to be patient, etc.) which may or may not be related to physical violence is evidence we have over-egged the pudding; on the contrary, we simply recognize that Paul's exhortations prevent retaliation up to, that is to say *all the way up to*, self-defense. Enduring "lesser" offenses may be "less" non-violent than enduring a physical assault, but it is not unrelated. If one is untrained in responding non-violently to "minor" offenses, how could one be expected to cope with the temptation to live a retaliatory lifestyle in everyday matters?

8. Thompson, *Clothed with Christ*, 96. Cf. Neirynck, "Paul and the Sayings of Jesus," 270; Michel, *Der Brief an die Römer*, 305: "Wir haben feine genaue Wiedergabe, sondern eine targumartige Paraphrase des Jesuswortes vor uns."

9. So-called parallels between Romans and Matthew are marked with double underlining; parallels between Romans and Luke are identified with a single underline. The

Romans: "Bless <u>those who persecute you</u>, <u>bless</u> and do not <u>curse</u> them."

Luke: "Love your enemies, do good to those who hate you, <u>bless</u> those who <u>curse</u> you, pray for those who abuse you."

Matt: "Love your enemies and pray for <u>those who persecute you</u>."

Numerous proposals for Paul's "rearranged" wording have been made,[10] but the fundamental point is best summarized by Dunn. He suggests that the differences in the wording of the sayings illustrates that Jesus' teaching was part of an early "living tradition" in which some flexibility was allowed, so long as the proper point was still being made.[11] The amount of data available for comparison makes it rather difficult to reach a firm conclusion about Paul's source(s), especially since he may have been working with something more fluid than a written form of Q. But as some recent work on oral tradition has shown, one of the chief characteristics of oral tradition is the flexibility permitted within the fixed tradition.[12] In short, a word-for-word approach to comparisons adopts a literary model on what is at least *partly* an oral phenomenon. At points Romans 12:14 is closer to Matthew's gospel, in other respects it follows Luke more closely, but whatever its parent (that is, whether literary text or oral tradition, or both), Paul's expression arguably echoes Jesus' saying. The malleability of 12:14 supports the view that this saying could have been remembered from the beginning in a number of different forms. The differences do not indicate a corruption or change in the logia over time. Rather, it is more likely that Jesus said similar things on different occasions, increasing from the start the diversity of the earliest traditional material. Dunn concludes: "The fact

---

comparrison was originally drawn from Dunn, *Romans*, 2:745.

10. For a full discussion, see Thompson, *Clothed with Christ*, 96–105. Romans 12:14 shares Luke's verb (εὐλογεῖν), but Matthew's object (οἱ διώκοντες).

11. Dunn, *Romans* 2:745. See also his considerably expanded defense of this position on the flexibility of living tradition in Dunn, "Jesus Tradition in Paul," 155–78 (esp. 174), and the work cited in the next footnote.

12. See, e.g., Bauckham, *Jesus and the Eyewitnesses*, 240–318. See also Dunn, "Altering the Default Setting," 139–75. More importantly, oral tradition "subverts the idea(l) of an *'original'* version" since the tradition is "at best the *witness* of the event, and as there were presumably several witnesses, so there may well have been several traditions, or versions of the tradition, *from the first*" (153). Both Dunn and Bauckham build on the work of Bailey, "Middle Eastern Oral Tradition," 363–67, and Bailey, "Informal Controlled Oral Tradition," 4–11, and an ever-growing field of literature related to the oral transmission of traditions. See also Vansina, *Oral Tradition as History*.

that [Jesus'] exhortation was remembered in different versions simply underlines the extent to which Jesus' sayings formed a living tradition where the expression of the sense was more important than a particular form of words."[13]

OBJECTION ON THE GROUNDS OF OLD TESTAMENT "BACKGROUND"—A great deal of literature that antedates or is contemporary with Paul's letters gives similar instruction without depending on the teachings or example of Jesus.[14] Nonetheless, something *is* unique about Romans 12:14. The traditional Jewish sapiential antonyms, *bless* and *curse* (εὐλογέω and καταράομαι), are combined by Paul in an unusual way. In the Old Testament the two actions are often contrasted, but blessing is not directed toward the one who curses. For instance, Psalm 108:28 reads (LXX):

> They will curse (καταράσονται), but you will bless (εὐλογήσεις)
> Let my opponents be put to shame,
> but your slave will be glad.

In other words, the psalmist is cursed by his opponents, but blessed by God. In this case too, the psalmist happens to pray that the curse of the accusers is revisited upon their own heads (108:17–20). This pattern is so common in the ancient world that Michael Thompson claims that "*nowhere in pre-Christian Greek literature do we find humans (or God) responding to* καταρᾶν *or* λοιδορεῖν *with* εὐλογεῖν. The evidence from vocabulary therefore strongly supports an echo of Jesus [at Rom 12:14]."[15] While Paul's ethical instructions in general have a great deal of Jewish tradition informing them (as do Jesus' own), Jesus' ethic of *enemy love, non-retaliation,* and *blessing of persecutors* which has been preserved in both Matthew and Luke

---

13. Dunn, *Romans*, 2:745. Thompson's question (*Clothed with Christ*, 99–100) seems to get at the heart of the form-critical issue too: "Clearly Jesus called his followers to love their enemies . . . Which is more likely, that he said something so unusual only once, with no explanation, or that its gist was a regular element in his preaching? He probably repeated this difficult to accept teaching and its applications on different occasions. We should not be surprised then to find different formulations in Matthew and Luke, and unfortunately we cannot speak with any certainty as to what has been created by the evangelists."

14. Thompson, *Clothed with Christ*, 96. Cf. Zerbe, *Non-Retaliation*, 165–73, for a summary of the presence of non-retaliation in pre-Pauline Jewish writings.

15. Thompson, *Clothed with Christ*, 97–98. "Vocabulary" may not be the best choice here. It is, rather, on the basis of a dissimilar (i.e., unexpected) application of categories of response that the claim for uniqueness (and therefore dependence on Jesus Tradition) is strong.

goes beyond "the more typically Jewish assumption that God would curse those who cursed his people. The inescapable conclusion is that the attitude inculcated here is distinctively Christian."[16] Many scholars come to a similar conclusion—Romans 12:14 is both uniquely "Christian" in the response it esteems and goes back, with a disputed degree of confidence, to a saying of the historical Jesus.[17]

Romans 12:17–21

OBJECTIONS: OLD TESTAMENT "BACKGROUND" AND THE PAUCITY OF PARALLEL WORDS—The same confidence among scholars is usually expressed for 12:17–21, though dependence in the particulars is less certain than in 12:14. One problem for showing Paul's dependence on Jesus Tradition is again the existence of non-Christian parallels that antedate his letters. Material from Proverbs is the most likely Jewish source of 12:17 (cf. LXX Prov 17:13, cited below), but there are no direct quotations of Proverbs until 12:20.[18] The obvious sapiential and dominical overtones have led some to posit that 12:17a is a dominical saying which itself was influenced by Proverbs 17:13.[19] However, the argument for Paul's dependence on a dominical logia runs into one more complication: 12:17a does not seem to have any saying of Jesus as its obvious referent. The similarities between Romans, 1 Thessalonians, and 1 Peter are quite clear, though 1 Peter's dependence on Paul is difficult to rule out. The direct connection with Matthew 5:38–39 and Romans 12:17a is minimal. The most obvious canonical parallels are collected below.

COMPARING THE SAYINGS AND THE PATTERN OF RESPONSE (ROM 12:17A, MATT 5:38–39)—The catena of passages gathered below represent the closest parallels to Romans 12:17a in (roughly) chronological order.[20]

---

16. Dunn, *Romans*, 2:745. After writing *blessing of persecutors*, it occurred to me that I myself conflated Matthew and Luke's differing traditions; Jesus instructs his followers to bless those who curse (Luke) and pray for those who persecute (Matthew). Evidently Paul's logion has shaped my own memory of what Jesus "said" more than I had realized.

17. For the majority, see, e.g., Cranfield, *Romans*, 2:640; Fitzmyer, *Romans*, 655; many recent commentators cite Thompson's work.

18. Other potential "background" texts: Jos. As. 23.9; 28.4, 5, 10, 14; 29.3; Apoc. Sed. 7.9; Ahiqar 2.19.

19. Thompson, *Clothed with Christ*, 107, and literature cited there.

20. One might also include (though it is rather more difficult to date) Jos. As. 29:3: "οὐ προσήκει ἀνδρὶ θεωσεβεῖ ἀποδοῦναι κακὸν ἀντὶ κακοῦ" "It does not befit a man who

- "Whoever repays evil for good//evil will not be moved from his house." (Prov 17:13)

- "See that none of you repays evil for evil." (1 Thess 5:15)

- "Do not repay anyone evil for evil." (Rom 12:17a)

- "Do not repay evil for evil." (1 Pet 3:9)

- "An eye for an eye . . . do not resist an evildoer." (Matt 5:38–39)[21]

Even allowing for the flexibility of oral tradition, it is difficult to base a positive conclusion on the parallel of only two words. More compelling, however, is the similarity in what *pattern of response* the instructions convey. Rather than living by a tit-for-tat ethic, Jesus' disciples and Paul's communities should seek to fulfill the law through the love of neighbor *and* enemy (Rom 12:20; 13:10; Gal 5:14; Mark 12:31; Matt 5:17, 43–44). Returning evil for evil or gouging eye in place of eye is not the way of Jesus' followers. The words may be different, but the response envisaged is the same. Thompson concludes that there is no indubitable connection between 12:17a and Jesus Tradition; however, even if its origin is not dominical, the command "effectively summarizes" Jesus' teaching and behavior with respect to non-violence.[22] Individual links between Paul's letter and known Jesus Tradition are difficult to establish, in part because of the sometimes brief length of Paul's exhortations. Nevertheless, the instructions "could not but remind Christians whom Paul had never met of the characteristics of the one they confessed as Lord."[23]

---

worships God to repay evil for evil" or again 23:9 "καὶ οἴδαμεν ὅτι οἱ ἀδελφοὶ ἡμῶν ἄνδρες εἰσὶ θεωσεβεῖς καὶ μὴ ἀποδιδόντες κακὸν ἀντὶ κακοῦ τινι ἀνθρώπῳ" "and we know that our brothers are men who worship God and do not repay evil for evil to anyone."

21. The possible overlap for Matthew is less apparent in English. In Greek, two roots (in italics) align with Rom 12:17: ὀφθαλμὸν ἀντὶ ὀφθαλμοῦ . . . μὴ ἀντιστῆναι τῷ πονηρῷ.

22. Thompson, *Clothed with Christ*, 107. Cf. ibid., 109, "If the teaching of Jesus is not explicitly present in the passage, the example is implied." So also Dunn, *Romans*, 2:752.

23. Thompson, *Clothed with Christ*, 109–10. Since Paul was writing to a non-Pauline community and seems to have assumed enough knowledge of Jesus Tradition to hear his references to it even in Rome, then the memory of a non-violent Jesus was more widespread than is often recognized. Assemblies established by Paul and by other apostles transmitted traditions which preserved Jesus' sayings and example that related to non-violence. We will say more about the issue of the non-Pauline character of the Roman church at the end of the present chapter.

Demonstrating Paul's Behavioral Correspondence with Jesus Tradition (1 Corinthians 4:11–13)

At the beginning of this chapter, it was suggested that one way through the Jesus-Paul debate that has been explored insufficiently is the continuity in *both* the words (teaching) and *deeds* (example) of Jesus and Paul, specifically regarding their attitude towards violence. In the preceding analysis, we have tentatively provided one sample of evidence for Paul's continuity with Jesus on *teaching* a particular, non-violent response to hostile behavior for Christ's followers.[24] We must now ask: did Paul follow his own ethical advice?

In 1 Corinthians there is a clear instance where the politics of peaceableness intersects with the politics of violence. In one of Paul's peristasis catalogues, Paul boasts (N.B. the use of first person *plural*):

> Until the present hour we are hungry and thirsty, we are naked and beaten and homeless, and we grow weary from working with our own hands. When insulted, we bless; when persecuted we endure, when slandered, we conciliate. We have become like the refuse of the world, the scum until now. (translation mine)

This passage may be set in a highly rhetorical context, but one need not attempt to strip away the rhetoric to find the "historical" Paul. For present purposes, it is more important to identify the way Paul's claims align with or diverge from traditions about Jesus preserved in the gospels. To that end, we will focus on the threefold antitheses of 1 Corinthians 4:12b–13a.

Jesus and Paul Blessing the Ones Who Curse (1 Cor 4:12b and Luke 6:28)

How then, do the three antitheses stand up to a comparison with Jesus' teaching and example? Owing to their form (and brevity), the three

---

24. That Romans 12 addresses a situation facing Roman Christians is taken for granted at this point. The focus of Paul's teaching on non-violence has been purposely limited to his letter to the Romans. In the next section of the chapter, we will address the Corinthian correspondence, and in subsequent chapters we will draw out Paul's references to a non-violent ethos in Galatians (chapter 4), and 1 Thessalonians (chapter 5). The purpose in demonstrating this theme in all of these letters is more than providing evidence across a range of letters, but demonstrates too that the theme had a wide geographical footprint in early Christianity.

antitheses are difficult to identify as Jesus Tradition, at least in the classic sense of identifying literary dependence. However, all three demonstrate clear "continuities" with the Jesus Tradition that is preserved in Luke's gospel. So, in the first of the antitheses, only one word is shared (and that in differing person/moods), but the sense is virtually identical:

> "when reviled we *bless*" 1 Cor 4:12b
> "*bless* those who curse you" Luke 6:28[25]

Jesus instructed his disciples to bless the ones who curse them; Paul claims to have done that very thing when faced with people who reviled/slandered him.[26] Paul claims to have acted in a manner consistent with the teaching of Jesus. Although we know nothing of Paul's pre-Christian response to being the recipient of slander, I noted above the unprecedented response to being cursed advocated by Paul in Romans and Jesus in the gospels.[27] That is, blessing one's slanderers is not an obvious pre-Christian (Jewish) strategy. Paul follows Jesus in this peculiar response to slander.

It is not enough to compare Paul's *behavior* and Jesus' *teaching* alone, however. No less important is Paul's behavioral continuity with Jesus' *actions* towards those who slandered or reviled him. The synoptic passion narratives catalogue numerous instances of verbal abuse suffered by Jesus, and the consistent response of Jesus is silence. He is mocked, blasphemed, insulted, and reviled by various characters throughout his trial and execution.[28] Surprisingly, the authors of the gospels *refrain* from portraying Jesus as one who publicly blessed those who slandered, reviled, and abused him, creating an acute difficulty for demonstrating Jesus and Paul's behavioral

25. *Bless* being the only root shared in the Greek.

26. Fee, *First Corinthians*, 179, also points out the wording in Rom 12:14, where Paul shares another word with Luke 6:28, *curse* (καταράομαι): "Bless those who persecute you, bless and do not *curse*."

27. Thompson, *Clothed with Christ*, 97–98.

28. The *verbal* aspect of abuse experienced by Jesus is gathered here. In Matthew he is *mocked* (ἐμπαίζω, 27:29, 31, 41), *blasphemed* (βλασφημέω, 27:39) and *insulted* (ὀνειδίζω, 27:44) and offers no response from the cross except "My God why have you forsaken me?" In Mark he is *mocked* (ἐμπαίζω, 15:20, 31), *derided* (βλασφημέω, 15:29), and *reviled* by those crucified with him (ὀνειδίζω, 15:32), and yet he offers no response. In Luke he is *mocked* (ἐμπαίζω, 22:63, 23:11, 36), *blasphemed* (βλασφημέω, 22:65), treated with *contempt* by Herod (ἐξουθενέω, 23:11), and Jesus prays: "Father forgive them, for they know not what they do" (23:34). Rulers *scoffed* (ἐκμυκτηρίζω, 23:35), soldiers *mocked* (ἐμπαίζω, 23:36), one criminal *railed* (βλασφημέω), and he only prays "into your hands I commit my spirit" (23:46). Cf. John's gospel, where his dying word is not a bitter curse, but "it is finished." A catalogue of physical suffering follows below.

correspondence in blessing those who have reviled them. The prayer from the cross in Luke's gospel (23:34, see discussion below on 1 Cor 4:13a) is the exception that proves the rule. More typically, Jesus is silent when facing mistreatment or interrogation (cf. Matt 26:63; 27:12; Mark 14:61; 15:5; Luke 23:9). One must stretch as far "ahead" as 1 Peter 2:23 to find the claim about Jesus that one might have expected from the gospels:

> When reviled he did not return abuse (cf. Matt 5:39)
> Though he suffered, he did not threaten,
> But he entrusted himself to the one who judges justly
> (cf. Jer 11:20).

Although there is scant detail regarding the responses Jesus made to his own abusers, Paul claims to have offered blessing to his opponents when he was slandered. The nature of his letters provides us little in the way of evidence however, since they were not written primarily to report the abuse he suffered and the responses he made to mistreatment. While there certainly are examples to which one could point to demonstrate Paul's failure to bless his opponents,[29] Paul rhetorically portrays himself as consistently "walking towards the truth of the gospel" (Gal 2:14); he envisages not just his own imitation of Jesus (1 Cor 11:1; cf. 1 Cor 4:16), but also views his own life as animated by the risen Lord (Gal 2:19–20).

Jesus and Paul Enduring Persecution (1 Cor 4:12b)

The second antithesis of 1 Corinthians 4:12b ("when persecuted, we endure" "διωκόμενοι ἀνεχόμεθα") has no direct verbal parallel in Jesus Tradition, though conceptually it reflects the behavior of Jesus on display in the passion narratives.[30] Like the first antithesis, the second reappears in Paul's

---

29. Cf. Gal 5:12 (which we will discuss in Chapter Four) or the letter he wrote to the Corinthians that grieved them (2 Cor 7:8), to name just two possibilities. I will only say here that Paul's rhetorical excess, while understandable, need not be viewed as acceptable. At Gal 5:12, he has gone too far. Others will disagree, and the tradition of defending Paul here goes back at least to Tertullian, *An.* 16.6, but here I would rather affirm the view of Klassen, "'Love your Enemies,'" 21: "There is . . . a clear case of Paul's departure from the teaching of Jesus when he expresses the wish (in Gal. 5:12) that his enemies would accidentally castrate themselves."

30. Fee, *First Corinthians*, 180. During his trial and execution, Jesus faces numerous *physically* punitive measures; in Matthew he is *spat* upon (ἐμπτύω 26:67; 27:30), *struck* (κολαφίζω 26:67; τύπτω, 27:30), *slapped* (ῥαπίζω) (26:67), *flogged* (φραγελλόω, 27:26) and *crucified* (σταυρόω, 27:26ff) by the Romans. In Mark he is *spat upon* (ἐμπτύω,

ethical instructions or exhortations elsewhere, although not in the same form.[31] Like so many possible allusions to Jesus Tradition, this example suffers from its brevity. The phrase is not an identifiable part of the stock of Jesus Traditions, but Paul's response to persecution rehearses Jesus' own exemplary endurance of suffering, especially from Gethsemane to the cross.[32]

The primary concern is not in any case dependent upon confirming a dominical logion in Paul's letter, but instead we are interested in how Paul's behavioral response to suffering persecution is similar to and even modeled on Jesus' endurance of suffering. By his own account in Galatians, Paul inflicted great suffering on those he opposed, but once he became a "member" of the group he violently opposed, he evidently ceased engaging with opponents through physically violent means, and instead he recounts enduring physical suffering without resorting to physical retaliation. For example, we learn from one of his peristasis catalogues that he endured: countless beatings, 39 lashes on five occasions, being beaten with rods three times, and being stoned once (2 Cor 11:23–25). In Galatians, he asks "But why, brothers, if I am still preaching circumcision, am I still being persecuted?" (5:11; cf. 4:29), and refers to the marks of Jesus he bears on his body (6:17). He refers repeatedly through his letters of *affliction* (θλίψις) he and other coworkers endured, though he typically refrains from providing

---

14:65; 15:19), *struck*, and received *with blows* (κολαφίζω and ῥάπισμα, 14:65), *flogged* (φραγελλόω) (15:15), *struck* (τύπτω, 15:19), *mocked* (ἐμπαίζω, 15:20, 31), and *crucified* (σταυρόω, 15:20), and yet he offers no response. In Luke he is *beaten* (δέρω, 22:63) and crucified (σταυρόω, 23:33), and Jesus prays: "Father forgive them, for they know not what they do" (23:34). He also prays "into your hands I commit my spirit" (23:46). In John he is *struck* (ῥάπισμα) (18:22, 19:3) or (in Jesus' words, δέρω, 18:23), *whipped* (μαστιγόω, 19:1), *crucified* (σταυρόω, 19:16, 18) and his dying word is not a bitter curse, but "it is finished."

31. Cf. 2 Cor 4:9 "persecuted but not forsaken"; Gal 5:11 "Why am I still being persecuted?"; Phil 3:10–14 "I want to know Christ . . . and the sharing of his sufferings by becoming like him in his death."

32. Jesus' suffering in the Synoptic Gospels is rarely called persecution (John describes Jesus' suffering as persecution a few times), but Jesus did warn his followers that they would be persecuted or opposed just like their master (Matt 10:24–25; cf. Mark 13:9, 12–13, parallel Luke 21:12, 16–17). Of course, these "predictions" could be later additions to the tradition, i.e., they may reflect the interests of the authors of the gospels. On Matthew, Davies and Allison (*Matthew*, 2:193) consider these verses dominical, though they identify 10:25a as a dominical reformulation of a traditional proverb; cf. Bultmann (*History of the Synoptic Tradition*, 86, 99, 103), who considers the "possibility" that 25a was originally a secular proverb attracted to 10:24. Collins, *Mark*, 594–607, has a good summary of the competing views on the source and compositional history of Mark 13.

specifics of his suffering.[33] Rather than demonstrating Paul's correspondence with the "heroic autonomy" of Stoic perseverance, Thiselton argues that Paul endures persecution in a counter-cultural manner: "Paul follows Jesus' principle of non-retaliation, which . . . was regarded as weak or unmanly in the Roman and Graeco-Roman world of Paul's day."[34]

Jesus and Paul Speaking Kindly to Slanderers (1 Cor 4:13a, Luke 6:28a and Matt 5:11)

Slandered in 1 Corinthians 4:13a ("when slandered, we conciliate") occurs only once in the New Testament, but it is semantically related to the much more common *blaspheme* (βλασφημέω), to which Jesus was repeatedly subjected according to the gospels.[35] The antithesis of slander is offering kind words in response to an opponent's insulting speech.[36] Yet again, we are faced with a compact phrase which has little chance of being aligned with a specific Jesus logion, but we are likewise faced with the pattern of response which was clearly a part of Jesus' teaching and yet quite remarkable in comparison with a more "instinctive" response to being the object of

33. Although Acts cannot be used as constructive evidence here, Luke's portrait largely confirms Paul's own outline. It may be that Luke has simply taken Paul's outline and created narratively interesting, if fictive, accounts of Paul's suffering, but it is important to point out that Paul's own terminology is enough to provide the following generalized statement—Paul once sought to destroy the church of God, a goal which probably included using physically violent measures (see chapter 4). Once Jesus was apocalypsed to/in him, he faced physical abuse on several occasions (whether from Jewish opponents, "Christian" opponents, or Roman/local civic authorities we do not know) and he claims to have endured those forms of suffering (presumably without retaliating). If we jettison Acts for historical reconstruction, nothing more specific can be said about Paul's violent behavior or his endurance of suffering.

34. Thiselton, 1 *Corinthians*, 363, 368.

35. Incidentally, *blasphemy* replaces *slander* at 1 Cor 4:13 in some manuscripts. On Jesus' experience of blasphemy, see Matt 27:39; Mark 15:29; Luke 22:65; 23:39. Other common words in the same semantic domain are: ὀνειδίζω κτλ. (seven occurrences in the Synoptics, see esp. Matt 5:11; Luke 6:22; Mark 15:32), λοιδορέω κτλ. (ten occurrences in the Synoptics), and καταλαλέω κτλ. (eight occurrences, though none are in the Synoptics).

36. BDAG, 765n5. Other uses of παρακαλέω in Pauline letters cover a wider range of meaning to express: a summons to aid (2 Cor 12:8), the making of an appeal (Rom 12:1; 1 Cor 4:16 *et al.*), a strong request (2 Cor 12:18; Phlm 10), comfort or encouragement (2 Cor 1:4; 7:6 *et al.*) or speaking to one in a friendly manner (1 Thess 2:12). The final definition makes the most sense of the antithesis at 1 Cor 4:13; it is the semantic opposite of being spoken against or insulted.

slander. Jesus urged his followers to "bless those who persecute you" (Luke 6:28a) and Luke has Jesus himself bless those who finally crucified him when he prays for their forgiveness from the cross (Luke 23:34).[37] Although the gospels fail to record how Jesus publicly responded to insults or slander in line with his own imperatives, at the crucial moment of experiencing horrendous physical torture and severe verbal abuse, the gospels, despite whatever redactional interests each author might have, consistently perpetuate the memory of Jesus' silence and endurance of suffering without returning evil for the evil he experienced.

Paul faced nothing quite like Jesus' passion, at least by the time of writing 1 Corinthians (although he does claim to have been stoned at 2 Cor 11:25, which *could* have occurred before he wrote 1 Corinthians). And there is not a historically reliable extant record of how he responded in what is traditionally thought to be his death as a martyr. Still, Paul claims to have encountered his share of hostility to which he responded after the pattern of Jesus. In 2 Corinthians Paul famously catalogues the afflictions he (and Timothy[38]) experienced as servants of Christ (6:4–10); among them he lists beatings and imprisonments, and in response he lists the qualities which commend their ministry: patience, kindness, and truthful speech.

As evidence of Paul's intimate knowledge of Jesus Tradition, 1 Corinthians 4:12–13 may be circumstantial or even merely suggestive, but when taken with other more clear parallels or allusions to Jesus Tradition, it supports the view that Paul knew details of the teachings and example of Jesus, and he implored his communities to become imitators of himself just as he was of their Lord (1 Cor 4:16; 11:1).

---

37. It should of course be noted that Luke 23:34 reflects Luke's redactional interests and cannot with confidence be traced back to the historical Jesus. It is, after all, unique to Luke. Moreover, the verse itself is suspect, not included in many early witnesses. Metzger, *Textual Commentary*, 154, noted that this bracketed saying, "though probably not a part of the original Gospel of Luke, bears self-evident tokens of its dominical origin, and was retained . . . in its traditional place where it had been incorporated by unknown copyists relatively early in the transmission of the Third Gospel."

38. It is worth pointing out that one avenue of future research along these same lines would be to trace where Paul's letters make claims about the endurance of suffering of his coworkers. That is, my thesis is focused primarily on how Paul changed from a violent persecutor to non-violent apostle, but it is worth considering whether support for my thesis can be garnered through viewing how Paul's coworkers responded to persecution. It would be rather surprising for all of his coworkers to have responded to strong opposition (possibly violent opposition) non-violently unless non-violence was a fundamental commitment of early Christians generally.

PRESERVATION AND TRANSMISSION OF JESUS TRADITION IN EARLIEST CHRISTIANITY

I want to return finally to a point which was hinted at but not developed earlier: that Paul, in writing to the Christians in Rome, alludes to domini-cal logia *and* assumed their prior knowledge of this Jesus Tradition which preserved Jesus' orientation to peacemaking. Paul cannot assume their knowledge of this tradition, however, in the same way he can for a church that he founded. For instance, for the churches in Thessalonica and Galatia, Paul knew what knowledge they had of Jesus Tradition because he himself would have been among the first to deliver it.[39] Not so with a church he had never personally visited. In other words, Paul could assume that Jesus Tra-dition, in particular those traditions which recalled the non-violent politics of Jesus, had reached the Christians in Rome independently of Paul's own mission. Paul expects the Roman churches to recognize Jesus as the ideal model of non-retaliation, as the one who overcame evil with good.

Without assessing the way in which the traditions were passed from one group to another, how can we know whether the echo or allusion would have been heard? That is, alluding to the presence of Jesus Tradition in Paul's letters raises the questions of the method and content of trans-mission of Jesus Traditions. While I cannot afford to adjudicate between the many models available regarding the issue of transmission methods, I will identify the model I have chosen to adopt, focus on the content of Jesus Tradition in Paul, and reconsider the significance of Paul's letter to the Romans on the question of transmission of Jesus Tradition in early Christian circles.[40] In surveying the *content* of Jesus Tradition in Paul's

---

39. That Paul was in some way or another a recognized tradent will be argued below. Rather than claiming that Paul was the first or most significant bearer of Jesus Tradition to those communities, I recognize that Barnabas (in Galatia) or Silas/Silvanus (in Thes-salonica) may have played an equally if not more important role than Paul in this regard.

40. The question of the transmission of Jesus Tradition is an important one for my thesis, arguing as I do that non-violence was a cornerstone of the message of Jesus from the very beginning. If Jesus' non-violent teaching and actions stem from traditions which can be characterized as straying from the "truth" of the historical Jesus, my own thesis regarding the centrality of non-violence would be imperiled. If, however, the traditions reflect, as I believe they do, the surest account of Jesus' life among the disciples, then the content of those traditions can serve as a point of comparison for the traditions which may be detected in Paul's letters. In short, I follow the model of transmission proposed by Bauckham, *Jesus and the Eyewitnesses*, 264–318, in dialogue with sympathetic ear-lier approaches (e.g., Gerhardsson, *Memory and Manuscript*; Bauckham, "Unwritten

letters, I will demonstrate the centrality of the Sermon on the Mount/Plain in early Christianity, regardless of a particular community's origin. Since attempts to prove allusions to Jesus Tradition in Paul have failed to secure a consensus,[41] perhaps illustrating Paul's continuity with virtually every other early Christian author will go some way to establishing *these* as dominical allusions to non-violence in Paul's letters.

Evidence for "Transmission" in Paul's Letters

Technical Terms for Receiving and Handing on Jesus Tradition

Before attending to the content of Jesus Tradition in Paul's letters, I will identify the way in which we can see traces of the process of transmission of Jesus Tradition in Paul's letters. Paul repeatedly uses the technical terms for receiving and handing on tradition (παραδίδωμι and παραλαμβάνω, respectively); it appears that there was indeed a formal process of control of these traditions in the earliest Christian writings. In a variety of places Paul employs the technical terms which give the unmistakable impression that Paul received traditions from a "qualified traditioner."[42] First Corinthians 15:3 (and 11:23–26) makes explicit what is elsewhere implied by the technical terms: Paul "handed on" what he "in turn had received." In other words, Paul doesn't name the source of the tradition,[43] but he makes the two-step

---

Jesus Tradition,"; Dunn, *Jesus Remembered*, 210–49. Cf. some recent work on the genre of the gospels which seeks to recover the "historical" character of the traditions: Burridge, *What Are the Gospels*; Byrskog, *Story as History*; Stanton, *Gospels and Jesus*, 13–18; Hengel, "Eye-witness memory," the bibliography could be greatly expanded here, not least in the area of those who would disagree with the model chosen, but this list serves as the tip of the proverbial iceberg.

41. Dunn, "Jesus Tradition in Paul," 159, laments "there is little point in rehearsing the debate on whether allusions to Jesus Tradition are present in the Pauline letters. It never succeeded in achieving a widespread consensus in the past and is hardly likely to do so now."

42. Bauckham, *Jesus and the Eyewitnesses*, 264. The t.t. for handing on a tradition: παραδίδωμι 1 Cor 11:2, 23; 15:3; cf. παράδοσις, 2 Thess 2:15; 3:6. T.t. for receiving a tradition: 1 Cor 11:23; 15:1,3; Gal 1:9; Phil 4:9; Col 2:6; 1 Thess 2:13; 4:1; 2 Thess 3:6. Deppe, *Sayings of Jesus*, 175n58, notes that the "objects in Paul's writings include 'the gospel' (1 Cor. 15:1; Gal. 1:9), 'the word of the message . . . the word of God' (1 Thess. 2:13), 'the things which where learned, heard, and seen' (Phil 4:9), 'the tradition' (2 Thess. 3:4), and 'Christ' (Col. 2:6)."

43. Cf. Watson, "'I Received from the Lord,'" 103–24, where he attempts to take

process clear: Paul received tradition, Paul handed it on; Paul "places himself in a chain of transmission."[44] The chain of transmission is evident not just in Paul's letters, but also in a variety of other early Christian writings, as we should expect.[45] That Paul uses the technical terms for receiving and handing on tradition is yet more counter-evidence to the widespread view that Paul made little use of Jesus Tradition. It is better to separate the issues of Paul's apostolic authority or his authority to preach the gospel from the authority that was attached to the testimony of Jesus' disciples.

Paul's Visit to Jerusalem

Despite whatever protest Paul might make against our quest to discover what "really" happened, scholars have traditionally not shied away from proposing his visit in Jerusalem with Peter (Gal 1:18–19) as the perfect opportunity to avail himself of all the traditions about Jesus he required. The details of the fortnight-long visit with Peter are notoriously sketchy, and one scholar has quipped: "We may presume they did not spend all the time talking about the weather."[46] If we insist that the visit could *only* have been for the purpose of getting to know Peter (as opposed to getting information *from* him), we make good sense of the context in Galatians of Paul's defense against preaching a gospel which was derivative of Peter's or Jerusalemite testimony (cf. Gal 1:11–12, 16–17; 2:6), but the risk is that so restricting the purpose of Paul's visit obviates what in fact would have been (at least) a secondary benefit—Paul's access to the eyewitness *par excellence* of Jesus' life during his public ministry.

A related issue adds corroborating evidence to this view of the first meeting between Peter and Paul, and to our understanding of the early transmission of Jesus Tradition more generally. First, if early Christians did

---

seriously Paul's claim at 11:23–26 to pass on what he received as direct revelation from Jesus.

44. Bauckham, *Jesus and the Eyewitnesses*, 265.

45. E.g., Luke 1:2, Acts 16:4; Jude 3; Did 4:13; Barnabas 19:11.

46. Dodd, *Apostolic Preaching*, 16; quoted in Bauckham, *Jesus and the Eyewitnesses*, 266. See also Dunn, *Galatians*, 71–74, and Dunn, "Relationship between Paul and Jerusalem," 461–78, and Longenecker, *Galatians*, 37–42. But Martyn, *Galatians*, 171–3, recognizing the equally positive philological grounds for the two traditional approaches to explaining the purpose of the meeting (and translations of ἱστορέω), insists that the context "almost certainly" excludes the purpose of the visit as one which was concerned with receiving traditions about Jesus. See also Walter, "Paul and Jesus-Tradition," 64–66.

wish to guard closely their testimony to the words and deeds of Jesus, then a face-to-face meeting with one of the twelve would be crucial for establishing Paul's own authority to pass Jesus Tradition along to the churches he helped establish. Paul may have already become familiar with a great deal of Jesus Tradition that was (presumably) circulating among Christians in Damascus or Antioch,[47] but a trip to Jerusalem to see Peter would guard against accusations that the *content* of Paul's Jesus Tradition had been distorted through multiple instances of transmission. His chosen course of action (i.e., a visit with Peter in Jerusalem)[48] created a different problem for him in Galatia, namely, that his gospel was derivative, an accusation which he doggedly argues against in his letter to the Galatians (cf. Gal 1:1, 11–12).

Churches and Individual Teachers as Recipients of Jesus Tradition

Any account of the earliest transmission of Jesus Tradition, especially in Paul's churches, would be incomplete if it failed to account for the role of teachers in Paul's (and other early Christian) communities.[49] That they are described as teachers (διδάσκολοι) of course raises the question: of what? Exposition of scripture presumably would have been a critical task assigned to such teachers, but so also the reception, preservation, and passing on of traditions about the figurehead who had shaped the identity of these minority communities. Any individual teacher became in effect a "walking reference library" for the sake of becoming the community's living aid to memory.[50] To show the balanced achieved between individual and community control of the transmission process, a lengthy quotation from Bauckham is apropos:

---

47. Taylor, "Paul and the Historical Jesus," 105–26.

48. Dunn, "Relationship between Paul and Jerusalem," 465–6, notes that the difference between ἱστορῆσαι Κηφᾶν and ἰδεῖν Ἰάκωβον is that Paul would have wanted to spend the most time with Peter because he was closer to Jesus.

49. E.g., Acts 13:1; Rom 12:7; 1 Cor 12:28–29; Gal 6:6; Eph 4:1; Heb 5:12; Jas 3:1; Did 15:1–2. Cf. also 1 Cor 4:17 and, though pseudepigraphal, 2 Tim 2:2 recommends establishing just this kind of link: "And what you have *heard* (ἤκουσας) from me through many witnesses *entrust* (παράθου) to faithful people who will be able to *teach* (διδάξαι) others as well."

50. Quotation from Vansina, *Oral Tradition*, 37, quoted in Dunn, *Jesus Remembered*, 177. Here Bauckham (*Jesus and the Eyewitnesses*, 269) and Dunn agree on the importance of teachers in the Christian community.

> Paul transmitted traditions to each Christian community as a
> whole [and probably] also transmitted the traditions to a few des-
> ignated persons in each community, people with the skills and gifts
> necessary for preserving the traditions and for being a resource
> for the traditions that belonged to the community as whole. Thus,
> even within the Pauline communities, we should reckon with the
> role of specially authorized guarantors of the traditions, and thus
> a more formal process of preservation and transmission of the tra-
> ditions than Bailey's model envisages. *The rather important result
> is that designated persons in each Pauline community knew the Jesus
> Traditions through a chain of only two links between themselves and
> Jesus himself, namely Paul and the Jerusalem apostles.*[51]

We have already noted above that other apostles and Christians served
alongside of Paul, possibly even as examples of Jesus' non-violent lifestyle
by their own endurance of suffering. There are several named associates
of Paul who might have been official bearers of Jesus Tradition on their
own merit. Barnabas, John Mark, and Silvanus/Silas[52] were all "prominent
members of the Jerusalem church"[53] who had access to the Jesus Traditions
of that mother church and would have been entrusted with assisting in its
transmission and control as they accompanied Paul (or as he accompanied
Barnabas, as in Acts 11:25–26; 13:2–5) on their missionary journeys.[54]

---

51. Bauckham, *Jesus and the Eyewitnesses*, 270, emphasis added.

52. Barnabas was sent by the Jerusalem church to the church in Antioch in Acts
11:19–26, where he became one of their principle teachers (cf. esp. vv. 22 and 26); at
13:1 he is included among the *prophets and teachers* of the Antioch Church. At 15:35,
Barnabas is one who was teaching and proclaiming the good news at Antioch (with Paul
and others). John Mark accompanied Barnabas and Saul on their first missionary journey through Cyprus as an assistant (Acts 13:5, 13). Although Paul (according to Luke)
deemed him unfit to be included in their next journey, Barnabas took John Mark along
for a subsequent visit to the churches in Cyprus (Acts 15:37–39). John Mark's mother's
home also seems to have been an important meeting place for the Jerusalem "church,"
as people are gathered there to pray when Peter was arrested (Acts 12:12). In Acts 15:22,
Silas is described as a leader (ἡγούμενος) among the brothers. He is a prophet (15:32);
a trusted companion of Paul's (15:40; 17:10) who faced persecution for the gospel with
Paul (16:19, 25) and co-sent 1 Thessalonians (1:1) and 2 Thessalonians (1:1; if it is not
pseudepigraphal). The author of 1 Peter (5:12) calls Silas/Silvanus a "faithful brother."

53. Bauckham, *Jesus and the Eyewitnesses*, 271.

54. An important, potentially analogous parallel to passing on Jesus Tradition is the
dissemination of the decision of the Apostolic Council. In that incident (as Luke reports
it), the apostles selected Silas and Judas to accompany Paul and Barnabas to pass along
and confirm the decision reached by the council (Acts 15:27, 30, 32–33, 35). It seems fair
to assume, *mutatis mutandis*, that a similar equipping and sending of official tradents

Paul also sent Timothy to Corinth when he could not go himself, for the express purpose of "reminding" the Corinthians of Paul's "patterns of life in Christ Jesus, *just as I teach everywhere in every church*" (1 Cor 4:17). According to Luke,[55] others who served alongside Paul in Antioch as prophets and teachers were Barnabas, Simeon (called Niger), Lucius of Cyrene, and Manaen (Acts 13:1). The conclusion that teachers played an important role in early Christian communities is inescapable, and one of the key components of their teaching would likely have been the preservation and transmission of Jesus' teachings and example preserved in the Jesus Tradition authorized by the Jerusalem church.[56]

What Traditions Were Transmitted by Paul?

It almost goes without saying that the *content* of the Jesus Tradition that was passed through the lines of transmission would have been of utmost importance. When we analize early Christian literature, significant trends become apparent in the use of synoptic tradition. Individual sayings from the Sermon of the Mount (or Plain), and motifs and imagery from the Passion traditions, figure prominently in a significant number of allusions or echoes of Jesus Tradition.[57] The traditions that finally become fixed in the

takes place to spread Jesus Tradition to newly established Christian communities. That Silas and Judas are sent together with Paul and Barnabas in no way diminishes the fitness of the latter pair for being seen as authorized tradents; the "unbiased" reporters are only needed presumably because the decree (as Luke reports it), if Paul and Barnabas alone delivered it to Antioch, more closely aligns with their own position.

55. Although I have alternated between Pauline and Lukan references in these paragraphs, I do not wish to give the impression that I am collapsing the two sources. The importance of teachers in early Christian circles is so self-evident that I don't suspect I should encounter skepticism regarding Luke's value in describing (broadly) the role of teachers in the early church. That is, individual instances of teaching/transmission (i.e., the historical accuracy of the transmission of the Apostolic Council mentioned in the footnote above) may be examined for their historical value, but the overall portrait of many teachers in the early church is certainly not a Lukan fiction. For a longer note on the relationship between Luke and ancient historiography, see note 35 in chapter 5.

56. Did 4:13 ("You must not forsake the Lord's commandments, but must guard what you have received [παραλαμβάνω], neither adding nor subtracting anything") and Barn 19:11 ("You shall guard what you have received [παραλαμβάνω], neither adding nor subtracting anything") show that emphasis on preventing alteration to Jesus' commandments became a formulaic warning (adapted from Deut 4:2) in early Christian literature.

57. See Thompson, *Clothed with Christ*, 37–63 (here 60): "The only citations of dominical logia in the extra-Pauline NT Epistles appear in one of the latest letters,

Sermon on the Mount/Plain and the Passion are widely regarded as very early and probably stood alone before their inclusion in the larger narratives of the gospels.[58] Despite the widespread agreement among scholars today that the traditions which eventually became the Sermon on the Mount/Plain and Passion had an early, independent existence from the written gospels, the consistent trend among early Christian authors is to *refrain* from direct quotation of traditions as we find them now in the gospels. Significantly, this is the overwhelming tendency among nearly *all* New Testament authors, not just Paul but also the authors of James, 1 and 2 Peter, Hebrews, 1 John and many of the Apostolic Fathers. Rarely do they cite the words of Jesus overtly and where allusions or echoes of Jesus Tradition do occur, the majority of the sayings are parallel to those found in the (later and final-form) Sermon on the Mount/Plain or the Passion, most likely the former.[59] In other words, the core teaching that would have been particularly important to Gentile converts to a Jewish Messiah, which gave them guidance on new norms for social behavior in God's empire,[60] were words

---

1 John. . . . The sayings [whether citation, allusion, or echo] usually parallel logia in the SM or in the Olivet discourse." So too in the Apostolic Fathers: "Again most of the citations and echoes parallel the SM."

58. Nolland, *Matthew*, 7–8, identifies the Sermon on the Mount as one example of a "body of linked units of source material" for Matthew's gospel. Although the canonical form of the sermon is a "Matthean collection," the material probably comes to Matthew (through Q) in a different (i.e., longer) form than that received by Luke. Bauckham, *Jesus and the Eyewitnesses*, 243, stresses the early (40s CE), "connected narrative" of Mark's passion. Theissen, *Gospels in Context*, 166–99, recognizes the limits of our knowledge of the *scope* of a pre-Markan Passion story (169), but proposes Jerusalem as its origin (due to the use of protective anonymity, 188–89) and "critical shaping" of the narrative sometime between 30 and 60, "probably" between 41–44 CE (198–99). Cf. Bauckham, "Gospel Traditions Outside the Canonical Gospels," 378: "One of the . . . surest results of studies of writers who probably knew Synoptic tradition independently of the Synoptic Gospels is that they knew, not simply independent *logia*, but particular 'blocks' of tradition. For example, the central part of the Sermon on the Mount/Plain material of Matthew and Luke seems to be independently attested as a disconnected series of *logia* by Paul, 1 Peter, James, Didache 1:3–6, 1 Clement 13:2, Polycarp, Phil. 2:3; 12:3, and perhaps Justin (1 Apol. 15–16). Though the precise range and form of the Sermon material attested by each of these writers differs, *their common testimony to the fact that some such block of material was widely known in the early church is very impressive*" (emphasis added).

59. Thompson, *Clothed with Christ*, 60–62: "The important question that emerges . . . is not why the tradition is absent, but why a writer uses it when he does. What causes him to break the 'normal' pattern of relative silence?"

60. The first half of this sentence is largely influenced by Dunn, *Jesus Remembered*, 180: "Particularly important for Gentiles taking on a wholly new life-style and social

and deeds which shaped a community of peace in a world all too familiar with a politics of violence.[61]

If we turn our attention to Paul and what Jesus Tradition is found in his letters, we realize that like many other early Christian authors, Paul's allusions tend to group around logia which have become fixed in the Sermon on the Mount/Plain (cf. 1 Cor 7:10–16; Romans 12–13) and the Last Supper (cf. 1 Cor 11:23).[62] We have already detailed one aspect of Paul's deployment of the Sermon on the Mount/Plain material (the section on Romans 12 above), and here we simply point out that the claim that Paul knew of something like the Sermon(s), whether as an oral tradition or a written block of tradition (proto-Q SM/SP) is well supported by the evidence. Paul's knowledge of Jesus Tradition was not limited to Jesus' teaching on non-retaliation. Rather, Paul's use of Jesus Tradition extended to Christians participating in litigation,[63] divorce,[64] and judging.[65] Furthermore, although it is not usually adduced as evidence for Paul's use of Jesus

---

identity would be guidelines and models for the different character of conduct now expected from them. Such guidelines and models were evidently provided by a solid basis of Jesus Tradition which they were expected to remember, to take in and live out."

61. A complete discussion in the present chapter of Jesus Tradition in all the other New Testament documents would take us too far afield, but I will simply point out Thompson's *Clothed with Christ* as a fine introduction to the issue. According to Thompson [39–60], Paul's default practice of employing allusion and echo was hardly unique. Rather, this was common among the first group of Christian authors who in any case had not written with the purpose of transmission of Jesus Tradition. It can only be noted in passing that the Petrine letters, Hebrews, and the epistle of James all broadly correspond to what we find in Paul. See Thompson, *Clothed with Christ*, 39–60, who summarizes, besides the witnesses mentioned above, the Johannine letters, Jude, 1 Clement, Barnabas, Didache, The Epistles of Ignatius, Polycarp's Epistle to the Philippians, and 2 Clement.

62. This does not challenge the claim in Allison, "Pauline Epistles and Synoptic Gospels," 11, that Paul displays knowledge of "a handful of relatively brief, well-defined sections" of early Jesus Tradition. Allison notes (10–17) the blocks known to Paul were the Sermon on the Plain, the synoptic missionary discourse (Mark 6:6b–13; Matt 10:1–16; Luke 9:1–6; 10:1–12; 1 Cor 9), and Mark 9:33–50. For Allison, 12 of 21 Pauline allusions come from these three block of material. On a different table in the same article (cf. page 20), Allison lists 25 allusions, 11 of which correspond to material from the Sermon on the Mount/Plain.

63. It is at least arguable that Matt 5:40 is applied loosely by Paul to the situation in Corinth when they take their legal grievances against one another before a pagan court (1 Cor 6:1–8).

64. 1 Cor 7:10–11 = Matt 5:32; 19:9.

65. Rom 14:10 = Matt 7:1; Luke 6:37

Tradition, his knowledge of certain events in Jesus' life also implicitly point to Paul's knowledge of Jesus' passion. Paul clearly knows of Jesus' death on the cross, and his betrayal (known as part of his recollection of Jesus' last night with his disciples), his burial, and his resurrection from the dead.[66] So Paul's letters, corresponding to the pattern of virtually every non-narrative document in the New Testament, show a significant priority given to Jesus Tradition that underscores the non-violent character of Jesus' teachings (Sermon on the Mount/Plain) and example (the Passion). One can only conjecture that the same focus may have been perceptible in Paul's teaching when he first established his churches.

Why Paul's Letter to the Romans Is Important

In light of the evidence outlined above, it should be clear that not only for Paul, but for virtually every early Christian author, the memories of Jesus that were preserved and passed on to fellow Christians included what many consider to be the most startling and memorable aspect of Jesus' teaching.[67] This core emphasis on the ethical teaching of Jesus now preserved in the Sermon on the Mount/Plain, and in particular on living non-violently, or better still, living peaceably in a violent world, was uniquely *central* to the early Jesus movement—not completely novel in Judaism—and it was so fundamental that Paul, when writing to a group of Christians *whom he had never met*,[68] could take for granted that when he told them to eschew retaliation, they could affirm Paul's exhortation as one which aligned with their own understanding of the sayings of Jesus and which had been demonstrated perfectly in the peaceableness of their Lord.

In the present chapter we have examined the continuity between Jesus and Paul on the specific issue of non-violence. We have highlighted the pattern of the parallels between the two in both their teaching and lived

66. On Jesus' betrayal: 1 Cor 11:23; crucifixion: Gal 3:1, 13; Phil 2:6–8; burial: 1 Cor 15:4; resurrection: Rom 4:25; 8:34; 1 Cor 15:4.

67. Luz, *Matthew*, 1:274; Betz, *Sermon on the Mount*, 77.

68. Except, of course, *some* of those in the list of people he greets in chapter 16. Dunn, "Jesus Tradition," 177n70 notes: "That Romans has such a high proportion of such allusions is significant, since Paul could not have passed on such traditions to the Roman believers himself. He must have been able to assume, nevertheless, that the churches in Rome, or elsewhere, had been furnished with a stock of Jesus (and kerygmatic) tradition similar to that which Paul himself drew on. This tells us much about the breadth and relative fixedness of the Jesus Tradition passed on to new churches."

example and we have sought to understand the place or importance of this particular issue in a broad stream of early Christianity. We have shown that the traditions about Jesus were passed from authorized tradents to local Christian communities *and* their own individual members who were charged with the task of "remembering Jesus." In the specific case of Christians in first-century Rome, though we have no ability to identify founding missionaries,[69] we might imagine the founding missionaries in Rome as first-generation followers of Jesus or of the apostles, so that the Jesus Tradition which was transmitted in Rome was mediated through only one, or at most two, tradents.[70] Expanding our horizon in early Christianity, we should imagine that "more or less *from the first* those who established new churches would have taken care to provide and build a foundation of Jesus Tradition,"[71] and the evidence we have puts the Sermon on the Mount/Plain and Jesus' Passion at the heart of those traditions which were known to, and provided a behavioral norm for, a wide Christian audience within the life span of the first generation of Jesus' disciples. The evidence strongly suggests that the memory of Jesus as one who eschewed violent behavior as totally inappropriate to the character of God's children had a wide geographical footprint in earliest Christian circles and is best explained as one of the most salient features of the teaching and example of the historical Jesus, a feature which endured transmission because it was *this Jesus* who was recognizable as staying true to the living voice of Apostolic testimony.

69. Lampe, *From Paul to Valentinus*, 1, introduces his magisterial monograph on Roman Christianity thus: "The beginnings of pre-Pauline Christianity in Rome are shrouded in haze."

70. Secondhand testimony in the first century appears to maintain its "living and abiding" connection to the voice of the first-hand eyewitness. See Alexander, "The Living Voice," 221–47. Note the intriguing conjecture of Bauckham, *Gospel Women*, 165–86, that the Junia of Romans 16:7, a "compatriot" of Paul's who was "prominent among the apostles and . . . in Christ before I was" is the possible Latin equivalent of Jesus' disciple Joanna (Luke 8:3; 24:10). I do not wish to defend this conjecture here, but it does provide for the intriguing possibility of one of the first eyewitnesses to Jesus' resurrection (and an early companion in his ministry) to have been present among Roman Christians and available for authenticating (or rejecting) whatever testimony arrived in the capital regarding Jesus, Paul's included. Even apart from Bauckham's conjecture, the phrases Paul employs to commend Andronikus and Junia allow the possibility that they were eyewitnesses to the resurrection. See Jewett, *Romans*, 961–64.

71. Dunn, *Jesus Remembered*, 180, emphasis added.

4

Trajectories of Violence
and Peace in Galatians

Given the conclusion reached in the prior chapter, it is worth asking whether Paul dispensed with the non-violent image of Jesus when he penned the most "violent" letter in the Pauline corpus. By any account, the tone of his letter to the Galatians departs from the usual one found in Paul's other letters, which, with some exceptions,[1] tends to be encouraging or positive instead of being marked by the frustration and anger so evident in Galatians. It may come as a surprise, then, to read that although "Paul does not make an explicit call to nonviolence in Galatians, as he does elsewhere (Rom 12:14–21), nonviolent witness to the universal lordship of Jesus Christ is *everywhere implicit* in Galatians."[2] It is not the first half of Douglas Harink's statement which is surprising of course, but the second. Where, we might ask, are the implicit references to Christian non-violence? And how does one explain, if non-violence is a fundamental constituent of the gospel, the apparently "violent" tone and content at points in Paul's letter?

To examine Harink's claim, I propose the following: to let the issue of violence resonate beyond its usual parameters in Paul's letter. At Galatians 1:13, Paul wrote: "You have heard, no doubt, of my earlier life in Judaism. I was violently persecuting the church of God and trying to destroy it." My

---

1. The Corinthian correspondence at some points (e.g., 1 Cor 4:19–21) evince frustration too, but the scale in Galatians seems to be of a different order.

2. Harink, *Paul among the Postliberals*, 102, emphasis added.

concern is not to settle the debate regarding the kind of persecutions Paul participated in, nor the reasons for his action, worthy as those aims may be. I am rather more interested in whether Paul's past as a violent persecutor in a certain sense situates the non-violent witness to which he calls the Galatian churches. In other words, what happens when some of the prominent themes of Galatians are fed through the "grid" of Paul's violent past? In the present chapter, then, I will use Paul's violent past as a filter for tracing the trajectory of violence and peace in Paul's biography and in the biography of Paul's Galatian converts. Although some might consider the reason for his abandonment of violent tactics as obvious (i.e., quite simply, he became part of the group he had earlier tried to destroy), greater scrutiny indicates that this view of things is overly simplistic and fails to do justice to the text of Galatians.

A PRELUDE ON THE "AGITATORS"

Any interpreter who interacts with Paul's letter to the Galatians faces a number of challenges, and one of the most vexing issues must be the identity of the so-called agitators. I want to confront this particular issue early in this chapter in order to clear the ground of a few stumbling stones. It is important to flag a critical issue at the outset: from the moment one identifies the other "influencers" as Paul's opponents or as "agitators," as advocates of "another gospel," the effort to describe them is decisively based on Paul's rhetorical point of view, and does not necessarily reflect or correspond to the "historical" influencers' self-understanding, which is exceedingly difficult to reconstruct anyway.[3] Still, it is imperative for understanding his letter to make some comments towards identifying the agitators *as Paul characterizes them.*

Commonly labeled "the agitators" (derived from 1:7 οἱ ταράσσοντες ὑμᾶς and 5:10), we *might* conclude from Paul's letter that teachers or influencers emerged[4] in Galatia after his own visit, and added to his teaching

3. See Nanos, *Irony of Galatians*, esp. 110–99. Nanos's distaste for the label "agitators" is duly noted (127–30), and were I attempting to reconstruct the historical situation I might favor a more neutral label such as Nanos's own "influencers." For present purposes, I am content with identifying the rhetorical situation and reconstructing the agitators as Paul portrays them, and this label is possibly the least problematical of all the current options (e.g., Judaizers, opponents, rivals, teachers), though I do sometimes use "influencers" and "agitators" interchangeably. See ibid., 115.

4. Nanos's work has problematized the *origin* of the influencers, such that it cannot

in such a way that he thought amounted to a perversion of the gospel he preached (1:7). Paul accuses his opponents of a variety of more or less sinister activities, including: preaching "another" gospel (1:6–9); bewitching the Galatians (3:1); being improperly zealous for the Galatians (4:17); hindering the Galatians from obeying the truth through persuasion (5:7–8); troubling or agitating the Galatians (5:10, 12); being motivated to make a good showing in the flesh and avoiding persecution (6:12); and urging the Galatians to be circumcised (6:12). Paul's lopsided portrait of the agitators pulls no punches; they are rhetorically striped down of any redeeming qualities, and like "false brothers" he has encountered before (2:4), he paints (by association rather than by direct accusation) their so-called good news as hypocritical (2:13) and self-condemning (2:11) just to the extent that they are not, like Peter and Barnabas and others in Antioch, "walking towards the truth of the gospel" (2:14).[5]

If Paul's emotional response to the situation is anything to judge by, the agitators and their perversion of Paul's gospel have gotten under his skin; the stakes for Paul are clearly high. In the strongest possible terms, he denounces any (himself included) who would proclaim a gospel different from the one he originally announced to them (1:8–9). Paul also insists that the one who is unsettling them will bear judgment (5:10), and though ecclesiastical judgment could be entertained (not least because of Gal 6:1) the fact that for Paul, what is at stake is the very truth of the gospel suggests

---

be *conclusively* decided whether they arrived from outside the Galatian community or had been a part of it and only began to exert their influence after Paul's departure. Either way, their origin doesn't seem to be as significant to Paul as their effect: they are badly misleading the churches Paul left behind.

5. Nanos's work has agitated the consensus view on another key issue: whether the influencers were Christ-believing Jews or Jews (full stop), [or yet third and fourth alternatives, Gentile proselytes to Judaism, or Gentile proselytes to Jews who believe in Jesus]. Nanos, *Irony of Galatians*, 135, even raises the possibility that the influencers could be more than one group. Nanos points to Longenecker, *Galatians*, lxxxix, as representative of the consensus: the "almost uncontested view during the patristic and Reformation periods was that Paul's opponents were Jewish Christian Judaizers" and today they are most often described as Christian Jews who came to Galatia from Jerusalem. I raise the issue here because Nanos has demonstrated that, contrary to the consensus view, the evidence supporting the view of the influencers as Christians is not as strong as one might be led to believe. The nature of the influencers' "other gospel" would need to be reconsidered if they did not identify with Christ believers in Galatia. Despite Nanos's argument, I will loosely hold to the traditional view, recognizing that there is a possibility that the influencers had no part in trusting Jesus. My reason for holding to this traditional view is that I find the combination of 1:6–9, 2:4, and 2:14 to tip the balance in favor of *Paul* identifying the agitators as (pseudo-)Christ-believers.

that he considers the jugment that the agitator (in 5:10 the subject is in the singular) will face to be of an eschatological nature.[6] Another example where we can see that the situation in Galatia has struck a nerve is in his most infamous comment—a contender for the most disturbing image of the New Testament—when Paul declares "I wish those who unsettle you would castrate themselves!" (5:12).[7] In light of these three reference points alone, it would be difficult to overemphasize the severity of opposition Paul felt towards the message or influence of the agitators.[8]

Reconstructing the historical identity of the agitators and the historical situation that elicited Paul's letter would take us far beyond the scope of the thesis. In any case, a number of plausible competing paradigms for understanding the agitators could coexist alongside what is pivotal for the present chapter: the wide spectrum of views on the historical agitators is less decisive than the view one is able to reconstruct of the agitators *from Paul's own point of view.* I do not intend to present a "fair" historical reconstruction, but want instead to analize Paul's rhetorically constructed opponents and the situation "as he sees it" in Galatia.

6. Cf. Longenecker, *Triumph of Abraham's God,* 26n2.

7. The presence of 5:12 naturally places a question mark by my picture of a non-violent apostle. Gager and Gibson, "Violent Acts and Violent Language," 18, identify 5:12 (as well as 1:8–9; Phil 3:2 and 1 Cor 5:5) as an instance which betrays Paul's belief that violent action is not reserved for God alone, but that "he too is entitled . . . to act specifically against those who stand in opposition to his gospel." For Gager and Gibson (16) "the post-conversion Paul [was] still very much entangled in the coils of violence" because Paul was a "violent *personality,* in his actions, in his language, and in his ideology of Gentiles and their world as a world of violence." Although I agree in principle that (17) "violence is not just a matter of acts . . . but also a matter of words," I think care should be exercised in noting the differences between the two. Paul does not, after all, threaten to "cut off" his opponents, he wishes they would perform the act themselves. Splitting hairs, Gager and Gibson might protest, but the difference should be respected. Closer to my position is Gorman, *Inhabiting the Cruciform God,* 154: "It is of course true that words can harm and in that sense do violence to others, but this is a far cry from the violent activity of the pre-conversion Paul. To equate the two is to overestimate the significance of the former and to underestimate the significance of the latter." See also Jerome, *PL* 26:405C–D: "It is not surprising that Paul spoke this way once. He was, after all, only human, still enclosed in a weak vessel, one who saw in his body another law taking him captive and leading him to the law of sin. We often see saintly men fall in this way." The translation is from Plumer, *Augustine's Commentary on Galatians,* 92.

8. This does not say anything, however, about the attitude of the agitators towards Paul—we simply do not know whether they would identify themselves as Paul's opponents or adversaries. See Nanos, *Irony of Galatians,* 120–27; and Lyons, *Pauline Autobiography,* 79.

PAUL'S USE OF VIOLENCE

Paul's Violent End

From Galatians 1:11 to 2:14, Paul records the most detailed description of his own life. It is selective, covering some 14 or 17 years.[9] Indeed, he passes over most of them silently ("after fourteen years . . ." Gal 2:1).[10] Paul's violent past is recalled *twice* in only eleven verses—initially at 1:13, and again, at 1:23, where Paul indicates that the churches of Judea heard the report: "The one who formerly was persecuting us is now proclaiming the faith he once tried to destroy." In contrast to the many important events of his own life that he left out in his sparing narrative, Paul chose to reiterate his violent persecution of the earliest followers of Jesus.

The degree of violence in which Paul engaged has been questioned in the past, but even scholars who recognize a healthy measure of hyperbole in Paul's language tend to allow for varying degrees of physical persecution.[11] Rather than take up point by point the arguments of those who dispute the possibility of Paul's violence (or the extent to which he might have been violent), I will present a brief constructive argument which advocates seeing Paul's activity as persecutor of the "church" as violent. In presenting my argument, I will address several objections raised by those who doubt the veracity of holding such a view.[12]

As a way of entering into the matter, it is fundamental to establish a basic guideline from the start: Luke's account(s) in the Acts of the Apostles must not be the source from which one establishes the nature of Paul's activity. Although studies of the gospels sometimes illustrate that late texts

9. See Martyn, *Galatians*, 180–2 for a discussion of Paul's use of the adverb *then* (ἔπειτα) and its importance for dating Paul's visits to Jerusalem. Martyn ultimately decides for a cumulative perspective (14 years total), while Jewett, *Dating Paul's Life*, 52–54, decides on a consecutive perspective (17 years total), despite the difficulties this presents to other aspects of Paul's chronology.

10. It is a silence on 11 years if one subscribes to the cumulative view.

11. E.g., Bockmuehl, *Philippians*, 200, notes that "Paul himself clearly implies that his own approach was at the radical (and quite possibly violent . . .) end of the contemporary Jewish spectrum." Dunn, *Galatians*, 58, notes the "exaggerated" language, but confirms that "physical destruction" was real.

12. See, e.g., Menoud, "Le sens du verbe πορθεῖν," 178–86; Hultgren, "Paul's Pre-Christian Persecutions," 97–111; Crook, *Reconceptualising Conversion*; Murphy-O'Connor, *Paul*. I will make my own constructive case for the violent character of Paul's persecuting activity below, without reference to Acts of the Apostles.

may indeed preserve traditions that originate from periods that predate earlier texts, it is best to attempt to establish the nature of Paul's persecuting from what can be adduced from his own letters. This uncompromising preference for Paul is a double-edged sword for those who harbor doubts about the nature of Paul's activity: one cannot appeal to incredible elements in Luke's narrative (e.g., alleged letters from the chief priests) to accuse by association other elements presented by Paul himself. The possibility of Paul's violence rests with Paul's language and imagery alone. To put an unusual spin on the problem of the relationship between Acts and Paul's letters, I submit that if one should not appeal to Acts to fill in the narrative gaps, one also should not appeal to Acts in order to discredit what Paul himself writes about his activity as persecutor. We may consider ourselves unfortunate that Paul does not offer us a more detailed narrative of his pre-Christian existence, but the nature of his activity as a persecutor does come to us in the lengthiest biographical section in all of his letters, and the vocabulary used there provides us with some useful clues.

The earliest reference to Paul's persecution of Jesus' followers is in Galatians. Paul wrote:

> You have heard, no doubt, of my earlier life in Judaism. I was violently persecuting (καθ᾽ ὑπερβολὴν ἐδίωκον) the church of God and was trying to destroy it (ἐπόρθουν αὐτήν). I advanced in Judaism beyond many among my people of the same age, for I was far more zealous for the traditions of my ancestors (περισσοτέρως ζηλωτὴς ὑπάρχων τῶν πατρικῶν μου παραδόσεων). (Gal 1:13–14)

And a few verses later, he writes:

> I was still unknown by sight to the churches of Judea that are in Christ; they only heard it said, "The one who formerly was persecuting us is now proclaiming the faith he once tried to destroy (ὁ διώκων ἡμᾶς ποτε νῦν εὐαγγελίζεται τὴν πίστιν ἥν ποτε ἐπόρθει)." (Gal 1:22–23)

As with so many debatable interpretive possibilities, Paul's use of the verb *persecute* (διώκω) leaves the character of his activity an open question. In this sense, Phillippe Menoud[13] and Arland Hultgren[14] are not wrong to suggest that Paul makes no claims about the kind of activity he engaged in

13. Menoud, "Le sens du verbe πορθεῖν."

14. Hultgren, "Paul's Pre-Christian Persecutions," 97; 109: διώκω "carries with it the idea of both oral and physical abuse" when Paul uses it with the result that we do not know which it is in Galatians.

when he uses this generic verb.[15] However, context provides more color. Paul's persecuting is described as having the intent to destroy the church of God, a description which is difficult to square with a comparatively benign confounding of Christian arguments.[16] In Galatians 1:13 and 23, *destroy* (πορθέω) has a conative aspect, indicating what Paul set out to achieve, and while *persecute* (διώκω) is open to interpretation, the presence of πορθέω consistently "denotes violent action."[17] In almost every case, πορθέω is used to describe situations in which physical violence is presupposed.[18] A handful of representative examples ought to demonstrate the general picture of how πορθέω was used by authors roughly contemporary with Paul.

In 4 Maccabees, *destroy* (πορθέω) is used to describe the plundering of Jerusalem by Antiochus (4:23)[19] as well as the hellish torture inflicted on

15. If καθ᾽ ὑπερβολὴν is taken adverbially, the phrase may support a violent persecution, e.g., persecuted to utmost, i.e, to the extreme. But the phrase also has been read to describe Paul's enthusiasm. So Hultgren, "Paul's Pre-Christian Persecutions," 110: "He persecuted the church with an intensity of zeal (*not an intensity of violence*), which was beyond compare" (emphasis added). Although this is legitimate on grammatical grounds, I will show that at the level of syntax and, in view of the context, an adverbial reading is preferred. Furthermore, to try to deflect the possibility that Paul was violent as an exceedingly zealous individual only confirms that his action was possibly violent. That is, to say Paul was intensely zealous is, in practical terms, to say he probably approved of (and participated in) violent reprisals against gross offenders of the Torah. I will offer examples of this equivalency in the body of the text.

16. Hare, *Jewish Persecution of Christians*, 59, opines that "it seems highly probable that [Paul's] activity was primarily verbal."

17. Hengel, *Pre-Christian Paul*, 71. He notes the conative aspect in contrast to the durative aspect of the parallel imperfect verb ἐδίωκον, "persistently persecuted." So too Dunn, *Theology of Paul*, 352; and Martyn, *Galatians*, 154.

18. That I cannot say *always* may seem to weaken my point. It is true that sometimes the destroying relates to an argument or state of mind (see Philo, *Planting* 159; *Decalogue* 49; *Good Person* 38). However, the preponderance of usage points to *extreme* physical violence. Philo contains examples along these lines too. See Philo, *Confusion* 47; *Moses* 1:69; *Flaccus* 54; *Embassy* 114. In addition, the reports of Paul's turn from persecutor to proclaimer (Gal 1:23) would have been far less memorable if he had merely debated openly with the followers of Jesus.

19. 4 Maccabees 4:15–26 is a redacted version of 2 Maccabees 4:7–6:11. Although πορθέω is not used in the source text, the description of the sack of Jerusalem (its *destruction*, if we use 4 Maccabees' term) is embellished: Antiochus "commanded his soldiers to cut down relentlessly (κόπτειν ἀφειδῶς) everyone they met and to kill (κατασφάζειν) those who went into their houses. Then there were massacres (ἀναίρεσις) of young and old, destruction (ἀφανισμός) of women and children, slayings (σφαγαί) of virgins and infants. Within the total of three days eighty thousand were destroyed (κατεφθάρησαν), forty thousand in hand-to-hand fighting, and as many were sold into slavery as were killed." 2 Macc 5:12–14.

the seven brothers (11:4). This latter usage refers to the suffering of the first four brothers which included beating with scourges (9:12, 28), dislocating limbs (9:12–13; 10:5), being burnt alive (9:19–20), tearing away of the scalp (9:28; 10:7), and breaking fingers, arms, legs and elbows (10:6). When the "author" of 4 Maccabees used πορθέω, physical violence was very clearly in view.

Josephus too uses the word to describe the vicious burning of villages in Idumaea (Josephus, *War* 4:534) and the destruction of Jerusalem (Josephus, *Ant.* 10:135, cf. *3 Bar* 1:1), and the verb is commonly used by him in a formulaic description of the plundering or destruction of land by armies (e.g., *Ant.* 6:106; 9:253 "laid their country waste"). To proffer an example of what we might envisage when Josephus writes of a city being an object of πορθέω, he wrote that:

> Some places they burnt down, some they utterly demolished, and whatsoever grew in the country, they either trod it down or fed upon it, and by their marches they made the ground that was cultivated, harder and more untractable than that which was barren. In short, there was no sign remaining of those places that had been laid waste (τοῖς πορθουμένοις), that ever they had had a being. (*War* 4:537)

Josephus *invariably* uses the term to describe physical destruction, a consistency that may be unsurprising given the focus of much of his writing.

Although Philo provides several examples of the use of destroy (πορθέω) to describe the destruction of arguments (see Philo, *Planting* 159; *Decalogue* 49; *Good Person* 38), he also provides ample evidence that it most naturally connotes violent behavior. For instance, at *Confusion* 47, Philo writes that evil and foolish men: "do in peace every thing that is done in war; they plunder, they ravage, they drag into slavery, they carry off booty, *they lay waste* (πορθοῦσιν), they behave insolently, they assault, they destroy, they pollute, they murder treacherously, they murder openly if they are the more powerful." So while Philo can be adduced in support of the more benign image of πορθέω presented by Menoud and others, Philo also uses the term in an unmistakably violent sense.[20]

20. Another example: at *Moses* 1:69, Philo uses πορθέω to describe the unexpected reversal of circumstances which was to follow those led out of Egypt by Moses: "But when your enemies think most surely that they are destroying (πορθεῖν) you, then you shall most brilliantly shine out in glory." Though this passage is one illustration of Philo's allegorical interpretation at work, he is referring throughout to destruction that is quite real—the "destruction" is a reference to the perils faced by Israelites if they remained in

Paul uses the term only twice, both times in Galatians to describe the goal of his persecuting activity.[21] While we cannot squeeze any further details from these compressed uses of *destroy* (πορθέω), we should not overlook that, in addition to the violent activity that is telegraphed by Paul's use of the verb πορθέω, Paul's comment that he "advanced in Judaism" beyond many peers because he "was far more zealous for the traditions of my ancestors" hints at the possibility of violent activity too.[22] One must be careful to state that zeal did not *necessarily* need to be expressed through violence, in fact, examples of violence *identified* to be inspired by zeal among first-century Jews are difficult to find. Indeed, because Paul claimed to have acted with *exceptional* zeal, we should expect specific examples to be few.[23] Philo of Alexandria provides (possibly) the most illuminating comparisons.

Context is crucial when addressing the issue of zeal, since the word is used by Philo to advertise both positive and negative behaviors. However, for our purposes, it will be best to examine those cases where zeal is viewed positively and is seen as a virtue related to the (violent) punishment of those who transgress the Torah. Torrey Seland calls such cases establishment violence.[24] In three publications, Seland calls special attention to Philo's *De specialibus legibus* 1:54–57, not least because this passage is one in which the Phinehas episode from Numbers 25 is drawn upon by Philo to illustrate a warranted case of vigilante justice in Israel's Scripture.[25] We

---

Egypt: "You shall be saved rather than destroyed, by those who are desirous to destroy your whole race against their will." There are only eleven uses of the verb in the so-called Old Testament Pseudepigrapha, most of those occurring in the Syballine Oracles. The *exclusive* use of πορθέω in the Pseudepigrapha is to identify violent destruction, especially relating to the ravaging destruction of warfare. See *Sib. Or.* 3:510, 636, 639, 666; 8:31, 140; 11:57; 12:45; cf. 3 *Bar.* 1:1, "Nebuchadnezzar the king was permitted by God *to destroy* his city"; on 4 *Macc.* 4:23; 11:4, see above.

21. The only other New Testament occurrence is Acts 9:21, which I will refrain from appealing to since it relates to Paul's activity as persecutor.

22. Phil 3:6 also connects Paul's zeal with his persecution of the church.

23. Although the strong response Paul participates in was a minority viewpoint within first-century Judaism, we might expect it to gain greater notoriety *because* of its sensational or extreme aspects. That Paul's actions were *exceptional* is implied by his own description of his advancement among his peers by being περισσοτέρως ζηλωτὴς (Gal 1:14). Cf. Gager and Gibson, "Violent Acts and Violent Language," 17.

24. Seland, *Establishment Violence*, 84, quotes Rosenbaum and Sederberg's definition: "Establishment violence may be defined as 'acts or threats of coercion in violation of the formal boundaries of an established sociopolitical order which, however, are intended by the violators to defend that order from some form of subversion.'"

25. See Seland, *Establishment Violence*, 123–24; Seland, "Saul of Tarsus and Early Zealotism, 449–71, and Seland, "(Re)presentations of Violence in Philo."

will begin by looking at Philo's references to the Phinehas episode before querying whether Philo commends establishment violence in some cases of egregious Torah transgression among his contemporaries.

In *Spec. Laws* 1:56, Philo wrote:

> There is, in the history of the law, a record of one man [Phinehas] who . . . when he saw some men connecting themselves with foreign women, and . . . neglecting all their national customs and laws (ἀλογοῦντας μὲν τῶν πατρίων) . . . was seized with a sudden enthusiasm (ἐνθουσιάω) in the presence of the whole multitude; and . . . he slew one man who was so daring as to put himself forward as the leader and chief of this transgression of the law (παρανομίας) . . . and while he was openly performing sacrifices to images and unholy idols, [Phinehas] slew him, together with the woman who was with him.

In this section of *Spec. Laws*, Philo is treating specifically the first two commandments of the Decalogue. Like the passage in Numbers, Philo points out that the broad context of the vigilante action is a corporate disobedience of the first commandment, certain men (τινας) were neglecting/ disregarding their πατρίων—their ancestral or hereditary traditions. There was more to it than the actions of one man, but Phinehas [unnamed by Philo] killed the one who had been the "leader and chief of the wrongdoing" (*Spec. Laws*, 1:56).

Philo keys in on the neglect of ancestral traditions (πατρίων) and their taking part in rituals associated with foreign women. He claims that one man (Zimri according to Num 25:14) is so bold in his lawlessness as to sacrifice publicly to graven images. Numbers does not identify the specific action taken by Zimri ("One of the Israelites came and brought to his brothers a Midianite woman in the plain view of Moses and of the whole community of the Israelites" 25:6), but it is clear from the context he is one of those who is about to/intends to be joined with Baal Peor, an action that in the preceding verse warrants the punishment of death.

Although Philo does not seem to be pressing for a widespread implementation of the zealous judgment of Phinehas, he does call Phinehas's exploits "noble daring" (τὸ καλὸν τοῦτο τόλμημα) and obviously follows the tradition of upholding Phinehas' action as virtuous, repeating the scriptural declaration that God rewarded Phinehas by "crowning him with the gifts of peace and priesthood" (ἀναστέφει δωρεαῖς, εἰρήνῃ καὶ ἱερωσύνῃ) (*Spec. Laws* 1:57). Philo never directly promotes the specific action of Phinehas, but it is clear that Philo (along with virtually the entirety of extant tradition that received/commented on the Phinehas episode) believed Phinehas's decision to drive a spear through Zimri and Cozbi (Num 25:7–8) was the proper course of action in the circumstances.[26] Philo points out that his action "admonished a vast multitude of those who were prepared to commit similar follies" (*Spec. Laws*, 1:57). Phinehas' zeal-inspired violence was righteous not only for punishing the transgressions of the one man, but prevented (according to Philo) widespread and grave transgression of the first commandment.

Another passage in which Philo presents zeal together with (violent) reprisals for transgression of the Torah is in *Spec. Laws* 2:252–53. Reflecting on the fate of one who (foolishly) risks bearing false witness (and calling on God as a witness in the deed), Philo remarks that such a person:

> will never entirely escape [punishment], for there are innumerable guardians, zealots for the law and strict keepers of the ancestral traditions,[27] of rigid justice, prompt to stone such a criminal, and visiting without pity all such as work wickedness.

Philo does not offer specific examples of zealotic guardianship in this passage [indeed that is not the point of the treatise], but it is incredibly tempting to see in Philo's description a parallel with the self-description of Paul.[28] That Paul was once a strict guardian of ancestral tradition seems clear (Gal 1:14); that he was motivated to persecute because of his zeal for the Torah is certain (Phil 3:6). We can even easily imagine that Paul sought, through this course of vigilante action, to prevent widespread participation among kinsmen in the "church of God" from grave transgression of the Torah. Paul "saw himself as acting out the model of Phinehas, being zealous for the Law, even to the extent of using violence against overt perpetrators,

26. Phinehas turns up in many of Philo's works, always praised for his zeal (e.g., *Alleg. Interp.*, 3:242), reason, and love of virtue (e.g., *Cain*, 182).

27. "μυρίοι γὰρ ἔφοροι, ζηλωταὶ νόμων, φύλακες τῶν πατρίων ἀκριβέστατοι."

28. To clarify, we have no known contemporary examples of zeal-inspired violence from Philo; rather, evidence from Philo remains in the realm of historical description (as in the Phinehas episode) or rhetorical manuevering (as when Philo warns that there exist innumerable strict guardians of the ancestral traditions, willing to punish promptly and violently gross violations of the Decalogue). See Seland, "(Re)presentations of Violence," unnumbered paper, "Though we have no sources from Philo available that explicitly record actual cases of establishment violence, we have nevertheless his expositions of cases of gross non-conformity to the Torah in which he argues for coercive actions to be taken on the spot."

thus becoming a persecutor of the early Christians."[29] Which specific commands of the Torah is an open question; the evidence from Philo might push us towards expecting that Paul believed the church taught potentially idolatrous things about Jesus of Nazareth or spread false testimony concerning Jesus. The intensity of Paul's persecution will necessarily remain an open question too. No further Pauline evidence can be presented to convince those who doubt that Paul's persecuting veered toward the violent side of the spectrum. Seland recognizes the limits of our evidence, but offers a conclusion with which I agree:

> While we have no evidence in [Paul's] letters that he persecuted "into death" (compare Acts 22,4), the violent zealotic nature of his persecutions should not be under-interpreted. The evidence of Philo, as well as the zealotic activities of the various "revolutionary" groups in Palestine in Paul's times, provide a cultural context for understanding horrifying persecutions even if they did not always result in death. The early "Christians" is [sic] described in our sources as suffering zealotic persecutions almost from the very beginnings of their existence.[30]

To summarize my own case for seeing Paul's persecuting activity as situated firmly on the violent side of the spectrum of activity:

- The use of *persecute* (διώκω) by Paul does not tell us anything specific about Paul's activity as a persecutor in isolation, context is key in this instance.[31]

29. Seland, "Saul of Tarsus and Early Zealotism," 466.

30. Ibid., 468.

31. I have not extensively addressed the issue of hyperbole by Paul since the case for 1:13 being hyperbole flags when it is virtually certain Paul repeats at 1:23 a phrase that early followers used to refer to him—this is not a case of Pauline hyperbole, rather, he uses the language others have "given" to him. He has no need to exaggerate (*pace* Crook, *Reconceptualising Conversion*, 173–4); his reputation precedes him. In short, if 1:13 is believed to be a typical Pauline exaggeration, the use of πορθέω at 1:23 requires us to (re)consider the possibility of Paul's violent activity, and should cause us to rethink characterizing 1:13 as hyperbolic. Thurén, "'By Means of Hyperbole,'" 97–113, identifies Gal 1:13 as an example of καθ' ὑπερβολὴν functioning as an intensifier (98). Several of Crooks cautions are dead-on: many treatments of Paul's "conversion" are decisively influenced not only by a reading of Acts (rather than Paul's letters), but betray a psychologizing reading of the Lukan material, a "methodological miscue that is twice-removed from its subject" (153). But Paul does use rather strong language to describe his transformation from persecutor to proponent. After all, he does say that he has been "crucified with Christ" (Gal 2:19) and also exclaims "May I never boast of anything except the cross of our Lord Jesus Christ, by which the world has been crucified to me, and I to the world"

- As a rule, we cannot appeal to Acts, whether to corroborate Paul's language *or to discredit what we can infer from it.*

- Paul's use of *destroy* (πορθέω) points us down the path of seeing his actions as very likely violent, and extremely so.

- This is because *destroy* (πορθέω) is used consistently to convey the sense that activity characterized by the verb is extremely violent.

- Additional support comes from the picture Paul leaves that his persecuting activity was intimately related to his zeal (Phil 3:6), an image that corresponds to an *independent* image of zeal-inspired vigilante violence offered in the writings Philo of Alexandria.

Apocalypse! The End of the Violent Paul

Most scholars take for granted that the time period of which Paul speaks of God's "apocalypsing" of the Son "in me" (ἐν ἐμοί, Gal 1:15–16) is the same as that when Paul was intercepted by Jesus on the road to Damascus (Acts 9:1–9 and parallels).[32] Paul does not clarify this point, even though he does refer to *returning* to Damascus after a sojourn in Arabia (1:17), which seems to imply his receipt of the revelation in or near Damascus. Despite difficulties trying to locate definitively the *place* of that revelation (apart from a knee-jerk appeal to Acts), the portrait Paul paints in Galatians of his life is one of contrasting *periods of time*, and for the present argument this, rather than location, is key. Paul was once *formerly* a persecutor of God's church (1:13) which he tried to destroy (1:13, 23); however, once God "apocalypsed" Jesus in him, that activity, that period of his life, came to an end.[33] His one-time goal was terminated on the "Damascus road." The way ahead involved a serious alteration of his course.

(Gal 6:14). We do not need to collapse these statements into a description of Paul's "conversion" to see that to describe his current *modus vivendi* in this way is to paint a rather dramatic turn of events in his life. If someone wishes to describe his conversion with terms like "shattering," or "wrenching and decisive," I think Paul's language elsewhere in Galatians certainly gives us scope to be sympathetic to such views.

32. See, e.g., Lightfoot, *Galatians*, 82; Betz, *Galatians*, 74; Martyn, *Galatians*, 157–58; Schlier, *Galater*, 58–59; Hengel and Schwemer, *Paul Between Damascus and Antioch*, 38.

33. See Martyn, *Galatians*, 163–64.

The Subject of the Apocalypse—The Son

That Paul's violent life was shattered by the revealing of God's son should require some reflection on the person who was the subject of that apocalypse. Scanty are the references to Jesus' history in Galatians, but we have already noted that the lack of references to Jesus was a common feature of virtually all the non-narrative writing eventually collected in the Christian canon.[34] Apart from the few things which can be gleaned directly from the text of Galatians (e.g., Jesus' resurrection 1:1; self-giving 1:4; 2:20; Jesus' crucifixion/death 2:19, 21; 3:1, 13; 5:11; 6:12, 14; birth 4:4; Jesus was Jewish 4:4), scholarly discussion continues regarding whether there is a narrative substructure in Paul's letter(s) that can be used to reconstruct the "story of Jesus" in Paul's letter. One crucial feature of this narrative substructure is the theme of Jesus' own faithfulness.[35]

The Son of God revealed in Paul is foremost the crucified and resurrected Jesus. The risen Jesus who "terminated" Paul in the course of his violent mission was none other than God's Messiah who had himself refused to employ violence to achieve God's redemption of creation. For Paul, the messianic identity of Jesus seems to have been confirmed, in large part, by the fact of Jesus' vindication through resurrection; the politics of Jesus was secondary (not, however, non-essential), important for Paul only because Jesus had been raised from the dead. In other words, the violence or non-violence of any messianic claimant was not definitive for determining the messianic claim;[36] the "results" (i.e., crucified by the Romans) spoke for themselves, and by this measure Jesus, whether he had been violent or not, was an abject failure. This was likely the view Paul took before his "conversion" and I suspect that Paul's later non-violent position is taken not simply because Jesus and his followers were thus committed, but because

---

34. See chapter 3.

35. A lengthy defense of the presence of a narrative substructure in Galatians is beyond the scope of this chapter. See the second edition of Hays' seminal *The Faith of Jesus Christ*, and the collection of essays in Longenecker, (ed.), *Narrative Dynamics in Paul*.

36. Though not specifically addressing the issue of violence, see Wright, *Resurrection*, 244: "Neither Jesus' life, deeds and teachings on the one hand, nor his resurrection on the other, could by themselves have had the effect of making people say at once, 'He really was and is the Messiah.' But put them together . . . and the result is clear. A would-be messianic life would be an insufficient condition for such a result; even resurrection by itself would likewise be insufficient; but both remain necessary conditions for the claim to be made."

Jesus (who chose the path of non-violence) was God's Messiah. Paul's own non-violent praxis is therefore rooted in his christological commitments.[37]

The issue of Jesus' faithfulness is significant at just this point because if Jesus was thought to have been entrusted with the redemption of creation by the Father, his faithfulness to that task *and the means by which redemption is accomplished* bear the imprint of the divine will. Apart from the grammatical argument, which is contested and has led to an impasse in the reading of *faith in/of Jesus Christ* (πίστεως Ἰησοῦ Χριστοῦ at Gal 2:16 and elsewhere), the theological coherence of the subjective genitive reading tips the scales in its favor (in my view). Rather than being seized on the road to Damascus by an *unfaithful* messianic pretender, Jesus' resurrection firmly established for Paul Jesus' own fidelity to the God of Abraham, Isaac, and Jacob. This fidelity had at root a concomitant commitment to encountering and overcoming the anti-God powers without recourse to the violence that characterizes the *modus operandi* of those powers.[38]

The Violent Paul Co-Crucified

One is justified in asking not only who was revealed to Paul, but also what *action* Paul envisages occurring in the apocalypse of Jesus to and in him. The immediate consequence is that Paul "went away at once into Arabia" (1:17). But the *effect* of the apocalypse is distinct from the *subsequent activity of Paul*, that is, we perhaps have a better clue to what Paul believed to

37. On Paul's non-violent praxis, see Chapter Three. Gorman, *Inhabiting the Cruciform God*, 153 writes: "Paul needed a conversion from violence via a divine vindication of nonviolence—the resurrection—to conclude that nonviolence is the way of God and therefore also of the covenant people." Cf. Hays, "Narrate and Embody," 197: "So the christological case for pacifism is not merely a matter of explicating one or two of Jesus' sayings about renouncing anger and turning the other cheek. Rather, it is a matter of seeing the overall narrative of his life as the embodiment of human wholeness, and the narrative of his passion and death as a disclosure of the costly faithfulness and enemy love that leads to reconciliation (Rom. 5:10), rather than perpetuating the cycle of violence."

38. To suppose that Jesus was charged with the task of redemption of creation of course raises the question of whether the mode of redemption, i.e., crucifixion, is itself not only inherently violent but also belies the claim that the first person of the trinity is characteristically non-violent. Volumes could be written here; I suspect that Paul would have had little problem accepting the violent form which Jesus' sacrificial death took since the cross neither encompasses without remainder the redeeming activity of God in Christ nor does it demonstrate God's wrath without also revealing a fierce mercy as the characteristic effect of the pouring out of God's wrath on the cross.

have happened to him in the apocalypse at Galatians 2:19: "I have been crucified with Christ." In other words, the violent Paul was executed on the road to Damascus. This startling claim, the co-crucifixion of Paul's violent self, corresponds well with the *effect* the apocalypse had on Paul's new way of dealing not just with those in the "church of God," but with his enemies more generally. Of course, Paul's "co-crucifixion" with Christ is only half of the equation; he is also enlivened by the resurrected Jesus (see below). But at this point we should attend to the first part of that equation: the metaphor of being crucified with Christ.

The violent credentials of crucifixion are intuitively obvious, though primary source details are less gruesome than one might expect. Not only are the gospels themselves conspicuously sparing in offering details, but Roman literary sources also refrain from offering graphic descriptions.[39] J. Christiaan Beker claims that "whipping, torture, the burning out of the eyes, and maiming often preceded the actual hanging."[40] Whipping of the condemned and carrying of his own crossbeam have been posited as the basic procedures;[41] cruelty could no doubt only add to the humility and suffering. Indeed, Josephus (*War* 5:447–451 [Thackeray, LCL]) recalls the terrible fate of Jews caught outside the city walls in the siege of Jerusalem, when especially "citizens of the poorer class" found themselves "scourged and subjected to *torture of every description*" before being crucified opposite the city walls as a warning to those remaining in the city. Crucifixion, in this situation at least, became so mundane that the soldiers experimented with crucifying their prisoners in different postures in order to amuse themselves.[42]

Less clear to the modern reader may be the recipients of such violent punishment. In his seminal work on the subject, Martin Hengel shows that crucifixion in the Roman world was "almost always inflicted on the

39. See Green, "Crucifixion," 87–101. On account of this paucity of evidence (both literary and archaeological), one can almost forgive the editors of *CAH* 10, an otherwise exhaustive reference work on the Roman Empire from 43 BCE to 69 CE, which contains a measly two references (in the index) to the practice of crucifixion in the empire; Jesus of Nazareth predictably accounts for half of them.

40. Beker, *Paul the Apostle*, 206.

41. Hengel, *Crucifixion*, 22–32.

42. It is considered to be a typical exaggeration by Josephus, but the fact that he can even entertain that "so great was their number, that space could not be found for the crosses nor crosses for the bodies" suggests that at a certain point, the cruelty of crucifixion itself wasn't enough for the Roman soldiers; bored of the usual procedure, they amused themselves by devising new ways to torment their victims.

lower class (*humiliores*)."[43] It was a "horrendous, ignominious happening reserved for the scum of society, that is, traitors and runaway slaves."[44] The honor-stripping punishments could not, without significant reason, be performed against those of higher status (*honestiores*).[45] Brent Shaw sees both in Roman law and upper class attitudes a clear pattern of viewing the bandit (λῃστής) as a "non-person," one literally without legal identity—they were "out-law," "lumped together with . . . slaves and the insane."[46] Hengel suggests too that, in distinction from the Persian and Carthaginian use of crucifixion, elite Romans writers saw crucifixion as "the typical punishment for slaves."[47] For Paul to consider himself to have been, even if only metaphorically, crucified with Christ, he had to acknowledge the debasing reality of crucifixion. Is it a coincidence that Paul repeatedly refers to himself as a *slave* (δοῦλος) in his letters (e.g., Gal 1:10)?

That Paul did not die on a cross on the road to Damascus is obvious. However, the application of the metaphor is no less significant. Paul continues to live, but that life lived in the flesh he now lived in harmony with Jesus' own faithfulness, animated by Jesus' Spirit, in such a way that Paul's new life (ideally) recapitulates Jesus' own self-giving. The violent Paul died when Christ was apocalypsed in him; now Christ-in-Paul shapes Paul's life in the flesh into a cruciform existence.[48] Violence remains a part of Paul's life, but it is now violence inflicted on and received by the Apostle rather than performed by him. We might say that Paul's biography of violence received its death-blow on the road to Damascus, but that his new life (a new biography of sorts) *in Christ* continues to address the violence of the struggle

43. Hengel, *Crucifixion*, 34

44. Beker, *Paul the Apostle*, 206.

45. Hengel, *Crucifixion*, 34. Beker, *Paul the Apostle*, 206, goes too far in asserting that crucifixion could "never" be the punishment of a Roman citizen. In cases of high treason, the protection of citizenship could be overlooked. Indeed, in the later (sixth century CE) legal collection *Digest* 48.18.29, citizenship and freedom are said to be lost immediately by one sentenced to death. Brent D. Shaw, "Bandits in the Roman Empire," 3–52, identifies crucifixion along with being thrown to the beasts and being burned alive as punishments "members of the upper class believed that *latrones*" especially *deserved*. As a deterrent, "well-known bandits were to be executed and their bodies impaled on forked stakes in the same place where they had committed their crimes so that the mere sight would deter others from performing similar acts." The quotations are from pp. 20–21. Cf. *Digest* 48.19.28.10, 15; and Saller, "Status and Patronage," in *CAH* 10:852.

46. Shaw, "Bandits in the Roman Empire," 22–23.

47. Hengel, *Crucifixion*, 51.

48. See Gorman, *Cruciformity*, 178–213, esp. 194n42.

between the old and new ages, but from the perspective of receiving it and terminating its effectiveness through non-retaliation, rather than participating in its continual dissemination in a spiral of violence.

THE IMPACT OF THE APOCALYPSE OF JESUS IN PAUL: A CHRIST-ENLIVENED NON-VIOLENT PAUL

The subject of the personal effect of this co-crucifixion is one which has naturally received much attention in Pauline studies. Despite the flood of literature on the importance of Paul's call/conversion, few have called more than passing attention to the issue of Paul's violence in relation to his "death" and enlivenment.[49] And so, despite the numerous treatments of 2:19–20 already available, I will sketch the way in which Paul's belief that Christ living in him necessarily results in an Apostle who becomes conformed to the image of Jesus' non-violent life—even to the point of Paul's own death.

No Longer Do I Live, but Christ Lives in Me

> I no longer live, but Christ lives in me. But now the life which I live in the flesh, I live by means of the faithfulness of the son of God who loved me and gave himself for me. Gal 2:19–20 (translation mine)

The "startling" and "exaggerated"[50] language of Galatians 2:19–20 is fitting for Paul's attempt to convey the significance of the transformation he experienced in the apocalypse of Christ. The violent Paul of Galatians 1:13

---

49. Gorman's *Inhabiting the Cruciform God* (2009) and his *Reading Paul* (2008), as well as Harinck's *Paul among the Postliberals*, are the two authors who have attended to the importance of Paul's violent past in relation to his "conversion." Gorman, *Inhabiting the Cruciform God*, 158–9 writes: "Seldom . . . is his turn from violence *qua* violence (as opposed to his turn from persecuting the early church to promoting the faith) seen as a constitutive part of his conversion and new life, or as paradigmatic for, and therefore constitutive of, Christian conversion and new life more generally. *If the conversion of Paul*, grounded in the resurrection of Christ, *is paradigmatic, it is paradigmatic in multiple ways, not least of which is his conversion from violence to nonviolence.* Put differently, forsaking violence and embracing nonviolence is an essential part of Paul's theosis and of Christian theosis more generally" (emphasis added). The bibliography on Paul's "conversion" is immense and will not be catalogued here.

50. Dunn, *Galatians*, 145.

effectively "died" upon encountering the Messiah, and here Paul claims not just to have been incorporated into Christ's body, but in fact he claims to be enlivened by the non-violent Messiah Jesus. Paul's self is not obliterated; rather as John Barclay has pointed out, human and divine agency are held together "in a dialectical fashion" by Galatians 2:20 ("I no longer live . . . but now . . . I live").[51] The life Paul now lives, however, is one animated by the Christ who lived faithfully to God which was manifest in his self-giving love. Paul does not explicitly draw out the non-violent implications of being enlivened by Jesus, but the previous chapters demonstrated the widespread view of Jesus as a pursuer of peace who forsook violence. I do not wish to claim that this interpretation exhausts Paul's meaning, but when he claims that he no longer lives, the "I" to which he refers is the Paul who died to the law (2:19), and the law and the reputation of its giver were the things which he presumably sought to protect from corruption and misuse by the "church of God" through his violent opposition (1:13–14). When Paul claims that "It is no longer I who live," we ought to think foremost of the Paul engaged in violent suppression of the early Christian movement.

In the second half of Galatians 2:19, once again Paul's extraordinary, compact statement which asserts that Christ dwells in him deserves more attention than I can afford to give to it here. However, since I am concerned with how the indwelling Christ empowers and enlivens Paul *specifically in his ability to eschew violence where he once did not*, the focus is justified. Galatians 2:20 is clearly important for understanding Paul's letter, and for how Paul portrays the overall concept of Christ indwelling the believer.[52] We must probe how Paul's concept of being indwelled by Christ clarifies the way in which Paul and, in a corresponding way, other believers, become capable of refraining from violence.

Paul's statement, "it is Christ who lives in me," assumes that Christ's resurrection life elicits human faith or response. The power to elicit human response is found in Paul's extension of the sentence: "And the life I now live[53] in the flesh I live by faith, that is, by the faithfulness of the son of God

51. Barclay, "Paul's Story," 142–44, leaves untranslated the controversial phrase πίστεως Ἰησοῦ Χριστοῦ (2:16 twice; 2:20). One cannot help but notice how, by holding out both options of this slippery phrase, Barclay's insistence on the "dialectical" truth of "Christ lives in me" and "I live" comes closest to the ambiguity of the Greek original. However, Barclay does argue elsewhere for an objective genitive reading; see his *Obeying the Truth*, 78n8.

52. Cf. Rom 8:10; 2 Cor 13:5; Col 1:27; note also Gal 1:16 and 2 Cor 4:6.

53. Note here that Paul's image of being indwelled by Christ does not annihilate Paul's

who *loved* me and *gave himself* for me" (Gal 2:20).[54] Instead of living by means of one's own ability to conjure personal fidelity to God, Paul apprehends (or was apprehended by the fact) that in the apocalypse of Jesus, God now enlivens (*via* his Spirit) those whose faith has been elicited by means of the fidelity of God's own son.[55] Since the shape of the life Paul now lives is one patterned after the Christ who lived faithfully to God, the character of this Christ's life, which was manifest in self-giving love, becomes the normative pattern for Paul's new life as well. Since Paul thought that his new living to God was animated and enlivened by Christ, non-retaliation and peace became for him the new modes of engaging not only Christian brothers and sisters, but even his enemies who were under the sway of anti-God powers.[56] Such a pattern of existence was the template not for Paul alone, but for others whom he implored to imitate him in his imitation of the cruciform life of Jesus.

---

self; he may have been crucified with Christ, but he still acknowledges that he lives "in the flesh." Barclay, "Paul's Story," 143–44, could have called this Paul's dialectical agency: "'The agency of a 'new creature' in Christ is simultaneously the agency of the believer *and* the agency of Christ.'"

54. This translation is a modification of one offered by Hays, "Christology and Ethics in Galatians," 268–90. See Hays' arguments for the subjective genitive reading here at pages 278–80. Cf. also Longenecker, *Triumph of Abraham's God*, 148–50 and Hays, "Crucified with Christ," 240: "The community called to live 'in Christ' will necessarily live in a way that corresponds to the pattern of faith/obedience defined by Christ's death on the cross."

55. Cf. Congdon, "Trinitarian Shape of πίστις," 231–58, for a theological contribution to the πίστις Χριστοῦ debate. See esp. 255–56 for Congdon's focus on the Holy Spirit as the agent who elicits and empowers the faithful obedience of Christ's followers.

56. Describing his interaction with enemies this way raises the question of how his interaction with the agitators meets (or fails to meet) this description. In brief, it seems to me there are two alternatives: either Paul failed to live up to the standard of the ideal he presumed to teach, or what is at stake in Galatia requires *rhetoric* which demonstrates for the Galatians the seriousness of the issue at hand. If the agitators' teaching is "no gospel," then the Galatians are in danger of apostasy and possibly turning God's gift of the Law into an idol. Although I see merits for both views (and under duress would try to hold in tension the truth of both), I'm inclined to view the first as the more persuasive view of Paul's interaction with the influencers. Cf., however, Matt 18:6; Mark 9:42; Luke 17:2 for a comparatively shocking *rhetorical* statement made by Jesus.

The Cross-Centered Orientation of Life

If the immediate effect of the apocalypse is the death of the violent Paul, the extended effect is Paul's reorientation of all life around this new cross-centered existence. Galatians 6:14 illustrates where the cosmic and personal implications of the cross intersect: "May I never boast of anything except the cross of our Lord Jesus Christ, through which the world has been crucified to me, and I to the world." Coming as it does in the summary remarks of Paul's letter, Galatians 6:14–15 indicates the central and (creatively) explosive importance of Jesus' crucifixion for Paul and his transformed worldview.

To approach this "enigma"[57] from a fresh perspective, perhaps it is best to picture what Paul is describing. For Paul, those "agitators" who boast in the flesh of the Galatians (6:13) actually boast at the very point where Paul and the cosmos have been crucified. That is, it is as if Paul has replaced the two bandits crucified with Christ with himself and the cosmos. The agitators unwittingly boast of their participation in the violent crucifixion of the very thing which they presume to uphold, i.e., the law, which is a part of the cosmos. Or why should they boast in flesh when it and its opposite, not-flesh (i.e., lawlessness), have been crucified with Christ?

Since the cosmos has been crucified, then the *modus operandi*, or Paul's *old* way of living in it has been crucified as well. But it is not just Paul's way of living which has been transformed, but the *modus operandi* of the cosmos itself. At least this is how things "should" be. One of the characteristic features of Galatians is the motif of the identification of the time. That is, time stamps mark the breadth of the letter so that one of the keys to understanding how to act is by understanding what time it is. For Paul, to operate under the assumption that questions of circumcision and uncircumcision are paramount is to miss the event which relativized both of those old-world alternatives. By living under the sway of the Spirit of Jesus, the world's questions and its competition for power fall on (ideally, at least) indifferent ears, and the one enlivened by the Spirit of Christ is empowered to live for the sake of serving others and honoring others above any self-serving interest. The world that finds itself "crucified" to the disciple of Jesus finds its power to provoke violence broken. The trajectory of violence for Jesus' disciple is ruptured, and once they have been co-crucified, their transformed, newly enlivened bodies take on a power over

57. Minear, "Crucified World," 395–407.

violence which exercises its power-over-violence only because Violence cannot understand how it is defeated by weakness. The sway of the cosmos, the old-age *modus operandi*, led to Paul's violence, but Paul's new *modus operandi*, his new trajectory involves living into the new creation which has as its gravitational center the cross of Jesus.

Physical Evidence—Paul's Stigmata

Galatians 6:17 provides an interesting comment on Paul's co-crucifixion metaphor—Paul bears the "the marks of Jesus" (στίγματα τοῦ Ἰησοῦ) in his own body. The powers that violently opposed God's son, subjecting him to nothing less than the torture of crucifixion, still oppose God's purposes and thus oppose Paul in his current mission, with Paul's physical scars offered as proof. Paul carries on his own body the marks of the one who bore the distilled expression of the violence of Rome. A common conclusion is that those marks are the result of the various beatings, "from Gentile stones and from Jewish whips (2 Cor 11:24–26)" that Paul endured as a "soldier sent into the front trenches of God's redemptive and liberating war."[58] As such, those scars are Paul's commendation to the Galatians of the truth of the gospel that he proclaims, and the Galatians ought to "trouble" Paul no longer.

The stigmata effectively serve as the physical confirmation of the trajectory of violence in Paul's biography in two ways. First, Paul has been moved from being one who inflicted "stigmata" upon Jesus' followers to being a man whose obvious physical scars now evinced a servile, dishonorable character who submitted to violence against his body.[59] Second, the trajectory from violent persecutor to recipient of violent attack creates a corresponding trajectory of honor-abasement; whereas Paul's former life demonstrated his embodiment of the honorable, dominant male in Graeco-Roman society, his new life embodies the downward, dishonorable, self-abasing trajectory of being yoked to the son of God who "loved me

58. Martyn, *Galatians*, 568. Also Longenecker, *Galatians*, 299–300; Burton, *Galatians*, 360–61; Lightfoot, *Galatians*, 225–26.

59. Glancy, "Boasting of Beatings," 99–135, provides a nuanced account of how Paul's physical scars might have been perceived by his audience in Corinth or Galatia. Her chastening of the dominant view (Paul's sufferings are boasted about in order to inspire confidence in his manly endurance of affliction) can be summed up in two quotations: "Not every scarred body told an honorable story" (107); and "Vulnerability to corporal punishment signaled servility" to a Graeco-Roman audience (108).

and gave himself for me" (2:20). This reconstituted self was not counter-cultural in the usual sense (i.e., those who once were of no account are now to be valued), but radically redefines that which the world considers most shameful (the cross of Christ) to be the quintessential expression of true honor and worthy of praise.

THE COSMIC-CORPORATE EFFECT—NEW CREATION

The chapter thus far has focused on the *personal* effect of Paul's encounter with and enlivenment by the risen Christ. We have traced the contours of violence in Paul's biography: from the violence of his early persecuting activity, to his encounter with the risen Christ, his (metaphorical) death, to his enlivenment by the non-violent Christ. In the present section, we must examine whether Paul's personal death to violence corresponds to an equivalent death to violence for redeemed creation. In other words, the focus on Paul's biography will be expanded upon to see how Paul's biography vis-à-vis violence relates to violence in the "biography" of New Creation. While this shift in focus takes us beyond Paul's "biography" proper, his perception of violence (or the trajectory of it) in the cosmos sheds light on Paul's view of the legitimacy of violence in God's new creation.

Faith Working through Love

Insofar as the new creation is proleptically embodied by those who exist corporately in Christ, new creation is possible to participate in and is characterized by the work of faith expressed in love (5:6). Paul wrote: "For in Christ Jesus neither circumcision nor uncircumcision are valid, but what is valid is faith expressing itself through love."[60] Whereas the practices of circumcision and uncircumcision had once been expressions of faithfulness or lack of faithfulness, Paul now viewed the *requirement* of these practices as a mark of *unbelief* which has the effect of exclusion. In other words, there is nothing wrong with circumcision *per se*, what Paul now disputes is its requirement for Gentiles for being incorporated into Christ's fellowship. The new-age (new creation) marker of faith, rather than circumcision, is now the love which has been defined chiefly by Christ's self-giving on his cross.

---

60. Translation mine.

The agitators likely would have seen their insistence on circumcision as a mark of faith and as arising from no ill will towards the Galatians. Paul, however, interprets the effect of their persuasive influence as catastrophic—submitting to circumcision will cut them off from Christ. The dire result of the teachers' influence causes Paul to challenge their motive and even their incorporation into Christ.[61] But by including *uncircumcision* (ἀκροβυστία) in his formulation (5:6), Paul hedges against the counter-argument that he either anticipated or had faced regularly during his missionary efforts. If circumcision is not required of Gentiles, it might be inferred that the Torah as guiding-principle is dispensable too, and thus Paul unwittingly allows lawless self-indulgence for Gentiles while upholding strict law observance for Jewish Christians. One possible "use" of the law in Paul's time was the belief that submission to the law (Torah) was the means by which one fought against the flesh's desires.[62] It is possible that the agitators held this view. To abandon the Law was to lend hostages to fortune, and the failure of Paul to require circumcision of the (Gentile) Galatians was a failure to equip them with the God-given weapon to battle the desires of the flesh.

With his rhetorical sleight of hand, Paul suggests that the agitators, or any who would accuse him of advocating lawless self-indulgence, have missed his point altogether: he doesn't commend the opposite of law observance (uncircumcision), instead Paul apprehends that true fulfillment of the Law is accomplished through works of love which are rooted in faith. Again, the character of this love is self-giving to the core, and to insist that a life characterized by self-giving love is insufficient is to question the sufficiency of Jesus' own expression of sacrificial love. In a certain sense, to advocate circumcision in the aftermath of the resurrection is to do violence, unwittingly or deliberately, to the life, death, and resurrection of Jesus. For Paul, only a life—both individual *and corporate*—that recapitulates

---

61. It should be noted again that fairness was not a virtue in ancient rhetoric, and we have no reason to assume that Paul was himself attempting to portray his opponents fairly. See, e.g., Barclay, "Mirror-Reading a Polemical Letter," 367–82, and Johnson, "Anti-Jewish Slander," 419–41. I also note here that Gal 5:2 and 4 *seem* to indicate that the agitators are "Christians." If they were not (per Nanos' proposed reading), Paul's dire warnings about being cut off from Christ or of Christ being of no benefit would be irrelevant. If the agitators were not Christ-believers, they would have already told the Galatians that Christ was of no consequence whatsoever regarding their membership status in the people of God. Paul's warnings seem to me to be new information, a warning of the unrecognized effect of circumcision added to faith in Christ.

62. Martyn, *Galatians*, 524, 526, goes farther in suggesting that this is the position held by the "agitators." Cf., e.g., Sir 15:14–17; 1QS 4:15–16; 5:3–7; CD 3:2–3.

Christ's own self-giving love "counts"; and such a life, both communally and individually, in imitation of a peace-pursuing Jesus, necessarily will remove violence from the storehouse of "weapons" it employs in doing battle against the flesh.

Through Love Become Slaves to One Another

Paul rehearses this theme of self-giving love only a few verses later, and in doing so goes a step farther in proposing that the trajectory of life in Christ is one that advances in abasement: "For you were called into freedom, brothers and sisters; only not freedom as a pretext for the flesh, but instead, through love, become slaves to one another. For the whole law has been fulfilled in a single command, 'You shall love your neighbor as yourself'" (5:13–14, translation mine). Three observations must be made regarding these verses. First, as noted above, Paul anticipates the charge of antinomianism which is leveled against him. But rather than overturning the law, Paul's posture of abasement and service to others is one in which the whole law is summed up in a rather similar way to that of Jesus himself (5:14).[63] Second, Paul's admonition to become slaves to one another would jar any hearer in the first-century (Graeco-Roman) context, where public honor was seldom associated with the concept of slavery.[64] That is, in a setting in which the quest for public honor was a way of life, to debase oneself by acting as a slave to another was not just countercultural, but social "suicide." Competition for social prestige was ubiquitous and to act in any way that jeopardized one's honor invited public scorn.[65]

---

63. Cf. Matt 5:17–20; 7:12; 22:37–40.

64. Consider, e.g., Lendon, *Empire of Honour*, 96–97: "The natural assumption of men of the status of the jurists was that slaves had no honour. So utterly beneath consideration were they that one might put up with jocularities from slaves that one would never endure from free men." Nevertheless, despite their own assumptions, high-status authors recognized that "slaves grant each other honour in slavish eyes." While it is true that slavery to Christ Jesus (Rom 1:1; Phil 1:1) can be seen positively on the model of Old Testament examples of honored servants of Yahweh, the twin factors of service to others (i.e., not God) and the setting of writing to former pagans (rather than lifelong Jews) persuades me that the concept of service used by Paul in Galatians 5 is one that would have had dishonorable connotations for his audience. Cf. Hellerman, *Reconstructing Honor in Roman Philippi*, 119–20; 136–42.

65. Barton, "Savage Miracles," 45, demonstrates that "the person of honor was obliged to respond decisively to any threat to his or her boundaries."

Finally, Galatians 5:15 illustrates Paul's view of the "wages" of living not as slaves to one another, but as competitors in the quest for social prestige: "If, however, you bite and devour one another, watch out that you are not consumed by one another." Paul is hardly providing the Galatians with advice on how to avoid nipping each other to death, in the manner of wild dogs. This sarcastic remark shows the Galatians not only the serious threat of living life concerned with the flesh (in the manner of the Graeco-Roman preoccupation with gaining honor), but highlights how even the (possibly) well-meaning agitators reintroduce the habits of the self-destructive flesh by insisting on the removal of a part of their own flesh, quite literally. Thus, whether the Galatians "bite and devour" one another in a competition for public honor (their presumed old-way of life), or submit to the agitators' circumcision (the agitators' proposed way out of that old-way of life), in either case the Galatians would live a corporate life fixated on the flesh. The violence of the former way of life was obvious; the violence of the new way offered by the agitators was obscured, but Paul saw through the proposal of the agitators, not least because he experienced first-hand enmity and physical violence from people who operated from both ends of the horizon of life in the flesh.

The Opposition between the Spirit and the Flesh (Galatians 5:16–17)

Paul's deep-seated expectation of opposition and suffering for Christians surfaces in one of the more vexing passages from his letter. Galatians 5:16–18 expresses the cosmic opposition, the cosmic battle, which now rages and in which the Galatians find themselves caught up. If the apocalypse of Jesus has wrought with it many positive developments for those who are incorporated into his body, it has also inaugurated a new opposition on a cosmic scale. Although the trajectory of Paul's biography is one which is advancing towards peace, Paul is quite comfortable speaking of the continuing resistance of elements of the cosmos which violently oppose the invasive, transformative new-creation.

> But I say walk with the Spirit, and you will not[66] fulfill the desire of the Flesh. For the Flesh desires against the Spirit, and the Spirit desires against the Flesh, because these oppose one another, *with*

66. BDF §365; οὐ μή together with the aorist subjunctive constitutes "the most definite form of negation regarding the future." Cf. Barclay, *Obeying the Truth*, 111.

the result that[67] you do not do whatever you want. But if you are led by the Spirit, you are not under law.

The New Creation Antinomy

The first difficulty I will take up from these verses is the treatment of Spirit and Flesh as cosmic actors in an eschatological struggle. Rather than treating the desire of the Flesh as an impulse internal to the person, likening Paul's expression to the "evil impulse" common in contemporary literature,[68] Paul seems to describe the Flesh as an agent that, although operative or traceable in the individual and corporate body through its effects, still maintains its own agency that transcends its "expression" only in situations in which it is embodied.[69] In these verses in particular, the flesh appears to be an active agent working in opposition to the purpose of the Spirit sent by God. This flesh has *desire* (5:16), which in itself is perhaps nothing more than a creative anthropomorphism; but that it also *desires against* the Spirit and is described by Paul as being *opposed to* the Spirit suggests that something more than an anthropomorphism is intended. Instead, it is better to perceive the real opposition of (independent) agents in Paul's description. "Both the Flesh . . . and the Spirit awaken desires; both have their own plans for the human race; and their plans are so thoroughly at odds that they themselves are constantly at war with one another."[70]

Similarly, *Spirit* is used by Paul consistently in Galatians as the Spirit God has sent, i.e., Christ's spirit. That is, rather than speaking of a spirit internal to the human being, Paul writes about a spirit dwelling in the creature as a result of God's effort to transform creaturely existence. The Spirit in Galatians is one which they *received* (3:2, 14), which is *supplied to them* (3:5), and whom *God has sent forth* (4:6) into Christians. This Spirit with

---

67. Cf. Wallace, *Greek Grammar*, 473: the result ἵνα clause is where the "use of ἵνα + subjunctive expresses the result of the action of the main verb . . . a consequence of the verbal action that is *not intended*." So too Martyn, *Galatians*, 494n75.

68. I do not, however, want to restrict this concept to a wooden phrase. It could just as easily be an alternative to the (internal) idea of the Hebrew *yēṣer bāśār*, evil impulse/inclination. Cf. CD 2:14–16; 1QS 5:5; CD 3:2–3.

69. That is not to say that he *always* uses *flesh* (σάρξ) in this way, but that is the way I read it here. For the wider range on meaning in Paul's letters, see Dunn, *Theology of Paul*, 62–70.

70. Martyn, *Galatians*, 494.

which they are to "walk" leads them in such a way that the consequence is that they definitely will not fulfill the desires of that other cosmic agent which works against their transformation—the Flesh.

In an expression unique in Greek literature,[71] Paul speaks of the Spirit and Flesh, in turn, as *desiring against* the other cosmic power. This perplexing phrase is clarified (somewhat) by the clause which follows it: "for these (i.e., the Spirit and the Flesh) oppose one another." In an effort to illuminate the image Paul composed, Martyn appeals to the Letter of Polycarp to the Philippians (5:3), where Polycarp "translates" the Pauline expression into better Greek prose: "For it is good to be cut off from the sinful desires in the world, because every sinful desire wages war against the spirit."[72] Rather than the unusual Pauline expression, Polycarp offers a clearer picture of Desire *warring against* the Spirit. This oppositional contrast is not restricted to 5:16–17 either. "Both the Flesh and the Spirit are apocalyptic powers that do things not only *in* but also *to* the Galatians (5:13, 17, 19–21a, 22–23a)."[73] The opposition between Flesh and Spirit has as its origin the in-breaking of the Son into creation, the invasion of the Spirit into the realm of the Flesh. That is, the opposition between Spirit and Flesh is not a "timeless anthropological rivalry," but rather it is an apocalyptic battle declared by the Spirit against the Flesh.[74]

The Frustrated Wishes of the Galatians (5:17d)

The enigmatic clause at the end of 5:17 has occasioned many tortured interpretations, and John Barclay summarizes its vexing quality when he writes that it is "generally acknowledged to be one of the most difficult [clauses] in the whole letter."[75] Typical solutions to the problem have left something to be desired, but Barclay offers an interpretation that merits consideration: the new-creation communities created and transformed by the Spirit of Jesus constituted new communities whose behavior necessarily differed from those groups which did not walk by means of the Spirit.

71. Ibid., 493.

72. καλὸν γὰρ τὸ ἀνακόπτεσθαι ἀπὸ τῶν ἐπιθυμιῶν ἐν τῷ κόσμῳ, ὅτι πᾶσα ἐπιθυμία κατὰ τοῦ πνεύματος στρατεύεται.

73. Ibid., 528.

74. Ibid., 494.

75. Barclay, *Obeying the Truth*, 112. Riches, *Galatians Through the Centuries*, 264–83, provides a useful summary of the history of interpretation of Gal 5:16–18.

> For the Flesh desires against the Spirit
> And the Spirit desires against the Flesh
> For these are opposed to one another, with the result that you do
> not do whatever you want.

Interpreters differ on whether the preposition in the final clause (*with the result that,* ἵνα) is functioning here in a *telic* sense (result) or an *ecbatic* sense (purpose), but a firm commitment to *either* tendency might run roughshod over the possibility that Paul would not see a great distinction between the purpose and result of opposition between Spirit and Flesh.[76] In any case, the more troubling translation issue is determining whose wishes are frustrated. Three alternatives are usually advanced:[77] 1) the Flesh frustrates what the Spirit wants in the individual believer (an interpretation which often relies on Romans 7 for support); 2) the Spirit and Flesh each manage to frustrate the wishes of the other, producing a stalemate; and 3) the Spirit frustrates the Flesh, resulting in a "walk" according to the Spirit's guidance.

The first alternative, that the Flesh frustrates the wishes of the Spirit operating in the Galatians runs aground on the confident assertion of the previous verse. If the Galatians heed Paul's command and walk with (or by means of) the Spirit, *they are assured that they certainly will not fulfill the Flesh's desire.* More problematical still, this interpretation would "wholly undermine Paul's purpose in this passage"[78]—namely, to state his case that the Spirit provides the moral antidote to the desire of the Flesh, without the assistance of the Law.

The second alternative highlights the militant opposition between Spirit and Flesh of 5:17c. This interpretation too suffers from its deconstruction of Paul's overall purpose—to suggest that a stalemate has been reached would be to suggest that the Spirit is unable to deal decisively with the desire of the Flesh. With this interpretation, 5:16 would seem to offer a false promise, because one could never be sure that the desire of the Flesh was not being fulfilled.

The third option, that the Spirit frustrates the wishes of the Flesh, suits the confidence of 5:16 and aligns with Paul's overall purpose to vouch for

---

76. So Barclay, *Obeying the Truth,* 112, relying on Moule, *Idiom Book,* 142 and BDF §391.

77. For this threefold summary of positions, I am indebted to Barclay, *Obeying the Truth,* 113–14.

78. Barclay, *Obeying the Truth,* 113.

the moral sufficiency of the Spirit. However, it also fails to explain why Paul apparently thinks that the Galatians want to satisfy the desire of the flesh, rather than the wishes of the Spirit.

Barclay's compelling solution to the problem of translating 5:17d is to see it as Paul's response to the accusation of antinomianism which he probably faced from his opponents.[79] Only a few verses earlier (Gal 5:13), Paul reaffirms that the Galatians were "called to freedom," but he also clarifies that such freedom is not an opportunity to indulge the Flesh's desire. Rather than the unbridled freedom which would result from abandoning the Law, Paul says that total opposition between the Flesh and Spirit leads to two mutually exclusive "military" bases with the result that those who find themselves in the camp of the Spirit will discover that they are not free to do "whatever" they wish.[80] While "free" from the oversight of the law, they find themselves compelled to a "higher righteousness" (to borrow Matthew's phrase), to self-abasement (i.e., serving as a slave to one another, 5:13) and the outward orientation of neighbor love (5:14).

Glossing the clause in this way, the address remains open to every Galatian. That is, rather than restricting Paul's "you" to those who want to include law observance,[81] Paul also restricts the wishes of those who might understand the freedom in the Spirit as a license to satisfy the Flesh. In other words, freedom from the strictures of the law does not mean that one is therefore "in charge," there is still an ever more powerful authority to guide their steps—the Spirit.

Being Led by Christ's Spirit (5:18)

Having a new "general" to order their lives, the Galatians in Christ are no longer subject to the Law. Rather than leading to an undisciplined life, Paul views life in Christ to have its own charter for behavior. Paul's answer to the

79. Cf. Gal 2:17, 21; 3:21 for three possible instances in which Paul responds to charges made by his opponents.

80. I find no attempt to justify his "indefinite" reading of the relative pronoun in Barclay's treatment of 5:17. Wallace, *Greek Grammar*, 343, however, notes that "ὅς used with ἄν also has an indefinite force." *BDF* §293 notes that by the New Testament period, the definite relative and indefinite relative pronouns were "no longer clearly distinguished."

81. In the military camp metaphor, adding law observance to the gospel would seem to suggest that the Galatians were trying to march under the orders of two opposing generals.

question of what now do those in Christ possess to discipline the desire of the Flesh is the demanding leadership of the Spirit of Jesus. "But *if* you are led by (means of) the Spirit, *then* you are not under the Law." Incorporation into Christ rules out certain forms of behavior which are "authorized" by the Flesh; for Paul, certain characteristics are obvious in identifying to which camp one belongs (5:19–21). On the other hand, those led by Christ's Spirit observe a different kind of fruit from their (communal) life in Christ, and Paul declares "There is not a law against such things" (5:23) as love, joy, peace, etc. Not content to claim that those led by Christ's Spirit possess all they need to *overcome* the Flesh's desire, Paul makes the incredible claim (at 5:24) that those who walk with the Spirit "have *crucified* the Flesh" and its desires; Spirit-led communities have put to death that which the Law was thought to keep in check.

Life in the Spirit, Life in the Church

In the previous two sections of the present chapter, I have attempted to demonstrate the framework "constructed" by Paul's theologizing about the effects of the apocalypse of Jesus for individuals and for the cosmos (specifically in the church). In this final section I want to fill out that frame with a sketch of the practices (i.e., ethics) that describe the ideal community which Paul tried to birth (to using his own maternal imagery of Gal 4:19). Discussions of the ethical content of Paul's letters is quite congested, but in focusing on the ethics of non-violence, the present discussion is rendered more manageable and contributes a needed focus on the presence of a non-violent ethic in Paul's letter to the Galatians.

The Law of Christ (6:2)

The irony of beginning a discussion of Paul's ethics in Galatians with an investigation of his enigmatic appeal to "the law of Christ" is not lost on this interpreter. The law (νόμος) is a notoriously stubborn motif in Galatians and the rest of Paul's letters, not least at 6:2 where Paul writes, "Bear one another's burdens and in this way you will fulfill the law of Christ." This verse has been the subject of endless investigation, and it would seem to be the beginning of wisdom to shy away from holding too strong a view where other more capable interpreters sound warnings. Still, by running at the phrase from a slightly different angle, I hope to open a line of thought that could be accommodated easily by some of the dominant views of Paul's phrase.

Correction and Forgiveness rather than Enmity and Strife

It may be that the presence of the highly contested word *Law* (νόμος) has predetermined much of the discussion of this verse. For instance, though some interpreters mention its relationship to 6:1, exceedingly rare is the scholar who makes 6:1 the crux of their interpretation of 6:2.[82] Rather than fixing attention of the controversial phrase "the law of Christ," I want to attempt to understand 6:2 especially in relation to Paul's exhortation to restore gently anyone who is detected in a transgression. By (re-)locating within the church of the new creation the praxis of restoring one who has transgressed, we can recover the ethical bedrock of the practice of forgiveness for Paul's communities, and hazard sketching more specific contours of the "law of Christ." That is, rather than identifying the law of Christ as the law of love,[83] or more specifically, the love of neighbor as the fulfillment of the law (5:13–14), or even the law of love expressed in Christ's own self-giving (all of which are accurate to a point but do not define the "law of Christ" without qualification), the law of Christ fulfilled in burden-bearing is expressed in churches that practice confrontation and forgiveness non-violently, and its member-citizens can do that because the church is made up of ones who recognize that they have themselves been forgiven.

Before taking another look at the verse in Galatians, it is worth observing with C. H. Dodd that Galatians 6:1–5 bears some striking resemblance to Jesus' teaching on reconciliation between brothers that we find in Matthew 18.[84] Without attempting to construct rigid parallels that are not present, it is noteworthy that Matthew's gospel includes a fairly detailed explanation for the procedure of restoring a stumbling brother within the

---

82. Betz, *Galatians*, 299, is perhaps an exemplar here: Gal 6:2a, bear one another's burdens, "sums up [Paul's] teaching in Gal 5:13–14 and *is also related to* 6:1" (emphasis added). Betz comments no further on the relationship between the two verses, perhaps owing to his view that from 5:25—6:10 Paul composed *independent* "gnomic sententiae." Galatians 5:13–14 tends to play a more important role in interpreting 6:2 than does the verse that precedes it. Dodd, *Gospel and Law*, 64–83, and Strelan, "Burden-Bearing and the Law of Christ," 266–76, may be the two modern exceptions.

83. Cf. Luther, *LW* 27.113–14.

84. Dodd, *Gospel and Law*, 64–83, argued that Paul had adapted Jesus' teaching from Matt 23:4 and 18:15–16.

church.[85] Matthew's gospel outlines the internal governing practice of a new community in matters of corporate discipline. The praxis of ecclesial discipline is outlined in greater detail in Matthew's gospel than it is in Paul's letter, but the importance of the practice and its goal are readily apparent. In Matthew, Jesus' program is not a recommended course of action, but a command: "Go and point out the fault." Matthew's Jesus doesn't leave space for his followers to stew on the sin in the hopes of stoically rising above petty offenses. He commands his followers to go and confront. Similarly, Paul writes to the Galatians that if a person is detected in a transgression, the spiritual among the Galatians ought to *restore* (the imperative καταρτίζετε) the person gently.[86]

The final phrase of Matthew 18:15 clearly establishes the goal of Jesus' instructions. Jesus' followers are not commanded to point out transgression as an end in itself, but with the express purpose of regaining a brother. Though it is less explicit in Paul's exhortation, the restoration of the transgressor has the mending of fellowship in view. Without properly ordered relations, Paul's community had little hope of bearing one another's burdens (6:2). Commenting on Matthew's gospel, but equally fitting for Paul's letter, Stanley Hauerwas writes that Jesus

> assumes that conflict is not to be ignored or denied, but rather conflict, which may involve sins, is to be forced into the open. Christian discipleship requires confrontation because the peace that Jesus has established is not simply the absence of violence. The peace of Christ is nonviolent precisely because it is based on truth and truth-telling. Just as love without truth cannot help but be accursed, so peace between the brothers and sisters of Jesus must be without illusion.[87]

Conflict should be anticipated in Paul's churches, which like any other group is susceptible to corruption; but what sets the Christian response to conflict apart (i.e., its unique ethic) is that confrontation/restoration serves

85. We do not need to address the anachronism of Matthew here, if only because we are not attempting to argue that the practice of restoration (reconciliation) in Paul's communities was derived from Matthew's gospel. Remove our presuppositions of the word *church* (ἐκκλησία) from Jesus' proposal in Matthew's gospel and the *practice* remains intact.

86. The personal, private confrontation of Matt 18:15 is a suitable example of an attempt to restore a brother in a spirit of gentleness (Gal 6:1). We might wonder, however, how to understand Paul's public confrontation with Peter (Gal 2:14).

87. Hauerwas, *Matthew*, 165–66.

the goal of the corporate practice of bearing the burdens of even those who transgress against the church because it is itself made up of transgressors. If the immediate context of Galatians 6:2 is to offer any help in understanding Paul's phrase "the law of Christ," perhaps it should be in the praxis of mutual forgiveness commanded in 6:1 and commended by several different New Testament witnesses.[88] John Howard Yoder takes 6:1 as fundamentally important for understanding 6:2, drawing attention to the fact that the "linkage between our forgiving each other and God's forgiving us is restated elsewhere in the New Testament":[89]

- "Forgive us our sins as we forgive others." (Matt 6:14–15)

- "Forgiving one another, as God in Christ has forgiven you." (Eph 4:32)

- "Just as the lord has forgiven you, so also you must forgive." (Col 3:13)

- "If anyone among you wanders from the truth and is brought back by another, you should know that whoever brings back a sinner from wandering will save the sinner's soul from death and will cover a multitude of sins." (James 5:19–20)

Yoder understands Paul to mean that "the law of Christ" is this praxis of mutual correction and forgiveness. Paul "appealed to those of his readers who were 'spiritual' to initiate [correction] 'in a spirit of gentleness,' in the awareness of their own weakness (Gal. 6:1)" which at another time would require bearing too.[90] Although Yoder's interpretation is unique among exegetes, the identification of mutual correction and forgiveness would sit well *within* an interpretation that holds that the "law of Christ" is to be more generally regarded as self-giving or in some similar way the imitation of Jesus' own teaching and example.

---

88. Although 6:1 is not the key to interpreting 6:2 for Augustine, his comments on these verses do focus on the concern to practice mutual correction in love rather than violent retaliation in scorn for another's transgressions. Augustine, *Exp. Gal.* 56–58, in Plumer, *Augustine's Commentary*, 221–27.

89. Yoder, *Body Politics*, 4. Yoder is primarily concerned, however, with the passage in Matthew, not Galatians 6. Betz, *Galatians*, 299, does write that when the maxim of 6:2 (bear one another's burdens) is "applied to 6:1 [it] means that 'failure' by Christians should be regarded as part of the 'burden of life' and should be shared by the Christian community."

90. Yoder, *Body Politics*, 4.

If life in the Spirit was to be marked by the practices of correction and forgiveness, then Christian community was jeopardized by the enmity and strife that are censured in Paul's letter. This he does especially in the paraenetic section of Galatians, but not there alone. Translated variously as hatred, hostility, or *enmity*, ἔχθρα is a rare word in the New Testament. It occurs only six times, and only in Galatians does it appear in a list of "bad behavior." Elsewhere, it refers to the discord between two leaders (Herod and Pilate, Luke 23:12, ironically here, an enmity overcome by their mutual condemnation of Jesus), or between humanity and God (cf. Rom 8:7; Jas 4:4). The closest parallel is in Ephesians 2:14 and 16 where the hostility between Gentiles and Jews is overcome through Christ's cross. It seems that the hostilities to which Paul refers are between members of the churches in Galatia. Galatians 5:15 is one clue for describing the extent that hostilities characterized some relationships within the Galatian communities. Paul warns those who bite and devour (literally "tear to pieces,") one another to take care not to be destroyed or consumed by those who, it is assumed, will want to return the favor.[91] The irony, of course, is that such beastly behavior is unfitting for those who should endeavor to love their neighbor (5:14). Whether violent *actions* are implicit in Paul's use of "enmities" at 5:20 is difficult to determine, but such hostility certainly is moving towards a violent or destructive end, especially if the warning of 5:15 informs our picture of the situation.[92]

Not only does Paul warn the Galatians of the danger of enmity practiced among themselves, he levels a serious accusation at the agitators' feet. That is, enmity is precisely what Paul accuses the agitators of creating where peace and friendship once existed (4:15–16). What is worse, the enmity the agitators have created springs out of self-interest (4:17; 6:12–13), rather than from the interests of Paul's Galatian converts. The motives and consequences of the agitators on this score clearly diverge from the unity,

91. The argument that 5:15 indicates the situation "on the ground" is supported by Paul's syntax, in which the first class condition followed by a verb in the indicative "assumes the reality of the situation described," Longenecker, *Galatians*, 244.

92. One example, and there are many, which illuminates the violent trajectory of enmity is when Josephus uses *enmity* (ἔχθρα) to describe the reason for the (intra-Jewish) slaughter of even the peaceable (τῶν ἡσυχίων) bystanders in the temple during the siege of Jerusalem at Passover, 70 CE. "Many peaceable citizens from enmity and personal spite were slain by their adversaries as partisans of the opposite faction, and any in the past who had offended one of the conspirators, being now recognized as a zealot, was led off to punishment" (Josephus, *War* 5:103 [Thackeray, LCL]). Cf. the famous incident of Josephus, *Ant.* 20:118–36.

friendship, and gentle correction and forgiveness lauded by Paul. Where does Paul think the agitators have gone wrong? Since enmity and *sorcery* (φαρμακεία 5:20) appear together in the list of vices in Galatians, but not in any other Pauline vice lists, it is worth considering how the two are related, and whether they intimate something of Paul's view of the agitators.

Taking a cue from the prevalence of separation spells in Paul's day, Bruce Longenecker shows how Paul links the enmity-inducing agitators with the practice of sorcery. By creating the impression that they may have cast separation curses in order to "introduce enmity between previously allied parties," Paul manages to accuse the agitators, albeit indirectly, of harnessing demonic forces for their own personal gain.[93] In contrast to their prior willingness to go to extreme lengths to provide succor to Paul in his "weakness of the flesh," the Galatians, under the malicious influence of the agitators, now withhold their friendship from him, or so Paul intimates. This death of goodwill is bound up with the influence exerted by the agitators. For Paul, the toxic tactics of the agitators have taken root, killing off any desire the Galatians had in their earlier days of assisting Paul without considering their personal risk.[94] They once bore Paul's burden, but now they treat him as they would an enemy.

The agitators' influence has affected relationships among the Galatians too. Paul warns of the Flesh's work of generating strife, conflict which seems to have temporarily (at least) smothered the mandate of mutual forgiveness he commands in 6:1–2. *Strife* (ἔρις and its adjective ἐριστικός) finds its way into many early lists of behaviors unsuitable for Christians to practice, including Paul's letter to the Romans and both letters to the Corinthians.[95]

93. Longenecker, *Triumph of Abraham's God*, 155–56: A "scenario of demonically manufactured enmity between parties profitably informs Gal. 4.16–17, where Paul suggests that he has been made the Galatians' enemy (ἐχθρός, related to 'enmity', ἔχθρα), presumably due to the influence of the agitators, who are trying to separate the Galatians from association with him." See also Longenecker, "Until Christ is Formed in You," 95–96.

94. On Paul's "puzzling" (Betz, *Galatians*, 223) statement at 4:12 ("You have done me no wrong"), Schlier, *Galaterbrief*, 209, and Betz, understand Paul to mean that until now, the friendship between Paul and the Galatians has not been threatened by any "wrong-doing on the part of the Galatians." Longenecker, *Triumph of Abraham's God*, 159, and Wilson, *Curse of the Law*, 86, take it to refer to their initial reception of Paul, i.e., "you did me no wrong" when I first came to you in weakness.

95. Cf., e.g., Rom 1:29; 13:13; 1 Cor 3:3; 2 Cor 12:20; 1 Clem 9:1: "leaving behind our pointless toil and *strife* and the jealousy that leads to death"; 14:2; 1 Tim 6:4. Note that strife (ἔρις) is uniquely "Pauline" in the New Testament (only 1 Timothy and Titus employ the word outside of the undisputed letters of Paul); cf. Sir 28:11: "*Strife* being

Although Paul does not identify *strife* as the *source* of murder (φόνος) in Galatians (5:20), elsewhere the two concepts are closely related; in Romans, Paul strings together envy, murder, and strife (φθόνου φόνου ἔριδος) in a list of things that clearly "should not be done" (Rom 1:28–29). Paul does not relate one as cause and the other as effect, but the two seem to be related by more than *parechesis*.[96] An illuminating subsequent usage of the adjective is found in Didache (3:2), where being "contentious" is identified, together with being jealous (ζηλωτής) and quick-tempered (θυμικός) as a midwife to murder.[97] Rather than being characterized by strife and enmity that lead all too easily to interpersonal violence, Paul wants to see communities that respond to anger and offense in gentleness, correction and forgiveness.[98] This is the ethical praxis Paul seeks to birth in his Galatian converts.

Burden-Bearing rather than Competing

The above effort to highlight mutual correction and forgiveness is not, however, meant to be a claim that they exhaust the disciplines named in the slogan "the law of Christ." Since the motif of suffering-persecution runs throughout Galatians, the main figurative use of βάρος for "suffering" bears on Paul's usage here.[99] In this respect, the fruit of the Spirit which Paul calls *patience* (μακροθυμία) might profitably be identified as one of the founding disciplines of the community which comes to know suffering acutely. Finding their new brothers and sisters in sometimes quite literally unbearable circumstances, Paul's urging Christian converts to bear one another's burdens may have required demonstration in uncomfortably concrete ways. Economic assistance, "medical" aid, and mediation on behalf of a

---

hastened kindles a fire and a quarrel hastening pours out blood."

96. Jewett, *Romans*, 165, 185–86, insists the sequence "is associative rather than genetic" in Paul's list.

97. "My child, flee from every evil and from every thing like it. Do not be quick to anger, for anger leads to murder; and do not be jealous, nor quarrelsome, nor quick-tempered, for from all these things murders are begotten" (Did 3:1–2, translation mine).

98. Eph 4:26 does not complicate matters; Paul acknowledges the experience of feeling anger without condoning its expression in violent outbursts. Instead, Christians are advised: "Let not the sun set on your wrath," and should instead be ready to forgive in the same way that "God in Christ forgave you" (Eph 4:32).

99. Schrenk, "βάρος, κτλ," 1:553–61. On suffering-persecution as a theme in Galatians, see e.g., Baasland, "Persecution," 135–50, and Wilson, *Curse of the Law*, 80–86, and literature cited there.

social outcast are all scenarios that one might easily envisage as instances of burden-bearing by Christians for other Christians who found themselves suffering in the aftermath of conversion.[100] If these kinds of "burdens" afflicted the churches in Galatia, then it is indeed proper to understand the fulfillment of the "law of Christ" in relation to 5:13–14, where Paul equates the command "you shall love your neighbor as yourself" (Lev 19:18) with the fulfillment of the "whole law [Torah]." Under such circumstances, it was wholly inappropriate, in Paul's view, to compete for glory (5:26).

If burden-bearing and mutual correction and forgiveness begin to fill out our understanding of the ethics of Paul's communities, then alleviation of suffering and reconciliation of parties at enmity become concrete examples of the peacemaking practices of the churches Paul founded. In keeping with the picture of Jesus from Matthew's gospel, Paul urged his communities not to order their life according to the rule of a reciprocity of revenge, but instead implored them to order their fellowship according to the rule of a reciprocity of forgiveness. Such was one crucial aspect of the ethics of the church. If a group such as this one was to survive, its members needed unconventional "weapons" to create and sustain communal peace in a world where "peace" was normally the byproduct of violence.

The Fruit of the Spirit—Political Maneuvering in the Church of God

The next task in mapping the trajectory of peace in Paul's discourse is to show how several aspects of the Fruit of the Spirit mentioned by Paul not only implicitly exclude the use of violence, but build up its alternative, an alternative ethic founded on peace. In other words, Paul expects that all who become incorporated into this new-creation assembly will behave in ways which confirm that they indeed are under the sway of the Spirit of Jesus; those habits witness to the normative claim of the faithful life of Jesus for the community which bears his name and is enlivened by his Spirit. Like

100. Without sufficient space to develop the envisaged scenarios more fully, I point to a lengthy quotation in Barclay, *Obeying the Truth*, 58: "As Christian converts they had abandoned the worship of pagan deities (4.8–11) and this conversion would have involved not only massive cognitive readjustments but also social dislocation. To dissociate oneself from the worship of family and community deities would entail a serious disruption in one's relationship with family, friends, fellow club members, business associates and civic authorities." See also the plausible fictional account of suffering presented by Oakes, *Philippians*, esp. 77–102.

Jesus, their alternative manner of life resists devolving into a withdrawal from the cosmos, but also resists becoming a mirror image of the order of the cosmos. John Howard Yoder has described the role of the church vis-à-vis the world in this way:

> the will of God for human socialness [*sic*] as a whole is prefigured by the shape to which the Body of Christ is called. Church and world are not two compartments under separate legislation or two institutions with contradictory assignments, but two levels of the pertinence of the same Lordship. The people of God is called to be today what the world is called to be ultimately.[101]

The kind of political/ethical maneuvering Paul expects to find in the new-creation assembly is the focus of the next few paragraphs.

Paul wrote: "But the fruit of the Spirit is love, joy, peace, patience, kindness, goodness, faithfulness, gentleness, and self-control." Before attending to one of the specific marks which evince the Spirit's presence, we should recognize at least one point more broadly of Paul's list in Galatians 5:22–23. By listing them as the *fruit* of the Spirit, Paul has transformed them (like the works of the Flesh) from virtues to be cultivated (they are not actions or "good deeds," but characteristics seen chiefly through certain deeds) to those qualities of a community animated by the Spirit.[102] The fruit of the Spirit is descriptive rather than prescriptive. In other words, what is produced by the Spirit is the quality of love, etc., which can be seen in a variety of actions (e.g., such as "bearing one another's burdens" [6:2]).

Self-Giving Love, not Jealousy

Paul places love in the first position in the marks of the Spirit. Although some would have the meaning of love as Paul uses it here defined by the qualities that follow it, a more instructive case can be made by examining Paul's uses of the word, and its verbal equivalent, in the rest of his letter. This exercise points out some of the concrete actions Paul associated with the word in its most immediate context.[103]

---

101. Yoder, *Body Politics*, ix.

102. Martyn, *Galatians*, 499. Swartley, *Covenant of Peace*, 218, notes: "Paul does not *command* the fruit of the Spirit, as though it were within human capacity to embody it. Rather, he regards the fruit as *flowing* from the Spirit in one's life."

103. The occurrences in Galatians are as follows: ἀγαπάω 2:20, 5:14, ἀγάπη 5:6; 5:13; 5:22. It would be mistaken to jump too quickly to 1 Corinthians 13 to spell out Paul's

Three actions immediately come to the foreground of Paul's use of the ἀγαπ-word group in Galatians. Love is expressed in Galatians through *self-giving* (2:20); *obedience* to the truth (5:6–7, expressed negatively but implicitly here); and through radical *service* to others (5:13–14; where "through love serve one another" is the equivalent of "love your neighbor"). Naturally, the three expressions of love are interrelated. But for our purposes, it may be best to see radical service as an expression of love's ultimately self-giving character.

Paul's correlation of service with love requires elaboration. "But through love, serve one another." Galatians 5:13–14 is but one example of the paradox of Paul's gospel. Although Christ "has set us free" (5:1), it is a state of freedom that enables each one to "slave" for another. Not to do so runs the risk of handing that freedom over to the Flesh, to be enslaved once again by something that is not a god (4:8). In Paul's letters, of course, servant language is ubiquitous. It is particularly frequent in Galatians due to the many negative references to being "enslaved to" something or being "slaves" in 4:1–5:1.[104] But at 5:13, Paul *positively* identifies love with service. Although he doesn't flesh out here in Galatians what he means by the plea "through love be slaves to one another" (διὰ τῆς ἀγάπης δουλεύετε ἀλλήλοις), it is instructive to compare Paul's other statements, both negative and positive, concerning behavior towards *one another*. In the immediate context, Paul warns the Galatians that "if [they] bite and devour *one another*, [they should] watch out so as not to be consumed by *one another*" (5:15). They are also admonished not to compete against or envy *one another* (5:26). That is, provoking and envying one another "is the opposite of 'love' and of 'serving one another.'"[105] This seems to be the contrast posed by Paul: walking in line with the Flesh results in competing with one another and envy which breeds vicious fighting; or, living by the spirit seeking not to gain honor and servants, but to give honor and to serve that creates communal harmony without recourse to violence. The negative image portrayed by the terms *bite* and *devour* (προκαλούμενοι and φθονοῦντες) is one of hostile contestants engaged in battle or sport. Rather than behaving in this divi-

---

meaning in Galatians. Other letters may indeed provide useful evidence in support or in conflict with the model developed here, but establishing its use in the context of Galatians should be of first importance.

104. The frequency is as follows: δουλεύω, four times (4:8, 9, 25; 5:13); δοῦλος, four times (1:10; 3:28; 4:1, 7); δουλεία, twice (4:24; 5:1); δουλόω, once (4:3).

105. Betz, *Galatians*, 295. Such competition for honor is characteristic of the Roman world. See below.

sive, arrogant manner, those who "march in line following the Spirit as the leader"[106] will eschew a boastful spirit and instead seek to help those who with them belong to Christ.

If self-giving service to others was the target towards which Paul pointed his communities, he understood from personal experience that zeal/jealousy could blur the lines between giving oneself and sacrificing the "other." Paul's own expression of zeal played a vital role in his violent persecution of the Church (Gal 1:13; cf. Phil 3:6). However, one must not assume a mechanistic correspondence between Paul's biography of violence and all "forms" that zeal might take; in other words, zeal does not *necessarily* lead to violence. Of course, English translations treat these verses (1:13; 5:20) differently. In the former, it is understood that Paul's violence was motivated by *zeal*; in the latter, the work of the Flesh is *jealousy*. Despite the neat distinction between these two dispositions afforded to English speakers, in Greek there is no fundamental difference between them. Whether we translate ζῆλος as *jealousy* or *zeal*, the term often expresses a disposition or motivation which potentially leads to or encourages violence.

If Paul's own biography, for example, points to the possibility of violence arising out of *zeal*,[107] other ancient Christian authors highlight the possibility of violence caused by *jealousy*. For instance, 1 Clement (especially chapters 4–6), contains a catalogue of stories highlighting the role of jealousy (ζῆλος) in stories with undeniably violent outcomes. The author of 1 Clement "traces the vicious role of human ζῆλος . . . through the biblical history to the martyrdom of Peter and Paul, with additional illustrations from general history."[108] The stories identify jealousy (and envy paired with it) as the root or cause of: *murder* (Abel, 1 Clem 4:7); the *flight* of one brother from another (Jacob from Esau, 1 Clem 4:8); the *persecution to the point of death* and *selling into slavery* of Joseph (1 Clem 4:9); and the *torments and tortures* endured by "a great multitude of the elect" (1 Clem 6:1–2a), to name just four examples. The author of 1 Clement drew an explicit connection between jealousy (ζῆλος) and violence—and violence between *brothers*, no less. Just as 1 Clement pairs jealousy with envy (ζῆλος with φθόνος) in identifying the motivation for violence, Paul dutifully includes

---

106. Ibid., 294.

107. Other pre-Pauline examples could be added; e.g., Phinehas, Elijah, the Maccabees.

108. Stumpff, "ζῆλος, κτλ," *TDNT* 2:882.

the same *envy* (φθόνος) in his own list of the works of the Flesh (5:21).[109] So, zeal (ζῆλος), especially when it is paired with envy (φθόνος), is quite out of step with the Spirit of Jesus who enables Christians to orient their actions around self-giving love and service to others.

Gentleness, Not Outbursts of Anger

Gentleness is quite the overlooked "virtue" from Paul's lists. In Betz's commentary, *gentleness* (πραΰτης) merits nothing more than possible glosses (*humility* and *meekness*) and a footnote with cross references.[110] Vouga offers three sentences with extensive references to primary sources, a laudable accomplishment by comparison with those named in the previous note. Schlier and Longenecker are two of the most thorough, offering extensive treatment and documentation.[111] Perhaps it is the flatness of the quality of gentleness that has banished the characteristic from extensive attention, but when gentleness is viewed together with its semantic synonyms and antonyms, a more robust quality emerges.

First Corinthians 4:21 is one of the most illuminating Pauline usage of gentleness (πραΰτης), where Paul asks the Corinthians whether they prefer he comes to them with a stick/staff (ῥάβδος), or "with love in a spirit of gentleness." The contrast between the envisaged (violent) discipline of the stick and the happy reception of Paul in a gentle spirit is fairly clear, although the line between warning and threat is a fine one indeed.[112] A thematic parallel occurs in Galatians 6:1, too, when Paul offers instruction concerning correction and discipline within the community. Paul commands: "You who are spiritual should restore such a one in a spirit of gentleness." Paul wisely

109. Although the variant reading at 5:21 is rightly discounted as being influenced by Rom 1:29, the wordplay φθόνοι φόνοι is found in a number of reliable manuscripts.

110. Furnish, *Theology and Ethics*, 86–89, makes even less of gentleness, eliding its character into the broader concept of love. In Martyn, *Galatians* 499, πραΰτης virtually disappears. Hays, "Galatians," 328, offers an apology, claiming "Not every item in Paul's catalog of fruit requires comment," before ignoring seven items in Paul's list, including gentleness.

111. Vouga, *Galater*, 140; Schlier, *Galaterbrief*, 260–61; Longenecker, *Galatians*, 262–63.

112. Thiselton, *1 Corinthians*, 378–79, maintains that Paul's expression is "an illocutionary speech-act," a warning, rather than a "perlocution," a threat. Gorman, *Inhabiting the Cruciform God*, 154, dismisses the possibility that 1 Cor 4:21 constitutes a real threat, since "he is obviously speaking metaphorically."

refrains from providing his Galatian churches with the option of the stick for their own exercise of communal discipline, but like 1 Corinthians 4:21, highlights the need to correct in a spirit of gentleness.

Yet another place where Paul uses gentleness (πραΰτης) in conjunction with discipline is at 2 Corinthians 10:1–6. I do not want to become side-tracked here by leaving Galatians, but a few words about these important verses will help explicate Paul's references to gentleness. Although there are many difficulties with chapters 10–13 in 2 Corinthians (not least the issue of whether they constitute a separate letter altogether),[113] two points are readily apparent. First, Paul indirectly announces an impending (third) visit to the Corinthians in 10:2. He will not address the problem only from afar, but will eventually be present with the Corinthians to address the issue of whether he is timid in person and brave when away. Second, if (we take the consensus view that) he is responding to charges of being of no account in person, then we can see that Paul is framing his so-called timidity in a different light. He "corrects" the Corinthian perception, claiming that his timidity when face-to-face ought to be seen/understood as a manifestation of Paul's living after the "meekness and clemency of Christ" ("παρακαλῶ ὑμᾶς διὰ τῆς πραΰτητος καὶ ἐπιεικείας τοῦ Χριστοῦ.")

It is curious that in a situation which might otherwise provoke an *outburst of anger* in Paul (i.e., some Corinthians adopt a point of view of Paul that challenges his suitability as "their" founding apostle), Paul should refer to a quality that Matthew's Jesus applies to himself, especially as those qualities relate to the manner in which Jesus exercises authority: "Take my yoke upon you and learn from me, because I am meek and gentle in heart." Matthew does not divorce this "gentle" portrait of Jesus from a dose of rather more severe rhetoric (see Matt 11:20), and neither does Paul. Paul virtually begs the Corinthians to respond to his appeal in such a way that he needn't be "bold" when he visits them again.

I do not intend to argue that Paul is quoting or alluding to Jesus Tradition here, but it does strike me as exceedingly improbable that the authors use this particular *pair* of terms *in similar circumstances* without there being some relationship between them. Furnish dismisses the possibility that this is a dominical allusion, instead preferring to see Paul and Matthew to be drawn to the same messianic themes.[114] However, to read the

---

113. Martin, *2 Corinthians*, 298, claims that attempts to explain the transition from 2 Corinthians 9 to 10 "present the reader with a bewildering variety of choices."

114. Furnish, *2 Corinthians*, 460.

gentleness and clemency motif as referring to the preexistent one's humility in "assuming the human condition" is to miss the use to which Paul (and indeed Matthew!) puts the phrase.[115] Paul himself claims to act in gentleness and humility in a manner like Christ, *not in his preexistent graciousness* (how could he do that?), but in his earthly exercise of authority over those whom he disciplines. That is, just as Christ (Paul's term) *is* gentle and humble in leading his disciples, so Paul endeavors to be gentle and clement too. The fact that the Corinthians have failed to recognize Paul's gentleness and humility as qualities that mirror Jesus' own only underscores that they have failed to grasp the fundamental transformation of Paul from violent opponent to non-violent apostle as an effect of the apocalypse of Jesus in Paul.

Although many recognize the emphasis Paul has attached to this plea in 2 Corinthians (e.g., Matera,[116] Furnish, etc.,) very few would consider Paul's gentle and clement interaction with the Corinthians to have the same "weight" as the issue of circumcision in Galatia. I agree with those who see a defense of Paul's apostolic authority in these chapters; but I think it is equally important to note that Paul is defending a peculiar "style" (for lack of a better word) of apostolic authority. It is just as important to Paul that he be recognized for being an apostle as it is that he is recognized as a *gentle and clement* apostle. I think the importance Paul has attached to gentleness in his own dealings with the Corinthians should cause us to look again at this fruit of the spirit that is much neglected in recent scholarship.

It is possible that we can begin to understand the importance of the motif of gentleness in Paul's letter by viewing this characteristic in contrast to the dominant Graeco-Roman ideals for those exercising authority. As Kathy Ehrensperger has put it:

> Only apostles who were willing to "take up the cross" and risk their own lives... who were willing to be πραΰς and ταπεινός (2 Cor. 10.1); who were willing to become ἄτιμοι (1 Cor. 4.10); accepted the risk of being beaten up and humiliated in their male honour (2 Cor. 11.23–25); in the context of a society which was dominated by cultural values and social codes which advocated aggressive, competitive and dominating behaviour of men in an

---

115. Carter, "Take My Yoke Not Rome's," 108–29, provides a thorough critique of prevailing interpretations of Matthew 11:28–30, and correctly identifies the theme of authority (within imperial discourse) in the passage.

116. Matera, *II Corinthians*, 220.

all-pervasive quest and defense of honour, could be trustworthy messengers of the gospel of the kingdom of God.[117]

This Pauline summary of the character of the ideal apostle provides confirmation (outside of Galatians) that gentleness was not only Paul's personal "style" in ministry, but he believed it to be incumbent upon all disciples (and apostles) to behave in a way that expressed the meekness and gentleness of Christ rather than demonstrating one's enslavement to the appetite of the flesh for outbursts of anger.

Other uses of *gentleness* (πραΰτης) and its antonyms in antiquity confirm what has already been said about this neglected virtue. Discussing the Greek general and king Pyrrhus, Plutarch describes his forceful usurpation of resources. Finding himself in need of support to carry out a labor-intensive task, Pyrrhus acquired resources "not by fair and *gentle* dealing (οὐκ ἐπιεικῶς ἐντυγχάνων οὐδὲ πρᾴως) with the cities, but by force in a haughty and insolent way, and menacing them with punishments" (Plutarch, *Pyrrh.* 23.3 [Dryden]). Plutarch's adverbial usage of *gentle* (πρᾴως) stands in antithesis to Pyrrhus's own methods of persuasion—force and the menace of punishment. Plutarch traces the decline of Pyrrhus however, insisting "at first he had not acted thus, but had been unusually indulgent and kind, ready to believe, and uneasy to none; now of a popular leader becoming a tyrant by these severe proceedings, he got the name of an ungrateful and a faithless man." Gentleness and kindness are the qualities Plutarch contrasts with Pyrrhus' violence, haughtiness, insolence, and menace.

Plutarch is not alone. In various texts gentleness (and its cognates) is contrasted with *violence* (βίαιος, Plato *Leg.* 1.645a), *severe, stern* (χαλεπός Plato *Resp.* 2.375c); and *violent, insolent persons* (ὑβριστής, Dio Chrysostom 3 *Regn.* 40). In Esther 13:2b (LXX),[118] Artaxerxes announces his plan, one that he characterizes as embodying the virtues of *kindness* and *gentleness* (ἐπιεικέστερον δὲ καὶ μετὰ ἠπιότητος/πρᾳότητος) for all people who desire peace. His "gentle" plan was to secure lasting tranquility through

---

117. Ehrensperger, *Paul and Dynamics of Power*, 115. See also 112–13: "These values [gentleness, humility] differed radically from the values promoted in and by the dominating elite culture, rendering problems and conflicts almost inevitable when the movement spread into the Graeco-Roman non-Jewish world. . . . The fact is that these early Jesus Traditions (admittedly transmitted in written form later than Paul) clearly emphasize that, within the realm of the kingdom of God, leadership and the exercise of authority ought to be of a radically different kind than that promoted and exercised in the dominating Roman imperial order."

118. This is a variant which reads πρᾳότητος for ἠπιότητος.

the annihilation of all those who alone oppose all of humanity (13:5), putting every one of them throughout the empire to the sword (13:6).[119] In short, violence, severity, and menacing behavior are repeatedly contrasted with gentleness (in the last case it is, naturally, genocide masquerading as gentleness). When this range of antonyms is seen within the context of strained relations in Galatia, the impression of serious interpersonal conflict in the churches, possibly conflict leading even to violence, grows stronger. Rather than passing too hastily over gentleness in Paul's list, it is worth reconsidering whether it indirectly confirms a picture of severe, possibly violent conflict in Paul's churches which he took to be marks not of the Spirit at work among them but as signs that they were in danger of fulfilling the Flesh's desire to generate community strife where peace once reigned.

It is hardly surprising then, to see *outbursts of anger* (θυμοί) among those works of the Flesh that Paul reminds the Galatians to avoid. In using the plural form, Paul shifts the focus from human *feelings* of anger to *actions* carried out in a state of anger. Since Paul uses the plural form, a fitting translation is *outbursts of anger*.[120] As with strife (ἔρις), Paul does not attempt to identify the way in which outburst of anger are organically related to the other works of the Flesh, but the effects of each are patently clear—both are detrimental to the life of the community which should instead be bearing the fruit of the Spirit.[121]

First Clement (45:7), on the other hand, broadcasts the close relationship between outbursts of anger and violence: "Those who were hateful and full of every evil were roused to such a pitch of anger that they tortured those who served God with holy and blameless resolve." As noted in the discussion of strife above, the adjectival form of anger (θυμικός) is part of the trio of traits that give birth to murder (Did 3:2). In the same verse, anger (θυμός) is singled out as a disposition to avoid: "Do not be prone to anger, for anger leads to murder." Roman writers recognized the perils of

---

119. I owe these references to Schlier, *Galaterbrief*, 260n3.

120. BDAG, 461, no. 2.

121. Eph 4:26 does not present intractable difficulties. A quotation from LXX Ps 4:5, anger (ὀργίζω) has a legitimate place, but its pressure to lead to sin is to be strongly resisted. A few verses later (4:31–32), the Ephesians are told to remove anger and wrath (θυμὸς καὶ ὀργὴ) from their midst, and instead demonstrate kind, compassionate and forgiving behavior towards one another "just as God in Christ has forgiven you." Ephesians 4:26 then is no ringing endorsement of actions carried out in a state of anger, but a recognition that anger is a natural human emotion which is but another opportunity for the Christian community to work out in a reconciliatory fashion.

anger too. Seneca, for instance, dedicates one of his *Dialogues* to the topic, identifying anger as "the most hideous and frenzied of all the emotions" (Seneca, *Ira* 3.1.1 [Basore LCL]).

> For the other emotions have in them some element of peace and calm, while this one is wholly violent and has its being in an on-rush of resentment, raging with a most inhuman lust for weapons, blood, and punishment, giving no thought to itself if only it can hurt another, hurling itself upon the very point of the dagger, and eager for revenge though it may drag down the avenger along with it. (Seneca, *Ira* 3.1.1 [Basore LCL])

I do not wish to give the impression that *gentleness* and *outburst of anger* are precise opposites. Rather, I hope to have shown that gentleness is praised by Paul and contrasted with violence by numerous ancient authors, and that outbursts of anger are condemned by Paul and collated with murder, wrath, and torture in several instances. In sum, the Flesh breeds interpersonal conflict which leads to violence, whereas the marks of the community led by the Spirit of Jesus blaze a trail away from violent conflict via gentleness (πραΰτης).[122] The Spirit's community demonstrates self-giving love, peace, gentleness, patience, kindness, and excludes the violent settling of conflict. Conflict can be dealt with under the guidance of the Spirit, but it is to be encountered differently than it is when the Flesh provides the marching orders.

Peace of Christ rather than Pax Romana

Finally, we must look to Paul's inclusion of peace in his list of the fruit of the Spirit. Willard Swartley has summarized the importance of peace in Paul's writings in this manner: "Paul, more than any other writer in the NT canon, makes peace, peacemaking, and peace-building central to his theological reflection and moral admonition."[123] To make such a claim only raises the question: what does *peace* mean for Paul and his audience? Swartley addresses this question too, seeking to hold in tension the influence of the

---

122. The importance of gentleness is underscored all the more if the whole range of semantic equivalents is introduced. Of thirty-two occurrences in the New Testament of the semantic field of *gentleness, mildness*; sixteen occur in the Pauline corpus (and one in Acts is attributed to Paul in a speech).

123. Swartley, *Covenant of Peace*, 190.

Hebrew concept of *šalôm* on the one hand and the Graeco-Roman uses of εἰρήνη/*pax* on the other.

One aspect of *peace* that receives top billing in descriptions of its Old Testament background is the "personal wholeness" or well being characteristic of individuals and communities at peace.[124] This is only one aspect of the use of šalôm/εἰρήνη in the Old Testament, but it is a significant, perhaps even the dominant, meaning. Although I certainly want to avoid downplaying the Old Testament background of Paul's understanding of peace, it would be severely misleading not to focus on the interaction between the peace brought by the spirit of Jesus and the so-called peace brought and sustained by the Roman emperor(s).[125] Indeed, Dieter Georgi opines that the frequency of peace (εἰρήνη) in Paul's letters (44 occurrences if the Deutero-Pauline letters are included) makes it likely that Paul was "looking for critical engagement" with the Roman imperial ideology of worldwide peace established through Augustus and his successors.[126]

The parallel use of terminology, however, is insufficient to establish "critical engagement" as part of Paul's goal. In other words, the terminology is same, but what about the content? Or, as Crossan and Reed put the question: "How exactly did the peace of Rome differ from the peace of God? How exactly did the peace of the Lord Caesar Augustus, divine and Son of God, differ from the peace of the Lord Jesus Christ, also divine and also Son of God?"[127]

Grouping Paul's uses of peace (εἰρήνη) in its various guises, I have identified seven broad categories of usage. The easiest to identify and (tentatively) set aside for the present discussion are the uses of the word group in greetings and closings of his letters. These two categories alone account for 16 uses of the 44 "Pauline" uses (though two overlap with another category).[128] I will also pass over those times Paul uses peace in a quotation (twice, Rom 3:17 and 1 Thess 5:3), and when he uses it in a prayer for his communities (four occurrences; Rom 2:10; 15:13; Gal 6:16; 2 Thess 3:16).

---

124. So, e.g., Longenecker, *Galatians*, 261; Bruce, *Galatians*, 252.

125. Wengst, *Pax Romana*, 17, says of the peace secured and touted by the Caesars: "Despite all assertions to the contrary, the Pax Romana was not really a world of peace. This peace, gained by military force, had its limits at the limits of the Roman empire."

126. Georgi, *Theocracy*, 85.

127. Crossan and Reed, *In Search of Paul*, 74.

128. On greetings, see: Rom 1:7; 1 Cor 1:3; 2 Cor 1:2; Gal 1:3; Eph 1:2; Phil 1:2; Col 1:2; 1 Thess 1:1; 2 Thess 1:2; Phlm 3; 1 Tim 1:2; 2 Tim 1:2; Tit 1:4; on letter closings, see Rom 15:33; 16:20; Eph 6:23.

Although it is closer to my concerns, the moniker "God/Lord of peace" will also not receive more attention (used on seven occasions Rom 15:33; 16:20; 1 Cor 14:33; 2 Cor 13:11; Phil 4:9; 1 Thess 5:23; 2 Thess 3:16). The two categories to which I want to draw attention are those points when Paul uses *peace* in either a paraenetic context or to signal the result of peace established by the activity of God. Paul's letters (if the deutero-Pauline letters are included) contain ten uses of the *peace* (εἰρήνη) word group in paraenesis.[129] In certain places, Paul's expression is direct (e.g., Rom 12:18 "live peaceably with all"), in other cases, I have included less direct examples (e.g., Eph 6:15 "As shoes for your feet put on whatever will make you ready to proclaim the gospel of peace"). Paul tells his audience that peace ought to characterize their dealings with each other and with the world (Rom 12:18; 14:19; 1 Cor 7:15; 2 Cor 13:11; Eph 4:3; 1 Thess 5:13; 2 Tim 2:22) and, at one point he urges the Ephesians to ready themselves to preach the "gospel of peace"— *the gospel itself*, not just their relationships, *is characterized by peace*. Other associated qualities that further explicate the peace to which Paul exhorts his audience are *mutual upbuilding* (Rom 14:19; cf. 1 Thess 5:11), *agreeing with one another* (2 Cor 13:11), and *unity* (Eph 4:3; cf. Col 3:15). That is, in most of Paul exhortations to seek or demonstrate peace, foremost is his desire to see corporate unity among those in Christ.[130]

Much the same concern can be detected in Galatians 5:22. I have already attempted to show how strife and communal discord features throughout Galatians, and in the immediate context there is the list of the works of the flesh (consisting of several community-destroying attitudes and behaviors) as well as the "biting and devouring" intimated by Paul's comment at 5:15. Rather than participating in the community-destroying behaviors listed in 5:19–21, behaviors that Paul previously warned ("I am warning you, *just as I warned you before*") would exclude them from inheriting the kingdom of God, Paul claims that their communal life, if ordered by Christ's spirit, will be characterized by attributes which valorize peace and communal harmony.

Critics sometimes argue that such peace is achieved at the cost of "sameness" (Castelli) or the obliteration of particular (e.g., Jewish) ethnic identity (Boyarin). However, I am more persuaded by those who wish to describe a *negotiation* between the two poles of *solidarity* and *difference*,

129. Rom 12:18; 14:19; 1 Cor 7:15; 16:11; 2 Cor 13:11; Eph 4:3; 6:15; Col 3:15; 1 Thess 5:13; 2 Tim 2:22.

130. Cf. Horrell, *Solidarity and Difference*, 116–21, on the priority Paul gives to fostering unity in communities hindered by division.

to borrow the title of David Horrell's monograph on the topic.[131] It is a corporate, kingdom-of-God-peace that Paul is after, but it is not a coerced peace (or at least not coerced in the same way as peace was coerced by Rome, see below). The peace Paul lauds involves not conceit (κενόδοξος), envy (φθονέω), and competition (προκαλέω) (5:26), but self-giving love, patience, kindness, gentleness and self-control.[132] This kingdom-peace, or, in a more Pauline way of saying it, new-creation-peace, was not something Paul wished to attribute to human achievement, but to the effects of the activity of God in Christ, seen particularly (after the crucifixion/ resurrection) in the guidance provided by Christ's spirit. It is almost universally recognized now by commentators that Paul deliberately sets the fruit of the Spirit in opposition to the work of the Flesh—that is, he takes care not to attribute love, joy, peace, etc, to the power of the Christian to choose them, but to the power of the Spirit to cultivate them in the (diverse) community which is incorporated into Christ's body. To put it baldly, Paul's *unity* is not *sameness* nor is it the *toleration* of difference; neither of those paradigms is strong enough. Rather, both solidarity and difference fall under the earth-shattering category of Christ crucified. The peace of Paul's assemblies is not created by human tolerance or coercion, but is born through nothing less than the crucifixion of the cosmos and the new creation begun by Christ's spirit.

The above observation leads us naturally to address those places where Paul employs *peace* in a way that describes the results of God's activity. This type of usage might describe the opportunities available to those justified by faith (Rom 5:1: "let us have[133] peace with God through our Lord

131. See, e.g., Horrell, *Solidarity and Difference*, 124–32. Horrell's position (126) is that "corporate solidarity in Christ implies, for Paul, neither the *erasure* of previous distinctions nor merely their *encompassing* within a new sphere of belonging, but rather their *relativization* or revaluation, with real social implications." See also Lopez, *Apostle of the Conquered*, 148–49, and esp. 152, who sees in Paul's project the making of visible hierarchies "obsolete."

132. Lest one suspect that it is the "marginal" alone who are "exhorted" to display such selfless attributes, it is worth noting that it is the so-called "strong" in Romans who are told to curb their actions for the sake of the "weak." Those in danger of being marginalized are the ones Paul seeks to protect from coercion.

133. There is "far better external support" for the subjunctive ἔχωμεν. See Metzger, *Textual Commentary*, 452, and Jewett, *Romans*, 344, 348–49; the latter demonstrates the effect of this reading: "The subjunctive produces an admonition about the concrete embodiment of faith in the life of the congregation." In the plainest sense of the term, this reading fits under the exhortative context of peace; but I continue to include it under the effect of God's action since it is linked with the activity of justification in Christ.

Jesus Christ"), or it can be used to describe the character of life in God's kingdom (Rom 14:17: "the kingdom of God is . . . righteousness, peace and joy in the Holy Spirit"), or again it may describe the "horizontal" effects of God's activity in sending his son (Eph 2:14–15: "he is our peace . . . he has broken down the dividing wall, that is, the hostility between us").[134] In almost every instance there are numerous exegetical issues which deserve more attention, but the overarching point in these cases is sound: Paul views the effect of Jesus' life, death and resurrection as a source of peace for new creation—peace between humanity and God is achieved through Christ, peace between former enemies is possible, and the kingdom of God of which Christians are a part values peace (εἰρήνη) more than life's basic necessities (e.g., the "food and drink" of Rom 14:17). This last example is telling too, in that the food and drink to which Paul referred had created considerable tension between the so-called "weak" and "strong" at Rome (Rom 14:1–23).[135] In other words, peace was a more appropriate aim of kingdom fellowship (i.e., welcoming one another in Rom 14:1, 3) than was disputing over opinions (14:1); the Romans were exhorted to "pursue what makes for peace and for mutual upbuilding" (14:19), *an exhortation which grew out of the peace created by the self-offering of Christ* (14:15).

Before Paul's arrival in Galatia, the Galatians had experienced peace of another sort. I'm referring, of course, to the peace achieved by Caesar Augustus and maintained by his allies and successors.[136] Given the civil wars that had caused such instability and hardship on people across the empire, it is little wonder that the leader who "brought war to an end and has ordained peace" should be lauded publicly as a "savior," indeed, as a son of God.[137] This pax Augusti, or, as it was upheld by subsequent Caesars, this

134. The other uses I put in this category are Eph 2:17; Col 1:20; and Phil 4:7.

135. That Paul's letter addresses the circumstances in Rome is now (mostly) taken for granted, though of course the identity of the addressees is now a matter of debate. See, e.g., Horrell, *Solidarity and Difference*, 182–89; Dunn, *Romans*, 2:795; Fitzmyer, *Romans*, 76–77; 686–87, Jewett, *Romans*, 70–72.

136. See Foerster, "εἰρήνη," *TDNT*, 2:401. In general, εἰρήνη is used in a way that marks it as an antonym of war (πόλεμος); it named "an interlude in the everlasting state of war." Cf. Isocrates, *Ad Nic.* 2.24 (Norlin, LCL): "Be warlike (πολεμικὸς) in your knowledge of war and in your preparations for it, but peaceful (εἰρηνικὸς) in your avoidance of all unjust aggression."

137. From the Priene inscription *SEG* 4.490//*OGIS* 458; also found in Ehrenberg and Jones, *Documents Illustrating*, [hereafter *EJ*] no. 98, lines 32–37: "The Providence that has divinely ordered our life, has brought us regard and honour and arranged our life with perfect goodness when it brought to us Augustus, whom Providence has filled with

pax Romana, contrasts quite starkly with the pax Christi described above. Despite the longstanding tradition among ancient historians of extolling the benefits of the pax Romana without attending properly to possible detriments, the last few decades have seen a growing interest in reassessing Rome's so-called peace from the margins in, rather than from the perspective of the center of power.[138]

Like so many other topics with which we are concerned, the peace achieved and sustained in the "golden age" of the Principate deserves the voluminous attention paid to it, and we can do little more here than point out important features. The most important thing to flag in discussions of Rome's peace, in contrast to the peace characteristic of the community led by the spirit of Jesus, is the manner in which it was achieved. Rome's peace was created and sustained, unapologetically, by an active and fearsome military.[139] Peace was the result of victory, not diplomacy (certainly not conciliation), and it was proclaimed, like the name of the emperor who guaranteed it, "on seas stained with the bloodshed of victory and on battlefields piled high with the bodies of the dead" (Pliny, *Pan.* 12).[140] On the one hand, although Tacitus reported that during Augustus' reign some (no doubt elite) Romans felt that "very few situations had been treated by force [*vis*], and then only in the interests of general tranquility" (Tacitus, *Ann.* 1.9.5 [Moore and Jackson LCL]), he could also report that others noted that undoubtably "there was peace after all this [events leading to Augustus' rise to power], but it was a peace stained with blood" (Tacitus, *Ann.* 1.10.4 [Church and Brodribb]). The *modus operandi* of securing Augustan peace was etched in inscriptions discovered in three separate locations in Galatia (Pisidian Antioch, Ancyra, and Pisidian Apollonia)—his was a peace "acquired by victory."[141]

---

virtue for the benefit of mankind and granted to us and to those after us as our saviour [σωτῆρα] who has made war to cease and ordered the world with peace [τὸν παύσαντα μὲν πόλεμον, κοσμήσοντα δὲ εἰρήνην]."

138. Cf. Price, "Response," 176–77.

139. The latter quality was perhaps more important than the former for sustaining peace across such a vast empire. Lendon, *Empire of Honour*, 4, recognized the efficient use made of scarce resources: "Even where only a modest force was available, the Roman authorities stretched it as much as they could by inspiring terror: the governor progressed through his province dealing with malefactors in a way that locals would remember, by having them crucified, or burnt alive, or fed to wild beasts."

140. The translation of Pliny is from Wengst, *Pax Romana*, 16.

141. The Latin is "esset parta victoriis pax," *Res Gestae* 13. Augustus also touts his restoration of peace to the seas from pirates (*Res Gestae* 25, one supposes that he didn't ask

The benefits of the peace secured by Rome were legion, but, as Klaus Wengst sharply notes, the question of whether there was a "golden age" is an incomplete one unless we ask the related question: for whom?[142] Wengst closely follows the characterization provided by Harald Fuchs, who wrote one of the seminal works about the peace acquired by Augustus. Fuchs stripped away any sentimental view of the peace wrought by Rome, though he seemed to react too strongly in the other direction:

> The pax Romana was a hostile confrontation brought about by blood and iron and the use of every fighting weapon of the state imaginable against the whole earth, based on a politics of compulsion; and in each individual instance there lay behind it an unbounded desire to preserve its own advantage.[143]

The Galatians who heard Paul's letter, who were taught to look for the fruit of peace in their Spirit-led community, knew of a very different method for securing such fruit, and the Roman means of achieving peace had little to do with the self-giving love, gentleness, and forgiveness expected of those who found themselves in Christ.

Life in the Spirit contrasts in many ways with life in the Flesh. I have sought to demonstrate how Paul's ethics in Galatians identifies one such difference. Life guided by the Spirit of Jesus includes practices that actively attempt to build communities characterized by the peace of Christ. I have argued that activities such as correction and forgiveness, mutual burden

---

nicely), and the peace he restored to the provinces (Galatia named among them), 26. In the same place, Augustus recalls, "By my order and auspices two armies were led . . . into Ethiopia and into that part of Arabia which is called Happy, and the troops of each nation of enemies were slaughtered in battle [*caesae* from *caedo* meaning *hewn, cut to pieces, cut down*; the Greek is the same: κατέκοψεν ἐν παρατάξει] and many towns captured."

142. Wengst, *Pax Romana*, 10–12. The Homonadeis (or what was left of them after the "pacification" of the area by Quirinius), for instance, might have had a very different view of Augustan peace in Galatia than the colonial settlers in Pisidian Antioch.

143. Harald Fuchs, *Augustin und der antike Friedensgedanke*, 201. Quotation taken from Wengst, *Pax Romana*, 176n31. Cf. Greg Woolf, "Roman Peace," 171–94, who argues that rather than positioning oneself in one of two binary camps (e.g., Roman forces are seen as *either* "defenders" *or* "occupying forces"), we should attempt to "step outside the debate" and resist identifying with either Rome or its opponents (180–81). Woolf's (ibid., 185) balanced treatment nevertheless affords him room to recognize the realities of peace in the provinces: "The Roman peace did not mean that provincials had no experience of violence." Instead, it meant only that "provincials were spared the additional misery of warfare on top of the ill health, squalor, insecurity, poverty and low life expectancy that were the lot of most inhabitants of the ancient world. . . . Provincials were subject to the violence of landowners and of civic and imperial officials."

bearing, and serving, as well as attributes such as self-giving love, gentleness and peace serve to create and identify communities that witness to the faithfulness of Jesus' own non-violent encounter with the world through imitation of his non-violent, peace-producing behavior. Life under the sway of the Flesh, by contrast, is scarred by enmity, strife, jealousy, outbursts of anger, dissensions, factions, and quarreling. When peace is crafted in the Flesh, it is peace secured through threat, coercion, and ultimately "embodied" in violence. Although Paul does not attempt to explain the ways in which the works of the Flesh are interrelated, the generative relationships between enmities, strife, jealousy, outbursts of anger, envy and violence (specifically murder, persecution, and torture, to name just three examples) are explicitly posited in other early Christian authors, most notably 1 Clement and Didache. But by identifying the Flesh as a suprahuman power, Paul himself does not need to unveil the way the Flesh generates violence. Violence is as much organically connected to the works of the Flesh in the domain of the present evil age as peace is the natural produce of Christ's Spirit in the domain of those who are "in Christ."

A New Politics—Doing the Good (6:9)

Thus far I have attempted to demonstrate how Paul's *ethics* are distinctly non-violent, but in this final section, I want to explore one way in which Paul's ethics are constitutive of a new *politics*, indeed an "un-Roman" one. Like the division between religion and politics, the division between ethics and politics is a false one.[144] The behaviors, activities, and disciplines shared by a community *are* its politics, its way of ordering communal life together. Paul's assemblies (ἐκκλησίαι, a political term if ever there was one) are political bodies in at least this broad sense of the term. I want now to explore one more practice Paul urges his communities to participate in as part of a non-violent political body. Thus far, forgiveness and mutual correction, enduring hardship, burden-bearing, and self-abasement (through service) are some of the practices I have named as being commended and nurtured within the Christian community. They are practices that simultaneously identify its member-citizens and transform outsiders, by the enlivening work of the Holy Spirit, from allegiance to the politics of the Flesh into bearers of heavenly citizenship (πολίτευμα, cf. Phil 3:20; Gal 4:26). One more practice that Paul commends, by which the church fulfills faithfully

144. For further comments on the false division, see chapter 1.

its vocation to be an assembly of peace in a world of violence, is that of "doing the good."

Doing the Good in the Roman City

At Galatians 6:9–10, Paul urges the Galatians "let us not grow weary in doing the good, for in due season we will reap if we do not give up. So then, as we have opportunity, let us work for the good of all, but especially for the household of the faith."[145] It is the parallel expressions "doing the good" (τὸ δὲ καλὸν ποιοῦντες) and "working for the good" (ἐργαζώμεθα τὸ ἀγαθὸν) which may contribute to our understanding of the political import of Paul's communities. The expressions resonate with the politically freighted twin practices of euergetism and benefaction.[146] A full discussion of euergetism and benefaction is unnecessary, but two elements of these practices call for our attention. First, it is commonly assumed in secondary literature that the motive for performing good works in Graeco-Roman antiquity was, in general, not *primarily* philanthropic.[147] For those who could afford to bestow gifts on their city or private clients, the action may have been undertaken to secure an increasing profile of honor among peers.[148] The second aspect of

145. Translation mine.

146. Veyne, *Bread and Circuses*, 1, 10, 11. Veyne delineates euergetism from benefaction by pointing to the recipients of the action: euergetism is the giving of gifts by an individual to a community, whereas benefaction may have one client or a small group of clients in view. Noting that Paul's terminology here corresponds with the terminology used for benefaction or euergetism in no way commits one to argue that Paul is using a technical term for such practices or that he intentionally constructs a Christian alternative to the Greco-Roman practice. Significant differences remain, not least the fact that such activities as building an amphitheatre or aqueduct or hosting a city-wide banquet—common euergetistic gifts—are not presumably what Paul has in mind for his Christian communities. Rather, we might yet see another way in which the kind of activity Paul commends (doing the good) is sometimes indistinguishable from the activities of those outside the church, however different their motives may be. The comparison is still valid, differing "gifts" notwithstanding, when politics is defined by the church (ἐκκλησία) rather than by those powerful benefactors (εὐεργέται) who walk the halls of imperial or provincial power.

147. However, cf. Lomas and Cornell, "Introduction," 1–27, who warn that although evidence for euergetism is vast, it "is often . . . relatively limited in what it can tell us about the motivation for specific acts of euergetism."

148. Saller, "Status and Patronage," 847, assessing several of (the younger) Pliny's provisions of *pecunia* (money or assets), writes that, taken collectively, "Pliny's generosity illustrates how the aristocratic values of the Roman world encouraged the élite to deploy their wealth and influence as patrons of individuals and municipalities in order to

euergetism and benefaction that demands further comment is the fact that these practices are indelibly political—the practices construct the political inasmuch as they participate in creating, sustaining, and transforming the social and political fortunes of both those who give the gift and those who reciprocate with honor.[149]

Examples of the first point can be found, for instance, in writers such as Cicero and Pliny the Younger. In a passage meant to warn its audience of the corruption of the practice of euergetism-benefaction, Cicero writes:

> We . . . observe that a great many people do many things that seem to be inspired more by a spirit of ostentation than by heart-felt kindness; for such people are not really generous but are rather influenced by a sort of ambition to make a show of being open-handed. Such a pose is nearer akin to hypocrisy than to generosity or moral goodness. (Cicero, *Off.* 1.44 [Miller LCL])

But the context of Cicero's warning indicates that he does not attack the alleged lack of heartfelt kindness; instead, the apparently common enough practice of *giving beyond one's means* is the target of Cicero's ire. For Cicero, being generous beyond means is not faulted because it seeks honor, but because it engages in two corollary injustices: the gift beyond means necessarily cuts into the resources that would naturally (and justly) be given to or available for the gift-giver's kin, and second, "such generosity too often engenders a passion for plundering and misappropriating property, in order to supply the means for making large gifts" (Cicero, *Off.* 1.44 [Miller LCL]).[150] Evidently the practice of robbing Peter to pay Paul is a habit that predates the Apostles whose names color the famous expression.

---

achieve honour and social domination in personal relationships." Cf. Garnsey's "Generosity of Veyne," 167: "Euergetism is a display of superiority, a measure of the gap between ruler and ruled, a reminder of social hierarchies." Lendon, *Empire of Honour*, 86, 89, notes that "in Greek, one of the usual terms for a public benefaction was *philotimia*, an act of 'glory-love.'" The wealthy *euergetes* "devoted to the city his money and effort and got honour in return." This was done in part because the honor and prestige of one's city (of residence or of birth) "made up a part of its citizens' own individual honour."

149. In this I am closer to Garnsey's ("Generosity of Veyne," 168) gentle critique than to Veyne's assertion that (in Garnsey's words) euergetism does not "achieve or maintain political or social equilibrium . . . euergetism is neither a forced response to pressure from below, not an attempt to lull the masses into passivity." See the previous note.

150. It is worth pointing out the observation of Wood, *Cicero's Social and Political Thought*, 101, that generosity (*liberalitas*) was "rarely, if ever" thought of in humanitarian terms as a help for the poor. Instead, generosity was "an investment in friendship or a method of winning friends for the future."

Pliny too, has words of praise for the proper sense of humility that should accompany the performance of the good:

> I am sensible how much nobler it is to place the reward of virtue in the silent approbation of one's own breast than in the applause of the world. Glory ought to be the consequence, not the motive of our actions; and though it should sometimes happen not to attend the worthy deed, yet such a deed is none the less amiable for having missed the applause it deserved. But the world is apt to suspect that those who celebrate their own generous acts, do not extoll them because they performed them, but performed them that they might have the pleasure of extolling them. Thus the splendour of an action which would have shone out in full lustre if related by another, vanishes and dies away when he that did it tells the tale. (Pliny, *Ep.*1.8 to Pomeius Saturninus [Melmoth, LCL])

The irony of course is that the close reader of Pliny's letter begins to wonder whether Pliny affirms the ideal and casts aspersions on the boastful in order to flag his own consent to popular opinion while demurring from it in this particular instance. He is writing, after all, to a friend who has requested one of Pliny's orations which seems to have been delivered to a select audience (i.e., an audience on which Pliny would have to rely if he wanted his rhetorical prowess to be made public). There is a trace of special pleading near the close of Pliny's letter:

> Such is the disposition of mankind, if they cannot blast an action, they will censure the parade of it; and whether you do what does not deserve to be taken notice of, or take notice yourself of what does, either way you incur reproach. (Pliny, *Ep.* 1.8 to Pompeius Saturninus [Melmoth, LCL])

Such is the risk Pliny chooses to take by obliging his friend's request.

The second point, that euergetism is one among many public practices that both creates and sustains the social and political fortunes of people living across a wide spectrum of Graeco-Roman society is best illustrated by not only the ubiquitous competition for honor, but contention even over the manner in which it was to be gained. In J. E. Lendon's view, the path to honor and indeed its very value were "always in contention between rival communities of opinion in the Roman world, and the aristocratic conception of honour, broadly conceived, exerted a profound influence on how the rest of society conceived of honour."[151] Although the aristocratic norms exerted a powerful influence, there were

> innumerable communities of honour, many of which honoured qualities and achievements that aristocrats (whose standards varied from place to place, and who formed multiple communities themselves), might find strange or repulsive, and which constituted challenges to the way grandees conceived of honour.[152]

That is, we should conceive of honor as something negotiated within competing communities of public opinion, and performing the good, whether private benefaction or public euergetism, required political delicacy if one was to secure the desired end of praise rather than the shame that might visit the vain.

In a context of competition for honor, the performance of "the good" became a weapon deployed in self-interest to accumulate honor at the expense of all other competitors. Such competitive behavior, whether intentionally or not, reinforced the systemic violence that characterized so many social engagements in the Roman world.

Doing the Good in the Spirit

Paul, on the other hand, continued to attempt to persuade his churches to perform "the good,"[153] but categorically opposed the "lure of honor" and its implicit endorsement of the systemic violence of the empire. Doing "the good" was for Paul a mark of the community of faith and was motivated not by the opportunity for increased honor as were euergetism and benefaction among the Romans, but by imitation of or participation in the undignified, cruciform Christ.[154] At just this point the trajectory of peace intersects

151. Lendon, *Empire of Honour*, 90.

152. Ibid. That freedmen could be held as honored officials in Italian trade guilds, yet scorned by higher-born aristocrats (ibid., 98) is but one example of how the definition and path to honor was a contested issue, and that that honor could be had at levels of society far below an "aristocratic" one. Cf. Val. Max. 8.14.5, where of an "ordinary soldier" it is remarked: "There is no one so humble that he cannot be touched by the charm of glory [*gloria*]." Translation from Walker, *Valerius Maximus*.

153. Perhaps we again need to flag up the difference in "the good" for Paul. Rather than commissioning and funding buildings and public feasts, Paul's churches were called to do "the good" which is broadly outlined by the Fruit of the Spirit (Gal 5:22–26) and the bearing of one another's burdens (Gal 6:2).

154. Lendon, *Empire of Honour*, 92–93, recognized the "starkest possible challenge to

with the reality of tragedy. Paul and those who follow his example did not necessarily have a direct experience of the rewards of living peaceably, but continued to trust in the promise of reaping at the time of harvest. But between doing the good and reaping the harvest, the Christians in Galatia experienced opposition, possibly causing them to grow weary in their performance of the good. Paul exhorts them to remain steadfast in their working for the good of *all* and especially of their brothers and sisters in the family of faith, even when the harvest remains presently unseen. Paul's promotion of doing the good, rooted and defined as it is in being conformed to the self-giving faithfulness of the Son of God, is a politics conditioned by God's patience, most characteristically on display in the cross of Christ. Immediate results are not the goal (further subverting the idea that doing the good is aimed at accruing honor), but conformity to the Christ who enlivens every disciple is paramount. Doing the good without attempting to "make a good showing" (6:12) and doing so without the promise of immediate reward or result indicates the different politics embodied in the kingdom of God and in Paul's local assemblies.

CONCLUSION

In the present chapter, I have attempted to trace the trajectory of violence and peace in Paul's biography (and in Paul's Galatian converts more generally) in Galatians. Beginning with his self-portrait of his former life in Judaism as one which was conformed to the *modus operandi* of the unregenerate world, Paul calls attention to the violent politics in which he was a participant and by which he achieved a certain renown. The path on which he traveled, however, came to a dead-end in the revelation of the crucified and risen Son of God. The violent persecutor died at the apocalypse of the Son of God, but the biography of Paul took on a new trajectory, one that became increasingly conformed to the portrait of the Son of God. The new creation inaugurated by the advent of the Son set Paul on a new course, empowering him to gather new-creation assemblies that corporately sought to be conformed to the true lord (κύριος) of the cosmos who creates and sustains authentic and lasting peace. Such communities of peace could not ensure that violence would not visit them, and Paul warned his churches

---

aristocratic pagan attitudes" posed by Christianity. "Activities prompted by the lust for honour in this life were ruled out; ideally the whole proud, competitive, jostling ethos of the ancient city was abandoned."

that those loyal to the old-age *modus operandi* would burden them with trouble and tragedy. The new-creation way to encounter and overcome such hostility, however, was to reciprocate *good* for evil. To do so was to witness to the truth that what the church was called to be at present was what the cosmos was called to be ultimately. The trajectory of Paul (and the church) was movement from a politics of hostility and violence toward a politics of peace. If Paul and his churches ever strayed from the path left to them by Jesus, it might be more appropriate to put the failure down to the "foreignness" of the path rather than the capabilities of the guide or his followers. There is, after all, only one "native speaker" familiar with the grammar of Christian peacemaking.

5

Supporting Evidence
in 1 Thessalonians

In this chapter, I will identify ways in which 1 Thessalonians offers evidentiary support for my argument. Although a full account of my argument in Paul's first letter to the Thessalonians could potentially fill another volume, I haven't the space for such an extended treatment. What I offer here is more akin to a test of the present argument in outline form, which I hope to build upon in future work. In brief, I will attempt to show:

1. That the introduction of Paul's gospel in Thessalonica features thematic emphases that (arguably) appear to some ancient and modern interpreters to compete with the theo-political "gospel" of Caesar.

2. Rome's peace, featured in an imperial slogan in 1 Thessalonians, was understood by Paul to be different in kind to the peace of Christians.

3. Jesus Tradition features in 1 Thessalonians, and there is some evidence that the Sermon on the Mount/Plain material appears to be under consideration.

4. Three separate "biographies" of opposition against Paul, Thessalonian Christians, and Judean Christians identify a singular response, namely, returning good for evil.

In short, 1 Thessalonians confirms the necessarily political nature of Paul's gospel (without itself being derived from Roman politics as its mirror opposite), that, in contrast to the regnant political system, left no place for violence in Christian peacemaking.

Paul's Non-Violent Gospel

THEOLOGICAL POLITICS IN THESSALONICA

First-century Thessalonica was like any other thriving Mediterranean city of the era—though in significant ways it was independent, it always deferred to Rome whom it ultimately served. Still, it is important to identify *as far as possible* the presence, or degree of prominence, of the imperial power in the Macedonian capital. The limiting phrase of the last sentence is important; the ancient city of Thessalonica has, somewhat uniquely, survived at the same location since its founding in 316 BCE without extensive archaeological exploration.[1] Ancient buildings that are available to examine are from well after Paul's time there (second and third centuries CE) and first-century evidence is minimal by comparison with other cities in which Paul operated such as Corinth or Philippi. What is generally agreed about Thessalonica at the time of Paul's visit[2] is this: owing to its excellent location, it was one of the two most important cities of trade in Greece (the other was Corinth). Due to its commercial significance (it was situated near the midpoint of the *Via Egnatia*, on the Aegean Sea, with access to tributaries of the Danube River),[3] Thessalonica attracted a diverse population of between forty and one hundred thousand.[4] Although archaeological evidence for a Jewish presence in the first century is not strong, most scholars do not dispute the presence of Jews in the city at the time of Paul (as attested by Acts 17:1–13).[5] Thessalonica remained more "Greek" in its public expression than did, for example, Philippi under the Romans. The distribution of

1. Edson, "Cults of Thessalonica (Macedonica III)," 153; Meeks, *First Urban Christians*, 46. Cf. Vacalopoulos, *History of Thessaloniki.*

2. Tentatively placed between the summer of 49 and February of 50. See Malherbe, *Letters to the Thessalonians*, 73, and Riesner, *Paul's Early Period*, 364. Cf. also Jewett, *Thessalonian Correspondence*, 59–60.

3. Meeks, *First Urban Christians*, 46. Its unique location, at the junction of important routes in every direction, made it important for communication also.

4. Crossan and Reed, *In Search of Paul*, 155–57, gives the lower figure; Malherebe, *Letters to the Thessalonians*, 14, gives a range of sixty-five to eighty thousand within the city walls; Riesner, *Paul's Early Period*, 341, sets the upper limit at one hundred thousand. As to diversity, a third-century BCE complex dedicated to the Egyptian gods Sarapis and Isis suggest the presence of Egyptian traders; there is also early evidence for Italian traders, alongside a "local" population made up of Macedonians, Greeks, and Thracians.

5. Vacalopoulos, *History*, 9; Meeks, *First Urban Christians*, 46; Crossan and Reed, *In Search of Paul*, 157; Jewett, *Thessalonian Correspondence*, 119–20. Cf. Philo *Legat.* 281, who records that Jews inhabited all parts of the empire, including Macedonia. Josephus, *Ant.*, 14:115, writes that it is not easy to find a place in the entire empire (οἰκουμένη) that does not have a Jewish presence.

inscriptions between Latin and Greek in each city is a study in contrasts.[6] Its "Greek" character was preserved in more than just inscriptions; it remained a "free city" (*civitas libera*) after backing the victorious Octavian and Antony (42 BCE) during the Roman civil war, retaining its pre-Roman, republican form of government.[7] Octavian's benevolence (once he defeated Antony at Actium in 31 BCE) thus left Thessalonica with a measure of autonomy: no Roman garrison was stationed there (though inscriptions evince a significant number of Thessalonian veterans[8]), they maintained the right to mint their own coins, and the city retained its assembly of the people (ἐκκλησία τοῦ δήμου), council (βουλή), and the pre-Roman office of politarch (πολιτάρχης), of which there were probably five or six during the New Testament period.[9]

Roman Theological Politics in Thessalonica

Imperial Cult

By the time Paul arrived in Thessalonica, the imperial cult was well established.[10] During the reign of Augustus, a temple to Julius Caesar was built in the city, and coins minted (around 27 BCE) proclaim Julius Caesar a god (θεός).[11] On the reverse of one coin issue, Zeus was replaced by Octavian, and although the title "son of God" (υἱὸς θεοῦ) does not appear on any of the

6. Thessalonica: Greek, 1006; Latin 14; Philippi: Greek, 60; Latin, 361. Cf. Meeks, *First Urban Christians*, 45. However, see Oakes, *Philippians*, 35–40, on the dangers of making too much of the predominance of Latin inscriptions at Philippi.

7. *CAH* 10:574. Pliny *Nat Hist* 4.35, 36, 38.

8. Tellbe, *Paul between Synagogue and State*, 84n31.

9. Meeks, *First Urban Christians*, 47; Jewett, *Thessalonian Correspondence*, 123.

10. By using the phrase *the imperial cult*, I do not wish to minimize the local diversity of imperial cults throughout the empire. See Price, *Rituals and Power*, 61. For a cautious analysis of the cults in Thessalonica, see Hendrix, "Beyond 'Imperial Cult,'" 301–8. Naturally, the imperial cult was not the only one operating in Thessalonica. The cults of Serapis, Isis, Dionysus, and Cabirus all contributed to the "religious" character of the city. See Jewett, *Thessalonian Correspondence*, 126–32. However, as Gill, "Macedonia," 408, notes, the multiplicity of cults in the province found their "focal point" in the worship of the emperor.

11. Donfried, "Imperial Cults of Thessalonica," 217–18. Edson, "State Cults in Thessalonica (Macedonica II)," 133, estimates the temple to Julius Caesar was built as early as 26 BCE. Cf. *IG* X. 2, 31–32. Gill, "Macedonia," 415, posits that the "imperial cult was probably located in the western part of the city."

extant coins, his status as *divi filius* is implicit in his inclusion on the coin with his deified father (see example below).[12]

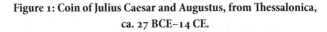

Figure 1: Coin of Julius Caesar and Augustus, from Thessalonica, ca. 27 BCE–14 CE.

Indeed, once the temple to Julius Caesar was built (sometime between 27 BCE and 14 CE), a "priest and agonothete of Imperator Caesar *son of god*" were established and are always mentioned first in inscriptions listing different priestly offices, indicating the priority given to the imperial cult.[13] Additional numismatic evidence from the first century CE indicates that

---

12. *RPC* I 1555, accessed on 31 December, 2009 on http://www.wildwinds.com/coins/ ric/augustus/RPC_1555.jpg courtesy of www.cngcoins.com and www.wildwinds.com. The coin's obverse is an image of Julius Caesar with Augustus on the reverse. From Thessalonica, between 27 BCE and 14 CE. ΘΕΟΣ is inscribed by the laureate head of Julius Caesar; ΘΕΣΣΑΛΟΝΙΚΕΩΝ, encircles the bare head of Augustus. Also found in *BMC* 58 or *SGI* 151. Donfried, "Imperial Cults of Thessalonica," 218, working from Holland L. Hendrix's unpublished ThD thesis "Thessalonicans Honor Romans," 170, only grants that the juxtaposition "may reflect Thessalonican awareness" of Augustus' status as son of God (υἱὸς θεοῦ). Subsequently, Hendrix, "Beyond 'Imperial Cult,'" 307, argued that the Thessalonian issue shows a *reluctance* by the Thessalonians to portray Augustus as a divine son. S. R. F. Price addresses the difficulties of distinguishing between the Latin *divi filius* and Greek υἱὸς θεοῦ in "Gods and Emperors," 79–95.

13. Hendrix, "Thessalonicans Honor Romans," 312; Donfried, "Imperial Cults of Thessalonica," 218–19; Crossan and Reed, *In Search of Paul*, 157. Edson, "State Cults in Thessalonica (Macedonica II)," 132–33, suggests "quite soon after the Battle of Actium" for the founding of the priesthood and agonothete of Augustus. Decker, "Agonothetes," describes the role of *agonothete* as one responsible for various aspects associated with the festivals and games in Greece.

Thessalonica accepted the divinity of the emperors from Julius Caesar to Claudius (d. 54 CE).[14]

Provincial Politics

The obvious enthusiasm for Augustus and his family demonstrated by the Thessalonian authorities betrays a civic insecurity—in the three most recent major Roman conflicts in which Thessalonica was involved, the city *initially* chose to support the eventual loser. It initially backed Pompey against Julius Caesar in 49 BCE,[15] supported Brutus and Cassius before it switched allegiance to Antony and Octavian before the second battle of Philippi (42 BCE),[16] and again backed Antony before the Battle of Actium (31 BCE).[17] Mikael Tellbe posits that it was this embarrassing history of supporting the "wrong" side that led the civic authorities of Thessalonica eagerly "*to cultivate the new emperor's confidence in the city's loyalty to him and his successors.*"[18] Civic embarrassment does not *fully* explain the desire to display their loyalty publicly, for very real benefits of imperial benefaction were also at stake. The issue of *imperial loyalty* was a crucial one for the profit of Thessalonica's citizenry, elite and non-elite alike. In this precarious situation, any who were seen to jeopardize imperial benefaction might understandably have been looked upon with great suspicion.

One way in which that loyalty could be demonstrated was by swearing the annual oath to the emperor, a practice that was widespread in the empire. Although a Thessalonian example of an imperial oath requirement is lacking, this is not surprising since the material record is comparatively

---

14. Crossan and Reed, *In Search of Paul*, 158. Tellbe, *Paul Between Synagogue and State*, 84, characterizes the number of coin issues honoring Octavian by the Thessalonians as "unusually high," suggesting eager participation by the Thessalonians in spreading imperial propaganda. On the divinity of the emperors from Julius Caesar to Claudius, see Jewett, *Thessalonian Correspondence*, 126, and Hendrix, "Thessalonicans Honor Romans," 108. At least one coin issue of nearby Amphipolis (through which Paul may have passed en route to Thessalonica) identifies Augustus as ΚΑΙΣΑΡ ΘΕΟΥ ΥΙΟΣ. See *RPC* 1626 / *BMC* 73 / *SGI* 29. *RPC* 1626 can be accessed on www.wildwinds.com.

15. Dio, *Roman History* 41.18, 44.

16. Their shift in allegiance properly situates, whether as cause or effect, the promise of Brutus and Cassius to their legions to have Thessalonica as booty after the battle at Philippi. Cf. Plutarch, *Brut.* 30; Crossan and Reed, *In Search of Paul*, 156–57.

17. Tellbe, *Paul between Synagogus and State*, 82, 84.

18. Ibid., 84. See also de Vos, *Church and Community Conflicts*, 143.

small. Representative of oaths sworn annually by provincial inhabitants are those that have been found at Paphlagonia and Cyprus.[19] The first text is cited at length below.

> In the third year from Imperator Caesar Augustus, son of the dei-fied Caesar (θεοῦ υἱοῦ Σεβαστοῦ) . . . on 6 March in Gangra[20] in [the market place], oath sworn by the inhabitants of Paphlagonia [and] by the Romans residing among them for business purposes.
>
> I swear by Zeus, Earth, Sun, all the gods [and] goddesses, and by Augustus himself that I will be loyal (εὐνοήσειν) to Caesar Augustus and his children and descendants for all the time of my [life], in word, deed and thought, considering as friends whom-ever they consider so, and reckoning as enemies whomsoever they themselves judge to be so; and that in their interests I shall spare neither body not soul nor life nor children . . . I shall endure every danger (πάντα κίνδυνον ὑπομενεῖν); and that if I see or hear anything hostile to them being either said or planned or carried out, this I will reveal and shall be the enemy of [the man] who is saying or planning or doing any of these things. And whomsoever they themselves may judge to be their enemies, these I will pursue (διώξειν) and defend (ἀμυνεῖσθαι) them against, by land and sea, by sword and steel.
>
> But if I do anything contrary to this [oath] or do not conform to the letter with the oath I swore, I myself bring down on my-self . . . and on my children and all my family and all that belongs to me utter and total destruction down to my every last connec-tion [and] all my descendants . . .
>
> All the inhabitant of [the countryside] also took the oath in the same terms in the shrines of Augustus in the districts at the [altar] of Augustus.[21]

Geographically, two things should be noted. Gangra lies some 80 km NE of Ancyra, the provincial capital of Galatia, a province in which Paul was active before composing 1 Thessalonians. Paphlagonia lies a further 100+ km NE of Gangra. I point out this detail simply to show the wide

19. Ando, *Imperial Ideology and Provincial Loyalty*, 359–60.

20. Gangra was the capital of Paphlagonia, annexed as part of Galatia in 6 BCE. The oath was taken three years later in the smaller city of Phazimon, where the inscription was found. *EJ* 315 [= *ILS* 8781; *OGIS* 532] translation is from Levick, *Government of the Roman Empire*, 141n129.

21. For the similar oath found at near Palaipaphos, on the island of Cyprus, and dated to the beginning of the reign of Tiberius, see Levick, *Government of the Roman Empire*, 142; and Mitford, "Cypriot Oath of Allegiance," 74–79.

distribution of the evidence of loyalty oaths from the provincial capital of Ancyra. If the oaths were made at the northern reaches of the province, it is probable that Paul would have encountered such oaths while working in (the south of) Galatia.[22]

Second, a similar oath was found near Palaipaphos, Cyprus. We learn from Acts (13:4–13) that Paul and Barnabas sailed to Cyprus, landing at Salamis, and worked their way to Paphos (= Palaipaphos) before sailing back to the mainland. The loyalty oath is dated towards the beginning of Tiberius' reign[23] (ca. 14 CE) and so would have been recited annually by the island's residents if Paul and Barnabas visited. While Paul's visit to Paphos is not substantiated by Paul himself, nothing in Luke's narrative is incredible; there is no compelling reason to doubt the historicity of the visit, especially given his companion Barnabas' Cypriot origins.[24] Rather, if Paul was unfamiliar with the practice of the oath of loyalty to Caesar, that would be remarkable.

The oaths of loyalty were widespread in the Roman Empire, and we should not "underestimate the eagerness of individuals to demonstrate loyalty . . . to placate, persuade, or dupe their Roman overlords."[25] The benefits of such loyalty were keenly felt by cities like Thessalonica whose loyalties were officially recognized by the emperor. Beginning with Augustus, cities undertook "urban renewal" projects, improving infrastructure (aqueducts, etc.) and raising new buildings (temples,[26] baths, theatres, porticos[27]) with direct Imperial assistance, usually in the form of tax relief or technical expertise.[28] Self-interest clearly played a role in demonstrations of loyalty, but communal benefits also accrued on account of communal demonstrations of loyalty and honors paid to the emperor and his family. Benefaction from the emperor fostered good will in the provinces, at the very least among

22. If Paul labored in North Galatia (rather than South), obviously that would put him geographically closer to the oath of Gangra.

23. Mitford, "Cypriot Oath of Allegiance," 79. The oath was believed to be cited at the temple to Aphrodite at Palaipaphos; ibid., 74.

24. Even e.g., Crossan and Reed, *In Search of Paul*, 230, who are routinely dismissive of Lukan details, consider the visit "basically historical." Cf. Acts 4:36; 15:39.

25. Ando, *Imperial Ideology and Provincial Loyalty*, 231.

26. The temple to Caesar at Thessalonica is attested in an inscription, but no remains of it have been found. See Hendrix, "Archaeology and Eschatology," 115, including notes 26–27. See *IT* no. 31 for the inscription.

27. Mitchell, "Imperial Building in the Provinces," 333–65 (esp. 336, 349–51).

28. Ando, *Imperial Ideology and Provincial Loyalty*, 306–7.

those for whom literary evidence survives (i.e., elite provincials).[29] If mid first-century Thessalonica was a typically thriving trade center receiving generous imperial favors, and all evidence suggests that it was, it does not strain credulity to imagine a vitriolic response to a few suspicious foreigners announcing good news about another son of God, born not into the Julio-Claudian line but in the line of Israel's greatest king, David. If this new "good news" compromised even a portion of the community's allegiance to Caesar, it threatened the favors that accompanied Caesar's beneficence.[30] Had they taken an oath similar to the ones found in Gangra and Paphos, the Thessalonians presumably could have considered any "policing" action in keeping with their oath to defend Claudius from his "enemies" by reporting the suspect "political" message of Paul and his companions.[31]

Increasingly, Paul's first letter to the Thessalonians, indeed his whole gospel, is being examined for ways in which it intersects with terminology and imagery employed by the imperial "gospel."[32] Conclusions have ranged from minimal or imperceptible engagement to outright hostility leading to martyrdom.[33] Arguments for a "political" understanding have been advanced for several key phrases or concepts from his letter: lord (κύριος), coming (παρουσία), meeting (ἀπάντησις), and "peace and security" (εἰρήνη καὶ ἀσφάλεια) are repeatedly identified as examples of Paul's use of imperial

29. Ibid., 306.

30. Barclay, "Conflict in Thessalonica," 515, highlights more broadly that disloyalty to the pantheon as a whole also threatened life outside of the control of the emperor (and by extension, his clients). Offending the gods might bring drought, famine, earthquake, or other disasters which were held at bay by placating the (sometimes) capricious gods. Cf. Lane Fox, *Pagans and Christians*, 109–17.

31. This is precisely the expectation that becomes codified much later (3rd to 5th century). A city lacking a "policing" Roman garrison would need to rely on individuals or municipalities "to detect, to pursue and to betray bandits to local authorities." See Shaw, "Bandits in the Roman Empire," 19, for primary sources.

32. E.g., Judge, "Decrees of Caesar," 1–7; Donfried "Imperial Cults of Thessalonica"; Koester, "Imperial Ideology," 158–66; Harrison, "Paul and the Imperial Gospel," 71–96; Oakes, "Re-mapping the Universe," 301–22; Smith, "Unmasking the Powers," 47–66; Hendrix, "Thessalonicans Honor Romans"; Crossan and Reed, *In Search of Paul*, 152–77.

33. E.g., Oakes, "Re-mapping the Universe," 318, concludes that 1 Thessalonians does not advocate the overthrow of Rome or rejection of the imperial cult, nevertheless, Paul's gospel supersedes the ideology of the empire; Pobee, *Persecution and Martyrdom*, 113–14, and Donfried, "Imperial Cults of Thessalonica," 349–50, consider it possible that those who have "fallen asleep" (4:14) were martyred for their faith. However, it seems more likely that Paul would have made more of their deaths had they been the result of persecution.

language. The paucity of evidence from first-century Thessalonica, however, forces us to broaden our material search elsewhere in the Greek East if comparisons are to be made between the imperial gospel and Paul's letter to the Thessalonians.

Christian Theological Politics in Thessalonica

Introduction of the Cult of Jesus

It is generally agreed that Paul was in Thessalonica around 49–50 CE, a date predominately given because he can be placed with some confidence in Corinth by the autumn of 50.[34] The only detail from Paul's letter about the circumstances of his arrival in Thessalonica is that he and his companions had been mistreated in Philippi before coming to Thessalonica (1 Thess 2:1–2). Although the travel narrative of Acts is suited to this detail in Paul's letter,[35] the manner in which he introduced the gospel is somewhat more difficult to identify.

---

34. Gill, "Macedonia," 398–99. Cf. Jewett, *Thessalonian Correspondence*, 59–60; Bockmuehl, "1 Thessalonians 2:14–16," 17–18; Riesner, *Paul's Early Period*, 363–64, places Paul in Corinth by February or March 50, with a stay in Thessalonica in late 49 lasting between one and four months.

35. Luke describes Paul and Silas being subjected to a severe beating with rods and a night in prison (16:23–24), before they departed Philippi and came to Thessalonica via Amphipolis and Apollonia (17:1). This corresponds to 1 Thess 2:2, though I do not wish to make more of the consistency here. Indeed, I have tried to make my case independently from Acts of the Apostles for the simple reason that the methodological questions that attend any appeals to Acts is fraught with problems. Perhaps a brief explanation of my view of the relationship between Acts and the letters of Paul is still apropos. While best practice advises us to be suspicious of Luke's portrait of events generally, with critical sensitivity to the Lukan agenda in the foreground, we can carefully assess whether individual episodes in Acts should be viewed as a reliable witness (albeit one that is biased and secondary) to "historical" events. That the state of research vis-à-vis Acts and its historicity has reached something like an impasse is now well documented. See, e.g., Phillips, "Genre of Acts," 365–96. See also Penner, "Madness in the Method?," 223–93. Since the question of genre has not settled the question of historicity—Pervo, *Acts*, 15, writes, "It has even become possible to say that, because Acts is a representative of historiography, one should not expect it to be factual,"—it would be best to treat the historicity question on a case-by-case basis. Cf. Alexander, "Fact, Fiction, and the Genre of Acts," 135: "It is much too simple to assume that identifying Luke's work on literary grounds with 'Greek Historiography' is an automatic guarantee of reliability." Dibelius, *Studies in Acts*, 107, wrote: "The historical reliability of Acts must be measured in each individual case, according to the material which Luke worked upon."

Paul, Silas, and Timothy's letter gives every indication that the church is composed mainly of Gentiles. Paul refers to the widespread reports about the assembly having "turned to God from idols" (1 Thess 1:9), indicating that they were pagans before their conversion. Paul would not characterize Jewish "converts" as turning to God; Gentiles worship idols, not Jews.[36] The lack of citations of Jewish scriptures seems to suggest the group was unfamiliar with Jewish scripture and traditions. Furthermore, the Gentile constituency is implied (for both the Christians *and* their opponents) by their placement in parallel to the churches in Judea and their persecutors—the "Jews who killed both the Lord Jesus [i.e., Jesus' compatriots] and the prophets" (2:14–15).[37] The Gentile compatriots who continued to worship the idols that the (Gentile) Christians had forsaken are those who afflicted Paul's assembly.[38] It is possible that Paul recognizes that just as Jesus was persecuted by his elite (i.e., priestly) compatriots, so the Thessalonians are being persecuted by their elite compatriots. The elite served as city officials or priests of local cults, sometimes occupying both offices.[39] We might suspect that if the elite opposed the recent theo-political turn of their Thessalonian compatriots, these same elite Thessalonians may have been responsible for Paul's sudden departure too (2:17–18).[40] Although

36. So, e.g., Bruce, *1 and 2 Thessalonians*, 46; Wanamaker, *Thessalonians*, 113; Malherbe, *Paul and the Thessalonians*, 47, 95; Meeks, *Origins of Christian Morality*, 47; Barclay, "Conflict in Thessalonica," 514; Still, *Conflict at Thessalonica*, 223–24n65.

37. So, e.g., Still, *Conflict at Thessalonica*, 224; Meeks, *Origins of Christian Morality*, 47; Wanamaker, *Thessalonians*, 113. First Thess 2:14–15 is not, of course, universally accepted as authentic. In spite of those who argue that it is an interpolation (e.g., Pearson, "1 Thessalonians 2:3–16," 79–94), I find the evidence for interpolation is weak at best, and has been shown to be unconvincing by, e.g., Gilliard, "Anti-Semitic Comma," 481–502; Weatherly, "Authenticity of 1 Thessalonians 2:13–16," 79–98; Bockmuehl, "1 Thessalonians 2:14–16"; and Smith, "Unmasking the Powers," 58–62.

38. Barclay, "Conflict in Thessalonica," 514; Still, *Conflict at Thessalonica*, 226–27; Bockmuehl, "1 Thessalonians 2:14–16," 12. Smith, "Unmasking the Powers," 60, submits that "given the strong pro-Roman atmosphere in Thessalonica . . . it seems likely that in 1 Thess 2:13–16 Paul is criticizing the pro-Roman aristocracy in Thessalonica by way of an analogy with the pro-Roman rulers of Judea."

39. *IT* 31, 32, 132, 133; cf. Hendrix, "Archaeology and Eschatology," 114–15: "Ascending in the pecking order was a new civic religious office established at the city in the last quarter of the first century BCE, a 'priest and agonothete of the Imperator Caesar Augustus son of god.' The office quickly assumed premier status in the hierarchy of civic offices at Thessalonica and superseded ultimately the priesthood of 'the gods,' which formerly had been at the apex of civic religious offices."

40. We have not discussed the variety of cults operative in the Thessalonica. For brief treatments, see de Vos, *Church and Community Conflicts*, 140–43, and Jewett,

Luke's story paints zealous Jews and low-life ruffians as Paul's opponents, it is the civic authorities (Luke correctly identifies them as politarchs) of Thessalonica who ultimately probably decide to get rid of Paul, especially when 1 Thessalonians 2:14–15 is factored into the discussion. Whether that occurred as banishment or as flight from death remains unclear; but it is obvious from Paul's letter that his sudden, forced departure from the church pained him (2:17–18).

Some distinctive features of the cult of Jesus Paul introduced at Thessalonica are important to consider. Paul's letter tells us that the Thessalonians turned from other gods (idols) to serve the living and true God (1 Thess 1:9); they awaited God's son who would come from heaven (1:10; 3:13; 4:15–16), the son of God for whom they waited was raised from the dead (1:10; 4:14–16; cf. Acts 17:3); the Thessalonians were warned of an impending wrath (1:10; 5:2–3); and were told of salvation which came "through our Lord Jesus Christ" (5:9). A few other themes from Paul's letter can be drawn (e.g., the expectation of suffering 3:3–4, cf. Acts 17:3), but I have tried to identify a few elements which point to a clear narrative arc in Paul's message. From these few verses then, we can conclude that Paul introduced the Thessalonians to the one true God of Israel whose son, the "anointed one," killed by his own compatriots, was raised from the dead by God, through whom the Thessalonians obtain salvation or deliverance from impending wrath which will occur after the son's return.

If these themes mark out a *theological* turn made by Thessalonian pagans, what can be detected of a corresponding *political* turn? Paul makes a comment about their new God who invites them into "his kingdom and glory" (1 Thess 2:12)[41] and warns them to take care of their own affairs so as not to be dependent upon anyone, especially outsiders (1 Thess 4:12). This latter point is a potentially jarring rejection of the common, politically-freighted economics of benefaction, a system that greatly benefitted the Thessalonians (especially elite ones) of Paul's day. If we include in our view of the political the way Paul expects the community to order its life together, we see that their political arrangements ought to be conducive to peace (5:13), to building up one another (5:11), and ought to include admonishing, encouraging and helping one another patiently (5:14), none

---

Thessalonian Correspondence, 126–32. We have focused on the conflict with the imperial cult due to its growing importance.

41. In Acts 17:7 we learn that Paul and his companions are charged with acting contrary to the decrees of Caesar and declaring that there is another *king* named Jesus. Cf. Hardin's "Decrees and Drachmas at Thessalonica," 29–49.

of which are to be attained through retaliation or coercion. Instead, they ought to seek to do good to one another and even to those outside their assembly (5:15).

There are clear points of contact between the arrival of Paul's gospel in Thessalonica and the fast-growing imperial cult there. I suspect that the debate about critical engagement with imperial politics cannot be settled here. Besides the complexity of the issue, there is the complicated matter of asking for whom might Paul's gospel have appeared anti-imperial? While I am more interested in what Paul thought about this question, the reception of his message is certainly not irrelevant. In his extant writings, naivety could scarcely be identified as characteristic of Paul's thought. I suspect that he was well aware of a number of ways his gospel flirted with subverting the imperial gospel in its local manifestations, wherever he happened to be. While Paul might not have set out to subvert the empire via his gospel (which would suggest that he adapted his message to emphasize the point), Paul does seem to determine his course of action and set out to achieve it, whatever the consequences. In other words, it seems far more characteristic of Paul to set before others his gospel, and walk towards its truth (to borrow his phrase from Galatians 2) even if some very powerful, very dangerous people warn him that he is flirting with disaster. So be it. That Paul's life is traditionally thought to be cut short by Nero's sword only fuels this suspicion.[42]

IDEOLOGIES OF PEACE IN THESSALONICA

One place where an intersection can be detected is in the competing ideologies of peace in Thessalonica. No stranger to conflict, Thessalonica was faced with the promise of peace from Caesar and his allies on the one hand, and Christ and his allies on the other. What are we to make of the peace set before them? I propose that the Thessalonians knew very well the kind

42. Eusebius, *Hist. eccl.* 2.25.5–8, is one of the earliest accounts of Paul's martyrdom. Cf. Tertullian, *Praescr.* 36. Intriguingly, the fourth- or fifth-century *Acts of Peter and Paul* (which matches the previous descriptions of beheading) records this significant, if somewhat tantalizing, detail: "And it happened also that Nero's wife Libia, and the yoke-fellow of Agrippa the prefect, Agrippina by name, thus believed, so that also they went away from beside their own husbands. And *on account of the teaching of Paul*, many, *despising military life*, clung to God; so that even from the emperor's bed-chamber some came to him, and *having become Christians, were no longer willing to return to the army or the palace*" (emphasis added).

of peace achieved and sustained by Augustus and his successors, and that Paul's gospel and his "God of peace" (1 Thess 5:23) looked rather different.

Violent Peace and Security in Thessalonica

It was long ago recognized that 1 Thessalonians 5:3 is better explained as a reference to a Roman imperial slogan than to some parallel to prophetic literature in the Jewish scriptures. Although Ernst Bammel made the case half a century ago, his proposal has only recently been resurrected in studies of Paul's letter. The case now is so strong that I suspect 1 Thessalonians 5:3 will regularly be read in light of an imperial slogan referring to the pax Romana.[43] After looking at the evidence for "political" uses of these terms, I will attempt to identify the difference Paul's theology makes in appeals to peace and security in God's kingdom.

Paul wrote: "When they say 'There is peace and security,' then sudden destruction will come upon them, as labor pains come upon a pregnant woman, and there will be no escape!" The phrase "peace and security" has long vexed those who searched for its elusive parent in the Old Testament. A common solution is to identify Jeremiah 6:14 ("saying 'Peace peace' and where is peace?" Cf. MT Jer 8:11) or Ezekiel 13:10 ("Saying 'Peace, peace,' and there was no peace") as background texts in which Paul has replaced a synonym, *security*, in the position of the second "peace" in the list, managing to coin his own paraphrase of the misguided false prophets.[44] One obstacle facing this solution is the fact that in the LXX, *security* (ἀσφάλεια) is *never* used as a translation of the Hebrew *šālôm*.[45] If the use of security

---

43. Crossan and Reed, *In Search of Paul*, 166, point out an altar from Praeneste (modern Palestrina, approximately twenty miles east of Rome), declaring the sacred Augustan *pax* and *securitas*. Bammel, "Beitrag zur paulinischen Staatsanschauung," 837; Donfried, "Imperial Cults of Thessalonica," 222; Wengst, *Pax Romana*, 77; Koester, "Imperial Ideology," 161–62; Hendricks, "Archaeology and Eschatology," 112; and Oakes, "Re-mapping the Universe," 315, 317–18, all at least concede that the imperial slogan is the probable referent for Paul's use of the phrase.

44. So, e.g., Holtz, *Thessalonicher*, 215; Wanamaker, *Thessalonians*, 180; Richard, *First and Second Thessalonians*, 260; Rigaux, *Les Épitres aux Thessaloniciens*, 558.

45. Recognition of this point doesn't stop Holtz, *Thessalonicher*, 215n364 from maintaining his position and (groundlessly) dismissing Bammel's case. Though it never stands in for *šālôm*, it does occur some 19 times in the LXX. These uses tend to relate to political treaties (e.g., 2 Macc 9:21) and to the security of strong city defenses (e.g., 1 Macc 14:37). The combination is used in Psalms of Solomon 8:18–19, though they do not appear together in the form of a slogan. Still, *peace* and *security* (εἰρήνη and ἀσφάλεια)

(ἀσφάλεια) is rare in the Pauline letters and is never used in the LXX in place of *šālôm*, it is striking that the term or its Latin equivalent occurs in a number of situations pertaining to Roman peace.

The altar to the peace and security of Augustus in Praeneste is perhaps the most notable example in the material record.[46] Though it is true that the altar is well beyond the reach of Paul's community in Thessalonica, the terms appear elsewhere too. Klaus Wengst claims that the terms refer to internal harmony (*pax*) and safety from beyond the empire's boundaries (*securitas*). Peace is had between allies; security is "protection against any threat from outside the boundaries of the empire."[47] Another inscription from Syria [*OGIS* 613] reads: "The Lord Marcus Flavius Bonus . . . of the first legion, has ruled over us in peace and given constant *peace and security* to travelers and to the people."[48] Separately, the two features are ubiquitous in coins, monuments, and public inscriptions. Holland Hendrix has conveniently gathered relevant evidence on this score. Not only is *pax* commonly celebrated on coins of Augustan issue (e.g., *BMCRE* 605, 612, 691), but Nero ("universal peace," 321), Galba (261) and Vespasian (558) each celebrated the "pax Augusti."[49] There are also stunning examples from Claudius' reign as well.[50]

---

are used in a reference to the ease with which Pompey entered Jerusalem.

46. See Crossan and Reed, *In Search of Paul*, 166, or Zanker, *Power of Images*, 307 (figs. 238–39), for images of the twin altars to *Pax* and *Securitas* from Praeneste. They are also found in *CIL* 14, 2898–9, or *ILS* 3787–88.

47. Wengst, *Pax Romana*, 19.

48. Quoted in Wengst, *Pax Romana*, 19.

49. Hendrix, "Archaeology and Eschatology," 113n16.

50. See http://www.wildwinds.com/coins/ric/claudius/i.html under RIC_0009/BMC 6, courtesy of Fritz Rudolf Künker GmbH (accessed on 29 December, 2009). The aureus is an issue from Rome in 41 or 42 CE. Obverse: TI CLAVD CAESAR AVG P M TR P, laureate head right. Reverse: PACI AVGVSTAE, Pax walking right, holding caduceus over serpent. There is a nearly identical denarius copy on the same website under RIC 10.

Figure 2: Coin of Tiberius Caesar and Pax, from Rome,
ca. 41–42 CE.

The *Ara Pacis Augustae* in the Field of Mars at Rome is another stellar example of the emphasis on the peace brought by Augustus to the entire empire, and it should not be forgotten that the magnificent exterior wall of the museum which currently houses the ancient altar is but a reminder of the *Res Gestae Divi Augusti* that was publicly displayed during Paul's ministry in Galatia. The only inscriptional remains of the *Res Gestae* come from Anatolia, and one location was Pisidian Antioch (in Galatia), a locale with which Paul was probably familiar (if Acts is to be trusted). Like the *Ara Pacis* in Rome, the *Res Gestae* likewise touts the worldwide peace and security established by Augustus. For instance, Augustus recalls that he "secured peace through victory" (2.13) and incorporated into the empire's boundaries several provinces "in/by peace" (ἐν εἰρήνῃ κατέστησα, 5.26). Velleius Paterculus (early first century CE) strikes a particularly appreciative tone in his list of Augustus' achievements when he rhetorically asks: "When were the blessings of peace greater? The *pax augusta*, which has spread to the regions of the East and of the West and to the bounds of the North and of the South, preserves every corner of the world safe from the fear of brigandage (*latrociniorum*)" (*Roman History*, 2.126.3 [Shipley, LCL]).

A letter of Claudius to the Alexandrians, sent November 10th, 41 CE, refers to two (presumably identical) gold statues, one for display in Rome and the other for procession in Alexandria. The two statues are said to represent "Claudian Augustan Peace."[51] The polite formalities found in

51. Hendrix, "Archaeology and Eschatology," 113n16. British Museum Papyrus no.

the first half of this papyrus give way to not-so-subtle threats, which only underscores the point that the much vaunted imperial peace was established not by goodwill alone, but by the threat of the emperor's wrath. In the second half of the letter, Claudius, having just accepted many of the honors proposed by the Alexandrians,[52] turns his attention to public disturbances relating to the Jews. He warns the factions that he will reserve "implacable wrath" for any who start the disturbance up again. "I tell you plainly, that if you do not put an end to this disastrous, outrageous frenzy against one another, I shall be forced to show you what a well-disposed Emperor is like when he becomes justifiably angry." One presumes the residents of Alexandria needed little skill to read between the lines.

Another ancient source that identifies peace *and* security with Roman rule is Josephus. In *Ant.* 14:247–8, Josephus records a decree from Pergamum which lauds the Romans for the risks they have taken to provide for security (ἀσφαλείας) for all humankind and their efforts "to make lasting peace" (βεβαία καταστῆσαι εἰρήνη, cf. *Res Gestae* 5.26 above) for their friends and allies. Tacitus too coordinates the sincere desire to establish *pax et securitas* by rival Roman generals Mucianus and Antonius (*Hist.* 3.53).[53]

Security, like peace, is touted on its own in similar fashion. Hendrix submits that *securitas/ἀσφάλεια* "figured prominently" in Augustan, Julio-Claudian, and Flavian propaganda.[54] Coins depicting the *securitas Augusti* or the *securitas* of the Roman people are in evidence, and in some prominent cases Caligula's sister Agrippina is represented as the goddess *Securitas*.[55]

1912; English translation and brief commentary in Levick, *Government of the Roman Empire*, 135–37.

52. It should be noted, however, that Claudius declines the proposed high priest and temples dedicated to himself, which he opines ought to be "rendered by every age solely and exclusively to the gods."

53. Cf. Cassius Dio, *History of Rome*, 55.10.17, where Gaius Caligula is said to have "assumed command of the legions . . . with peaceful intent. Indeed, he fought no war, not because no war broke out, but because he was learning to rule in quiet and safety."

54. Hendrix, "Archaeology and Eschatology," 113.

55. *BMC* 1, 36/*RIC* 33, accessed on 28 January, 2010 on http://www.wildwinds.com/coins/ric/caligula/RIC_0033.5.jpg, courtesy of www.cngcoins.com and www.wildwinds.com. Sestertius from Rome mint, struck 37–38 CE. Obverse: the laureate head of Caligula, C CAESAR AVG GERMANICVS PON M TR POT. Reverse: The three sisters of Caligula standing frontal, heads in profile, each draped and holding cornucopiae; Agrippina, as *Securitas*, rests hand on column. Drusilla (as *Concordia*) and Julia (as *Fortuna*) are also shown. Cf. *BMCI* 241 no. 212 (*securitas Augusti*); *BMCI* 1, 361 no. 266 and 3, 313 no. 570. Issues under Nero cast Poppaea in the same role. See Barrett, *Agrippina*, 61, who claims that the Roman coin struck by Caligula which depicted Agrippina as *Securitas*,

Coins only tell a story in shorthand. Augustus spells out his own preference for clemency in the midst of warfare: "The nations who *safely* could be pardoned, I saved rather than destroyed" [*Res Gestae* 1.3].[56] Such a comment would apply to Thessalonica, whose allegiance to Antony was well-publicised between Philippi (42 BCE) and Actium (31 BCE), but, after Antony's defeat, they understandably backed Octavian.[57] Like so many other provincial municipalities in the empire, Thessalonica not only depended on the emperors and their allies for peace and security, they were also well aware of the allegiance they owed to those whose magnanimity preserved them.

Christ's Peace and Security in Thessalonica

In contrast to the peace and security offered by Caesar and his clients, we should note the way Paul portrays God's peace and its infiltration of his Thessalonian assembly. If we were to restrict our picture to those instances in which peace or security are mentioned, however, there would be little to say. Instead, I will include those moments in Paul's letter that indicate

---

alongside Drusilla and Julia as *Concordia* and *Fortuna* respectively, pictured above, was copied in several places *including Judea under Herod Agrippa*.

56. "Τὰ ἔθνη, οἷς ἀσφαλὲς ἦν συγγνώμην ἔχειν, ἔσωσα μᾶλλον ἢ ἐξέκοψα." The adverb is used here, and the Latin is *tuto* rather than *securitas*. For our purposes, however, the Greek is more relevant.

57. See *IG* 10.2.1.83; Hendrix, "Thessalonicans Honor Romans," 36–37.

thematic relevance. Although there is a risk of over-egging the pudding here, I submit that the evidence I will present gathers tightly around two main interconnected features.

Peace (or some lexical form with the same root) occurs four times in 1 Thessalonians. Two of the occurrences can be set aside in the present discussion, because one usage is from the letter greeting ("Grace to you and peace"), and the other is from the Roman slogan ("when they say 'Peace and security'"). What do the other uses tell us of God's peace in Thessalonica? In the midst of the paraenetic section of the letter, Paul commands the Thessalonian Christians "be at peace among yourselves" ("εἰρηνεύετε ἐν ἑαυτοῖς," 1 Thess 5:13). This somewhat generic command is sandwiched between a double use of the verb νουθετέω (1 Thess 5:12, 14), which suggests that the peace which they ought to have among themselves does not consist of passivity towards one another, but includes mutual correction, warning, and exhortation to "walk in a manner worthy of God" (1 Thess 2:12; cf. Rom 14:15).[58] This worthy manner includes the exhortation of 1 Thessalonians 5:15, "See that none of you repays evil for evil, but always seek to do good to one another and to all."[59] Their mutual correction and encouragement includes, crucially, making sure an ethic of retaliation is not practiced by Christian believers. Rather, they are told to seek to do good to *everyone*, those in the assembly as well as those outside of it. The peace they are encouraged to enflesh is active rather than merely passive; Christ's peace is inextricably linked with admonition to, among other things, actively create peace.

A second theme which binds the peace and security of the Thessalonians is that of its eschatological point of reference. That is, peace and security are orientated towards both the character of God and the return of God's son. This second element can be found at the end of the paraenetic section, where Paul prays for the Thessalonians that "the God of peace" would sanctify them and *keep* them "until the coming of our Lord Jesus Christ" (1 Thess 5:23). The junction of the expression God of peace with the parousia of the Lord highlights the character of divine peace for Paul. Wanamaker suggests that the modifier (*of peace*) refers to the eschatological peace wrought by God, an image present in Paul's other letters as well.[60] The assurance of eschatological peace features earlier in the letter too. When

58. N.B. the similarity with Gal 6:1–2.
59. Again, note the parallel with Gal 6:10.
60. Wanamaker, *Thessalonians*, 205. Cf. Rom 2:10; 5:1; 8:6; 14:17; Phil 4:7.

Paul undermines the supposed peace and security hailed by others, it is the Thessalonian believers who are assured true peace and security:

> The day of the Lord will come like a thief in the night. When they say, "There is peace and security," then sudden destruction will come upon them, as labor pains come upon a pregnant woman, and there will be no escape! But you, beloved, are not in darkness, for that day to surprise you like a thief . . . For God has destined us not for wrath but for obtaining salvation through our Lord Jesus Christ. (1 Thess 5:2–4, 9)

Paul urges the Thessalonian Christians not to fear that day of the lord's coming, because they are appointed not to suffer wrath but to obtain salvation. The same concept appears towards the beginning of the letter too. For example, at 1 Thessalonians 1:10, Paul wrote that they wait for God's "son from heaven . . . who delivers us from the coming wrath." Although the terms peace and security do not appear here, it is the *safety* of assured deliverance that Paul underscores as a foundational part of the gospel the Thessalonians received. Finally, this eschatological orientation of peace and security informs Paul's prayer that the Thessalonians are strengthened in holiness so as to be blameless "before our God and Father *at the coming of our Lord Jesus*" (1 Thess 3:13). Once again, the words peace and security are not used by Paul, but the eschatological security of the Thessalonians lies at the heart of Paul's prayers for them. In short, the peace and security proclaimed by others is an illusion; true peace and security is possessed by Paul's assemblies who may anticipate deliverance when the true Lord of the empire arrives on the scene.

That is not to say, however, that Paul painted a rosy picture for the Thessalonians. Instead, Paul prepared the Thessalonian Christians for peace and security at the very point where it would be most fleeting. At 1 Thessalonians 3:4 he warned them beforehand of the persecutions they would (soon) face, indeed he says they are appointed/destined for them. Paul readied them for hardship, for experiences that would call into question the peace available to them as people allied to a different lord, even pointing out his own experience of affliction in preaching the gospel, experiences that did not deter Paul and his companions. Paul announced the gospel in Thessalonica with boldness, despite experiences that might otherwise recommend to him caution. Instead, Paul identified God as the source of their courage in spite of affliction (1 Thess 2:2). The identity of Paul's opponents is a matter of debate, but we need not settle the issue here to see that he points to real earthly opposition and real suffering, most recently experienced in Philippi.[61] Despite that opposition, Paul suggests that peace and security are not the products of one's circumstances, but are possessed by those who find their security in God's favor and the promise of deliverance at the parousia of the Lord.

In marked contrast to the Roman peace and security touted by coins, altars, and city assemblies, Paul announced a message that promised peace in the midst of present circumstances (peace that they helped to create through mutual correction and doing good), as well as the security that promised to endure every earthly kingdom or empire.

Jesus Tradition in 1 Thessalonians

An intriguing feature of the possible allusions to Jesus Tradition in 1 Thessalonians is that they are found mostly in the eschatological discourses of the gospels.[62] That is, whereas our earlier attention to this aspect of the argument showed a consistent use of material from the Sermon on the Mount/Plain and the Passion narratives, in 1 Thessalonians almost every individual verse or group of verses that has been seen as a potential allusion uses eschatological imagery or teaching. Rather than creating insurmountable tension, however, this discovery only strengthens the view articulated above that the (authentic) peace and security experienced by Paul's assemblies is had in the midst of current (or imminent) suffering and is promised to them beyond the reach of human ways of measuring time.

One potential allusion to the Sermon on the Mount/Plain is 1 Thessalonians 5:15. Comparing the *texts* leaves room to speculate whether Paul is indeed echoing Jesus Tradition in his letter, but as I argued in chapter three, a *textual* model for transmission is inadequate for understanding the living tradition Paul employed.[63] The *pattern of response* Paul advocates in 1 Thessalonians is close to the posture attributed to Jesus in the Sermon on the Mount/Plain; Paul tells the Thessalonian community to police its members in order to prevent them from engaging in a cycle of retaliation. They are to "pursue the good" for each other and for the outsider. By comparison, Jesus

61. Paul writes that the Thessalonians knew that he and his companions had been "προπαθόντες καὶ ὑβρισθέντες" in Philippi.

62. Tuckett, "Synoptic Tradition in 1 Thessalonians?," 163.

63. 1 Thess 5:15 bears almost no textual resemblance to either Matt 5:38–42 or Luke 6:27–31.

commanded his disciples "do not resist an evildoer." Rather than demanding the eye for eye reciprocity of the *lex talionis*, Jesus called on his disciples go the second mile (Matt 5:41) and do good to their enemies (Luke 6:35). In other words, the Jesus of Matthew (and Luke) bid his disciples to refrain from returning evil for evil, and wanted them instead to pursue the good for even their oppressors.

First Thessalonians contains several notable points of correspondence with Jesus Tradition as well as vocabulary that hints at the transmission of teaching to the Thessalonians. While there is no irrefutable proof that Paul is drawing directly from Jesus Tradition recorded (later) in the gospels at 1 Thessalonians 5:15, it does seem rather persuasive that he had knowledge of some form of Jesus' teaching about the eschatological return of the son of man.[64] Concerning the transmission process itself, Paul uses several terms that express either his previous teaching or passing on of information to the Thessalonians. For example, at 1 Thessalonians 1:6, Paul recounts how the Thessalonians received the word (δεξάμενοι τὸν λόγον) in much affliction. He also situates both the source and purpose of his proclamation in God. At 2:4, he writes that they "have been approved by God to be entrusted with the message of the gospel." Further, Paul tells of how dear the Thessalonians have become to him, so that he desired to share with them (μεταδίδωμι) not only the gospel of God, but his very self (1 Thess 2:8). He also refers to announcing (κηρύσσω) the gospel to them freely (1 Thess 2:9), uses the technical term for receiving tradition (παραλαβόντες λόγον; 1 Thess 2:13), and again at 4:1 the Thessalonians are said to have received instruction for how to live from Paul (καθὼς παρελάβετε παρ᾽ ἡμῶν τὸ πῶς δεῖ ὑμᾶς περιπατεῖν καὶ ἀρέσκειν θεῷ). They also "know what commands we gave you in the lord Jesus (οἴδατε γὰρ τίνας παραγγελίας ἐδώκαμεν ὑμῖν διὰ τοῦ κυρίου Ἰησοῦ; 4:2). Paul also transmits "a word of the lord" (1 Thess 4:15; cf. 1 Thess 2:13).

The overall impression from 1 Thessalonians is that a central feature of Paul's (and his companions') ministry was teaching his converts the content and consequences of the gospel about Jesus, and that, whether they were aware of its correspondence with early Jesus Tradition or not, Paul was already passing on, in his earliest extant letter, exhortations to his communities in which non-retaliation and peaceableness featured.

---

64. E.g., 1 Thess 5:1 (Matt 24:36); 1 Thess 5:2 (Matt 24:43–44; Luke 13;39; Gos Thom 21); 1 Thess 4:15–17 (Matt 24:30–31).

THREE BIOGRAPHICAL WINDOWS IN 1 THESSALONIANS

A recurrent theme in this work has been the expectation and experience of opposition for Jesus and his followers. In Chapter Two, the suffering and opposition against Jesus was highlighted, and in Chapter Four, I put a spotlight on opposition and suffering for Paul. In 1 Thessalonians, there is a tripartite narrative of opposition against Paul, Thessalonian Christians, and against the church in Judaea. I will briefly[65] identify this strand of opposition in three parts, and explain why this tripartite feature of the letter is significant for the present argument.

Opposition to Paul and His Response

Can we discern a pattern of opposition and suffering experienced by Paul when he wrote 1 Thessalonians? In a number of places, he refers explicitly to persecution or hardship experienced by himself and his traveling companions. For example, very early in the letter (1 Thess 1:6) Paul wrote that the Thesalonians "became imitators of us and of the Lord, because in spite of much affliction," they received Paul's gospel with joy. The sense is that, not only have the Thessalonian Christians experienced great affliction, but Paul (and the Lord) had such experiences before they had them. He refers to past suffering in 1 Thessalonians 2:2, where he reminds the Thessalonians that they were already aware of his prior suffering and the insults he endured at Philippi. Yet, "in spite of great opposition" Paul still declared the gospel of God to the Thessalonians. Whereas the first half of the verse points to the opposition he faced at Philippi, the natural sense of the second half of the verse refers to opposition at Thessalonica.[66] Although controversial, 1 Thessalonians 2:15 lends further support to the case of opposition faced

---

65. I will do so *briefly* for two reasons: it is hardly controversial to claim that 1 Thessalonians paints a portrait of opposition and suffering for Paul and his communities in Thessalonica (and beyond). It would only court controversy if I claimed to know *definitively* of what that opposition and suffering consisted. Second, in a monograph that could be expanded in every section, I hope this gesture towards one direction I hope to expand the present work will suffice for my argument.

66. It is possible that the second half too should be read with events at Philippi in view (e.g., as Rigaux, *Les Épitres aux Thessaloniciens*, 405, does), but it makes better sense contextually to understand the opposition to be in Thessalonica in order to illustrate Paul's courage to announce the gospel (i.e., despite *present* opposition). See Wanamaker, *Thassalonians*, 93.

by Paul. There Paul writes that the same people who killed Jesus and the prophets "drove us out;" as usual, Paul's expression is vague, but it is clear at least that he understood his lot to be one full of opposition and suffering.[67] At 1 Thessalonians 3:4, there is yet another hazy window on Paul's experience, where he wrote: "We told you beforehand 'we are about to be crushed,' just as you know it happened." Despite the onslaught of calamity and oppression, Paul and his coworkers found encouragement in the faith of the Thessalonians (1 Thess 3:7).[68]

Somewhat surprisingly, there is no concrete evidence set down in this letter that identifies Paul's response to the suffering and opposition he faced. The only possibilities are tenuous at best. At 1 Thessalonians 1:6–7, Paul intimates that he had received the gospel with joy despite much affliction, and in so doing had himself become an example for others to imitate. This would not necessarily exclude other responses, however. Further, at 1 Thessalonians 5:15, we might presume Paul would "take his own advice," so to speak. If he demanded that his communities returned good for evil, it seems probable that he aspired to behave in a similar manner when he was the recipient of hostility. But there is scanty evidence here.

Opposition to Thessalonian Christians and Their Intended Response

The letter is full of references to the suffering of the Thessalonians too. Just as 1 Thessalonians 1:6 flags opposition faced by Paul, so also it calls attention to the affliction experienced by his converts in Thessalonica. Paul points out that they suffered the same things as the church in Judea (1 Thess 2:14), and he sent Timothy to encourage them in the midst of the persecution they faced (1 Thess 3:3). The faith/faithfulness (πίστις) in which they continue despite persecution heartens Paul (1 Thess 3:7), and it may be that, with 3:8 in view ("you stand firm in the Lord"), we ought to read 3:7 as a reference to the Thessalonians' faithfulness in the midst of suffering. Finally, 1 Thessalonians 5:15, when read with the rest of the evidence of

---

67. See my earlier remarks about the authenticity of 1 Thess 2:15.

68. 1 Thess 2:3–4 indirectly corroborates the view of opposition faced by Paul. That is, since he claims to operate in a fashion which aims entirely at pleasing God *rather than* men, one might fairly conclude that Paul is indirectly confirming that his message elicits hostility among certain groups of people.

opposition experienced by the Thessalonians, offers corroborating evidence for their suffering.[69]

Opposition to Judean Christians and Their Response

Finally, I want to draw attention to the implied narrative of suffering experienced by the Church in Judea. Paul wrote: "For you, brothers and sisters, became imitators of the churches of God in Christ Jesus that are in Judea, for you suffered the same things from your own compatriots as they did from the Jews who killed both the Lord Jesus and the prophets." The point I want to underline is that Paul knows that the churches in Judea suffered at the hands of a particular group of kinsmen (i.e., "those who killed the Lord Jesus and the prophets"), and likens the Thessalonian suffering to that of the Judean Christians'. Markus Bockmuehl has sifted through the various proposals for what the suffering of the Judean churches looked like in the years spanning from the execution of Jesus to the writing of 1 Thessalonians, but such concerns will take us far beyond the evidence in Paul's letter.[70] It must necessarily be left open what Paul meant when he wrote of Judean Christian suffering. We can safely assume the Thessalonians knew of what he wrote, since he mentions that they suffered "the same things" as the churches in Judea.

The significance of this small correspondence between communities is easy to overlook, but I suggest it is a telling detail. By noting the suffering experienced by the Judean churches, 1 Thessalonians presses the evidence for the non-violent practices of the church back to its earliest foundation. In other words, while we have literary evidence for this commitment to non-violence as early as 50 CE (in this letter), this evidence points further back to the church in Judea that had suffered before them, and which they now imitate in their suffering and non-violent perseverance.[71] Paul himself

---

69. At 1 Thess 4:13, Paul refers to the death of some believers in Thessalonica. Although this could be viewed as a possible reference to death as a result of persecution, I suspect this is not the case since we should expect Paul to have emphasized the point if some in his churches were martyred.

70. See Bockmuehl, "1 Thessalonians 2:14–16."

71. Gal 4:29 also points to present suffering of persecution of Judean Christians (depending on the date of the letter, between 48–54 CE). Cf. Gal 4:25; 6:12. See Jewett, "Agitators and the Galatian Congregation," 340–42, for possible motives for persecution of Christians in Judea.

violently opposed the church in Judea in the early thirties,[72] and remembered the responses of the earliest Christians whom he sought to "destroy." If 1 Thessalonians points back to this period in the church's suffering, then evidence for a non-violent response to hostility existed at the earliest possible stage (ca. 31/32 CE) in a non-Pauline church, and as the gospel spread, the practice was adopted in every conceivable geopolitical context (Palestinian, Asian, Greek, and Roman Christianity), and by churches with different founding missionaries or figureheads (Paul and his coworkers; Peter and/or Apollos at Corinth; Rome; James in Jerusalem, etc.). Non-violence was not a Pauline preoccupation, but so central a part of the gospel that it was taught in virtually every community and virtually every community was encouraged to live non-violently after the manner of Jesus, who pointed his own disciples towards the non-violent politics of the Kingdom of God.

72. In contrast to the mistreatment he repeatedly recounts experiencing as an apostle of Christ, Paul never mentions experiencing physical retaliation at the hands of those whom he persecuted.

6

Conclusion

I have proposed that Paul's turn from violent persecutor to non-violent apostle was more than simply joining the group he once opposed. Instead, Paul's own language of dying to the law and being enlivened by Jesus necessarily included turning away from the *modus vivendi* he once embraced, following instead the *modus vivendi* of Jesus who was remembered by virtually all early Christians as one who confronted evil without recourse to violence. Violence was once a tool in Paul's arsenal of influence, but after the apocalypse of Jesus in him (Gal 1:16) Paul realized that God's messiah demonstrated his power in weakness rather than in a show of strength; his humiliation was his glory instead of a shattering of it. I have shown that this trajectory in Paul's life was one which he anticipated his own converts would follow too. Instead of bracketing his peaceableness as an ethical "implication" of the gospel, I tried to show that non-violence was a part of the political order for Pauline communities. They were expected to be a differently-ordered society since they had been corporately and individually enlivened by the spirit of the peace-producing Jesus, an enlivenment that, among other things, transforms violent human relationships into sites of reconciliation and peace. It remains to summarize four main points which have been advanced in the book that contribute to our understanding of the centrality of a politics of non-violence in the gospel from its very beginning.

Summary of the Argument

To put the argument of the first substantive chapter in its starkest terms, Jesus eschewed violence. Numerous methodological problems assail such a concise statement, but I attempted to deal with many problems in chapter 2. Although I sought to give a brief account of why I think it justifiable to hold the view that the historical Jesus was an advocate of non-violent interaction with enemies (a non-violent politics), I wrote the chapter principally from a narrative-critical standpoint. Taking this approach was not an attempt to sidestep the "historical" question, and indeed staying with Matthew's portrait required addressing certain theological tensions presented by the first gospel. What I tried to demonstrate was:

1. That the violence that is inscribed into many of the stories of Matthew's narrative comport with the ubiquity of violent experience in the first century (and here the difference between the 20s–30s in Galilee and 80s in Antioch, or anywhere else in the Roman world, are virtually nil).

2. Matthew's Jesus taught an ethic/politics that demanded peacemaking—it was not optional for his first disciples.

3. Matthew's gospel (following Mark, of course), preserves the non-violent praxis of Jesus, especially important in this regard is Jesus' restraint from employing (or even condoning) violence to defend himself in his arrest and crucifixion. He taught his followers to respond to evil with good, but he also put his theological-politics into action.

4. I directly addressed what many regard to be the stiffest challenge regarding my argument vis-à-vis Matthew, namely, the Matthean image of a God who judges the world violently. Ultimately, I suggest the tension created by this imagery is not fully resolved by Matthew even though Matthew appears deliberately to bracket violence out of the realm of possibility for Jesus' followers; furthermore, the images of judgment create the space for Matthew's implied reader to repudiate a politics constructed on violence.

In chapter 3, I addressed the contentious debate about Paul's knowledge of Jesus Tradition. Although there are many paradigms for understanding the transmission of Jesus Tradition in early Christianity, it was defended here that the likelihood that Paul evinces knowledge of Jesus Tradition—specifically Jesus Tradition relating to non-violence—is quite strong, not only because Paul arguably echoes Jesus Tradition related to *teachings* on non-retaliation, but because Paul's *praxis* corresponds to the praxis of Jesus when the two become the objects of violence. Jesus and Paul exhibit continuity in word and deed. Following my presentation of the evidence for this dual continuity, I outline my paradigm for the manner in which I envisage Jesus Tradition was exchanged in the earliest period. Another important aspect of the transmission of Jesus Tradition in the early church that I sought to highlight (though not in great depth) was the clear trend to use Jesus Tradition from the Sermon on the Mount/Plain or the Passion in the earliest Christian literature. That is, Paul, like every other early Christian writer, not only makes allusions (rather than many overt quotations) to Jesus Tradition, but the preponderance of Jesus Tradition alluded to in early Christian literature comes from two blocks of material that preserve the memory of a non-violent messiah and are widely regarded (not universally regarded) as traditions being circulated en block at a very early date, perhaps before Paul's own letters were penned. Finally, I pointed out that if we take a cue from Paul's allusion to Jesus Tradition in Romans 12, we may assume that Paul believed this particular theme to have been so integral to the gospel that he presupposed the Roman churches' familiarity with it even though he had not founded the churches or visited them prior to sending his letter. Although auditors may not have heard or recognized every allusion, the preponderance of allusions to Jesus' teaching on non-violence in early Christian literature would seem to suggest that, on this particular issue at least, we can assume virtually all Christians learned of Jesus' commitment to a politics of non-violence.

The aim in chapter 4 was to trace the arc of violence in Paul's life, moving from a time when he once used violence (a point argued for exclusively from his letters, rather than from details found in Acts) to his abandonment of such tactics. I argued that this change is attributable to more than Paul joining the group he once persecuted. I argued that his death and enlivenment by Jesus resulted in a corresponding turn away from using violence. I also showed how Paul constructed a picture of the Galatians that followed the same arc in the opposing direction. Once peace-producing in their warm reception of Paul, under the influence of the so-called agitators, the Galatians now created discord and division, perhaps unwittingly reproducing the politics of violence that characterize the Roman world.

If the first four chapters provide the bones of my argument, I wanted to put flesh on those bones by testing the thesis against what is widely held to be Paul's earliest letter. Not only does Thessalonica provide a more readily identifiable socio-political location (as opposed to, for instance, the letter of the Galatians), it also provides us with a chance to see if the themes of an alternatively ordered, violence-eschewing political body appear in Paul's earliest known writing. An important, though perhaps underdeveloped, feature of this chapter is the recognition that 1 Thessalonians preserves three parallel "biographical" windows onto suffering. In Paul's epistle, we become aware of opposition (leading to some kind of unspecified suffering) faced by Paul, by Thessalonian Christians, and by the Church in Judea. Indeed, he claims that the Thessalonians have suffered the "same things" that the church in Judea had suffered. His own claim points back to the time of Jesus' death, and (to our misfortune) Paul can leave out details because the Thessalonians know the suffering to which he refers. Although there is no clear indication in this letter of the motive for enduring suffering without violent retaliation, and no clear description of their non-violent engagement with those who mistreat them, it seems fair to assume (from 5:15) that Paul, the Thessalonian Christians, and the Judean church all endured suffering rather than reciprocating evil for evil. The implication of 1 Thessalonians is that the Thessalonian Christian community already was practicing non-violent engagement with antagonists, that they did so in imitation of Paul and his coworkers, and that both groups were descendants in this respect to the church in Judea. A theological-politics of peace, on this reading, began in Judea and spread to Thessalonica through the mission of Paul and those who traveled, taught, and transmitted Jesus Tradition with him.

My contention is that these individual chapters collectively provide a compelling case for the centrality of a politics of peace in the early church. Having just provided a summary of the arguments I have made, I would like to highlight a few key points that may help to identify the unique contribution my project makes to our view of early Christianity.

First, evidence for the presence of a non-violent theological-politics is quite early. Literary evidence exists as early as 50 CE in Paul's letter to the Thessalonians but, of course, I trace the genesis of this theme back to the ministry of Jesus himself. This is the perhaps least contentious point advanced by my argument. One key contribution that is made indirectly is that this aspect of the gospel is a central feature of "Christian" teaching. That is, if witnesses as divergent as Matthew and Paul can agree on the importance of Jesus' non-violent politics, we can be confident this was a core feature of Christian discipleship. Relatedly, this feature was non-negotiable. Matthew preserves or presents Jesus' teaching on this score as command—Jesus' disciples (and later, Paul's churches) are provided no escape clause to Jesus' challenging demands. There is not a more "realistic" alternative offered to loving enemies.

What may be the most significant corollary that is derived from the evidence I have marshaled is that non-violence is found in a geographically wide range of sources. Although this may initially score as a most pedestrian observation, I suggest that the payoff is significant. If we restrict ourselves to the primary sources treated throughout my argument, there is a high degree of probability that teaching on Christian non-violence occurred in multiple provincial capitals, e.g., Ephesus[1] (Asia Minor), Antioch[2] (Syria); Thessalonica (Macedonia), Corinth[3] (Achaea), as well as the capitol of the empire itself. If non-violence was as integral to the gospel as I have argued, then presumably every city in which Paul and his companions taught was exposed to this aspect of the gospel. If an analogy can be made with the strengths or weaknesses of textual variants, then it must be said that the geographic spread of witnesses to the non-violent core of the gospel is quite impressive.

Finally, I have shown the commitment to non-violence in early Christianity is not something that is to be confined to ethics, but has a political dimension as well. That is, non-violence in its many expressions is not merely an ethical implication of the gospel, but is itself constitutive of the politics of the gospel. Paul's theological-politics of peace consists of active engagement with people inside *and outside* the community for whom the Christian is actively to pursue the good. Rather than calling for a retreat from politics, Paul's Christian communities are called to participate in a new political order, one inaugurated by its lord, which starkly contrasts with the order of every other kingdom, including Caesar's. The political nature of the gospel has important ramifications for Pauline scholars who increasingly try to situate Paul's gospel within Roman imperial discourse.

1. Ephesus was the location from which Paul wrote 1 Corinthians. Cf. 1 Cor 16:8, 19–20. I presuppose here that the occasion(s) that elicited Paul's written response would have some effect on the content of his teaching in the city from which he wrote.

2. That is, if we observe with the majority of scholars that Matthew's gospel was (probably) composed for an audience in or near Antioch in Syria.

3. Corinth plays a significant role as a place *to* which Paul wrote, as well as a place *from* which Romans, possibly Galatians, and 1 Thessalonians were written. See Riesner, *Paul's Early Period*, 364, on Corinth as the probable location from which 1 Thessalonians was written.

This gospel challenges the status quo of the (Roman) political order, but not in a directly subversive way. Rather, it creates an alternative political body that seeks to overcome evil and enmity not by subduing it (as Romans *and their opponents* would have it), but by reciprocating good for evil. Such a strategy does not promise to be effective, nor does it promise to achieve desirable results by gentler means. Rather, Christian obedience to the command of Jesus to turn the other cheek and to love the enemy heralds to the cosmos that in God's kingdom, "the cross and not the sword, suffering and not brute power determines the meaning of history."[4] Jesus' disciples do not forsake effectiveness in principle, but announce to Romans and rebels alike that in Jesus of Nazareth, God has revealed "which kinds of causation, which kinds of community-building, which kinds of conflict management go with the grain of the cosmos."[5] Christians are called to be faithful to the teaching of Jesus to love neighbors and enemies in imitation of God who blesses good and evil alike. Theirs is a politics of gratuitous love, expressed in the most distilled form in the self-giving of the son of God, imperator of the cosmos, on a Roman cross.

SOME PROSPECTS FOR FUTURE RESEARCH

In light of the research presented in this monograph, I would like to offer a few prospects that I consider to be ripe for further research. Although I did not focus on the geographical distribution of the evidence I marshaled in support of my argument, I think it may be instructive to investigate further the geographical distribution of a gospel which promotes (or challenges) the theological politics of peace. In short, is there a locale that minimizes (or directly challenges) this aspect of the story of Jesus? Focusing on "Pauline" and "Matthean" communities has resulted in one particular geographical footprint, but it may offer an even more robust (or complex) portrait of non-violence in early Christianity if we expanded our picture to study the theological-politics of a Palestinian and/or Jerusalemite, or Coptic persuasion.

Relatedly, it may be illuminating to investigate whether the so-called extra-canonical gospels confirm or threaten to topple the picture I have constructed. I am thinking foremost of the Gospel of Thomas of course,

4. Yoder, *Politics of Jesus*, 232.
5. Ibid., 246.

but much of the non-canonical literature of early Christianity could become useful (not necessarily for historical Jesus research, but) for tracing the diverse reactions to the early church's (as we have represented from Matthew and Paul) "peace theology." I assume that tensions do exist. The key questions may be from where, and when do fissures begin to show, and what are the fundamental issues that lead to disagreement or eventually, a weakening of the stance against the use of force by followers of the Prince of Peace?

Another area that I think would be profitable to explore vis-à-vis my argument is to look further into canonical and extra-canonical traditions about Paul's coworkers. There is a small but growing body of secondary literature related to Paul's companions, and it is certainly worth asking whether they were subjected to the same persecution. Did they experience violent opposition? Did they retaliate? This discussion would, of course, need to be done in the context of assessing the question of historicity and rhetoric in any given source, but even if all we can say is that, for example, Paul constructs his coworkers to ascribe to the same theological politics, that would be evidence supporting my thesis. (Whether such evidence is persuasive would depend on what is there and the manner in which the case is made.) If we found evidence to the contrary, we would have to consider the way in which the evidence requires a reformulation of the present argument.

These three possibilities for future research obviously do not represent the full extent to which the present work can contribute to a constructive project on the theological politics of peace in early Christianity, but they do point to some of the paths to pursue along these lines. In spite of there being ever more paths to explore, I hope that my own first gestures towards the goal of this project convince the reader of this characteristic "varietal expression" of early Christian attitudes towards violence, peacemaking and "walking towards the truth of the gospel."

Bibliography

Alexander, Loveday. *Acts in Its Ancient Literary Context: A Classicist Looks at the Acts of the Apostles*. London: T. & T. Clark, 2005.

———. "Fact, Fiction, and the Genre of Acts." In *Acts in Its Ancient Literary Context: A Classicist Looks at the Acts of the Apostles*, 133–63. London: T. & T. Clark, 2005.

———. "The Living Voice: Skepticism towards the Written Word in Early Christian and in Graeco-Roman Texts." In *The Bible in Three Dimensions: Essays in Celebration of Forty Years of Biblical Studies in the University of Sheffield*, edited by David J. A. Clines et al., 221–47. Journal for the Study of the Old Testament Supplement Series 87. Sheffield, UK: JSOT, 1990.

Allison, Dale C. "The Pauline Epistles and Synoptic Gospels: The Pattern of Parallels." *New Testament Studies* 28 (1982) 1–32.

———. Review of *The Sermon on the Mount: A Commentary on the Sermon on the Mount, including the Sermon on the Plain (Matthew 5:3–7:27 and Luke 6:20–49)*, by Hans Dieter Betz. *Review of Biblical Literature*. Online: http://www.bookreviews.org/pdf/2235_1386.pdf.

Ando, Clifford. *Imperial Ideology and Provincial Loyalty in the Roman Empire*. Berkeley: University of California Press, 2000.

Andresen, Carl, and Günter Klein, editors. *Theologia Crucis, Signum Crucis. Festschrift für Erich Dinkler zum 70. Geburtstag*. Tübingen, Germany: Mohr, 1979.

Baasland, Ernst. "Persecution: A Neglected Feature in the Letter to the Galatians." *Studia Theologica* 38 (1984) 135–50.

Bacon, Benjamin W. *Studies in Matthew*. London: Constable, 1930.

Bailey, Kenneth E. "Informal Controlled Oral Tradition and the Synoptic Gospels." *Themelios* 20 (1995) 4–11.

———. "Middle Eastern Oral Tradition and the Synoptic Gospels." *Expository Times* 106 (1995) 363–67.

Bammel, Ernst. "Ein Beitrag zur paulinischen Staatsanschauung." *Theologische Literaturzeitung* 85 (1960) 837–40

Barclay, John M. G. "Conflict in Thessalonica." *Catholic Biblical Quarterly* 55 (1993) 512–30.

———. "Mirror-Reading a Polemical Letter: Galatians as a Test Case." *Journal for the Study of the New Testament* 31 (1987) 73–93. Reprinted in *The Galatians Debate: Contemporary Issues in Rhetorical and Historical Interpretation*, edited by Mark D. Nanos, 367–82. Peabody, MA: Hendrickson, 2002. References are to the 2002 edition.

Bibliography

————. *Obeying the Truth: A Study of Paul's Ethics in Galatians.* Studies of the New Testament and Its World. Edinburgh: T. & T. Clark, 1988.

————. "Paul's Story: Theology as Testimony." In *Narrative Dynamics in Paul: A Critical Assessment*, edited by Bruce W. Longenecker, 133–56. Louisville: Westminster John Knox, 2002.

Barrett, Anthony A. *Agrippina: Sex, Power, and Politics in the Early Empire.* New Haven: Yale University Press, 1996.

Barton, Carlin A. "Savage Miracles: The Redemption of Lost Honor in Roman Society and the Sacrament of the Gladiator and the Martyr." *Representations* 45 (1994) 41–71.

Bassler, Jouette M., editor. *Pauline Theology.* Vol. 1, *Thessalonians, Philippians, Galatians, Philemon.* Minneapolis: Fortress, 1991.

Bauckham, Richard. "For Whom Were Gospels Written?" In *The Gospels for All Christians: Rethinking the Gospel Audiences*, edited by Richard Bauckham, 9–48. Edinburgh: T. & T. Clark, 1998.

————. *Gospel Women: Studies of the Named Women in the Gospels.* Edinburgh: T. & T. Clark, 2002.

————, editor. *The Gospels for All Christians: Rethinking the Gospel Audiences.* Edinburgh: T. & T. Clark, 1998.

————. *Jesus and the Eyewitnesses: The Gospels as Eyewitness Testimony.* Grand Rapids: Eerdmans, 2006.

————. "The Study of Gospel Traditions Outside the Canonical Gospels: Problems and Prospects." In *The Jesus Tradition Outside the Gospels.* Vol. 5 of *Gospel Perspectives*, edited by David Wenham, 369–419. Sheffield, UK: JSOT, 1985.

Beker, J. Christiaan. *Paul the Apostle: The Triumph of God in Life and Thought.* Philadelphia: Fortress, 1980.

Betz, Hans Dieter. *Galatians: A Commentary on Paul's Letter to the Churches in Galatia.* Hermeneia. Philadelphia: Fortress, 1979.

————. *The Sermon on the Mount: A Commentary on the Sermon on the Mount, Including the Sermon on the Plain (Matthew 5:3–7:27 and Luke 6:20–49).* Hermeneia. Minneapolis: Fortress, 1995.

————. "The Sermon on the Mount: Its Literary Genre and Function." *Journal of Religion* 59 (1979) 285–97.

Bockmuehl, Markus, editor. *The Cambridge Companion to Jesus.* Cambridge: Cambridge University Press, 2001.

————. *The Epistle to the Philippians.* Black's New Testament Commentaries 11. Peabody, MA: Hendrickson, 1998.

————. "1 Thessalonians 2:14–16 and the Church in Jerusalem." *Tyndale Bulletin* 52 (2001) 1–31.

Bockmuehl, Markus, and Donald A. Hagner, editors. *The Written Gospel.* Cambridge: Cambridge University Press, 2005.

Bowman, Alan K., Edward Champlin, and Andrew Lintott, editors. *The Augustan Empire, 43 B.C.–A.D. 69.* 2nd ed. Cambridge Ancient History 10. Cambridge: Cambridge University Press, 1996.

Bowman, Alan K., Peter Garnsey, and Dominic Rathbone, editors. *The High Empire, A.D. 70–192.* 2nd ed. Cambridge Ancient History 11. Cambridge: Cambridge University Press, 2000.

Boyarin, Daniel. *A Radical Jew: Paul and the Politics of Identity.* Berkeley: University of California Press, 1994.

Brandon, S. G. F. *Jesus and the Zealots: A Study of the Political Factor in Primitive Christianity*. Manchester: Manchester University Press, 1967.

Brawley, Robert L., editor. *Character Ethics and the New Testament: Moral Dimensions of Scripture*. Louisville: Westminster John Knox, 2007.

Briggs Kittredge, Cynthia. *Community and Authority: The Rhetoric of Obedience in the Pauline Tradition*. Harrisburg, PA: Trinity Press International, 1998.

Brubaker, Rogers, and David D. Laitin. "Ethnic and Nationalist Violence." *Annual Review of Sociology* 24 (1998) 423–52.

Bruce, F. F. *The Epistle of Paul to the Galatians: A Commentary on the Greek Text*. New International Greek Testament Commentary. Exeter, UK: Paternoster, 1982.

Bultmann, Rudolph. *The History of the Synoptic Tradition*. Translated by John Marsh. Oxford: Basil Blackwell, 1963.

———. *1 and 2 Thessalonians*. Word Biblical Commentary 45. Waco, TX: Word, 1982.

Burridge, Richard A. *Imitating Jesus: An Inclusive Approach to New Testament Ethics*. Grand Rapids: Eerdmans, 2007.

———. *What Are the Gospels? A Comparison with Greco–Roman Biography*. Grand Rapids: Eerdmans, 2004.

Burton, Ernest de Witt. *A Critical and Exegetical Commentary on the Epistle to the Galatians*. Edinburgh: Clark, 1921.

Byrskog, Samuel. *Story as History – History as Story: The Gospel Tradition in the Context of Ancient Oral History*. Wissenschaftliche Untersuchungen zum Neuen Testament. Second Series 123. Tübingen, Germany: Mohr Siebeck, 2000.

Cadoux, C. John. *The Early Christian Attitude to War*. London: Headly, 1919.

Cancik, Hubert, and Helmuth Schneider, editors. *Brill's New Pauly: Encyclopaedia of Antiquity*. 10 vols. Leiden: Brill, 2009.

Carter, Warren. "Constructions of Violence and Identities in Matthew's Gospel." In *Violence in the New Testament*, edited by Shelly Matthews and E. Leigh Gibson, 81–108. Edinburgh: T. & T. Clark, 2005.

———. *Matthew and Empire*. Harrisburg, PA: Trinity Press International, 2001.

———. "Response to Amy-Jill Levine." In *Anti-Judaism and the Gospels*, edited by William R. Farmer, 47–62. Harrisburg, PA: Trinity Press International, 1999.

Castelli, Elizabeth A. *Imitating Paul: A Discourse of Power*. Louisville: Westminster John Knox, 1991.

Catchpole, David R. "The 'Triumphal' Entry." In *Jesus and the Politics of his Day*, edited by Ernst Bammel and C. F. D. Moule, 319–34. Cambridge: Cambridge University Press, 1984.

Cavanaugh, William T. "'A Fire Strong Enough to Consume the House': The Wars of Religion and the Rise of the State." *Modern Theology* 11 (1995) 397–420.

———. *Torture and Eucharist: Theology, Politics, and the Body of Christ*. Oxford: Blackwell, 1998.

Chase, Kenneth R., and Alan Jacobs, editors. *Must Christianity Be Violent? Reflections on History, Practice, and Theology*. Eugene, OR: Wipf & Stock, 2003.

Chilton, Bruce D., and Craig A. Evans, editors. *Studying the Historical Jesus: Evaluation of the State of Current Research*. Leiden: Brill, 1994.

Clines, David J. A., et al., editors. *The Bible in Three Dimensions: Essays in Celebration of Forty Years of Biblical Studies in the University of Sheffield*. Journal for the Study of the Old Testament Supplement Series 87. Sheffield, UK: JSOT, 1990.

Collins, Adela Yarbro. *Mark: A Commentary*. Hermeneia. Philadelphia: Fortress, 2007.

Collins, John J. "The Zeal of Phinehas: The Bible and the Legitimation of Violence." *Journal of Biblical Literature* 122 (2003) 3–21.

Collins, Raymond F., editor. *The Thessalonian Correspondence.* Bibliotheca Ephemeridum Theologicarum Lovaniensium 87. Leuven: Leuven University Press, 1990.

Congdon, David W. "The Trinitarian Shape of πίστις: A Theological Exegesis of Galatians." *Journal of Theological Interpretation* 2 (2008) 231–58.

Crafer, T. W. "The Stoning of St. Paul at Lystra, and the Epistle to the Galatians." *Expositor* 6 (1913) 375–84.

Cranfield, C. E. B. *The Epistle to the Romans.* 2 vols. International Critical Commentary. Edinburgh: T. & T. Clark, 1975.

Crook, Zeba A. *Reconceptualising Conversion: Patronage, Loyalty, and Conversion in the Religions of the Ancient Mediterranean.* Beihefte zur Zeitschrift für die neutestamentliche Wissenschaft 130. Berlin: de Gruyter, 2004.

Crossan, John Dominic, and Jonathan L. Reed. *In Search of Paul: How Jesus' Apostle Opposed Rome's Empire with God's Kingdom.* London: SPCK, 2005.

Davies, W. D., and Dale C. Allison Jr. *A Critical and Exegetical Commentary on the Gospel According to Saint Matthew.* 3 vols. International Critical Commentary. Edinburgh: T. & T. Clark, 1988–1997.

Davis, James F. *Lex Talionis in Early Judaism and the Exhortation of Jesus in Matthew 5:38–42.* Journal for the Study of the New Testament Supplement Series 281. London: T. & T. Clark, 2005.

Decker, Wolfgang "Agonothetes." *BrillOnline Reference Works.* No pages. Online: http://referenceworks.brillonline.com/entries/brill-s-new-pauly/agonothetes-e108380.

Deissmann, G. Adolph. *Light from the Ancient East: The New Testament Illustrated by Recently Discovered Texts of the Graeco–Roman World.* 4th ed. Translated by Lionel R. M. Strachan. London: Hodder & Stoughton, 1927.

Deppe, Dean B. *The Sayings of Jesus in the Epistle of James.* Chelsea, MI: Bookcrafters, 1989.

Dibelius, Martin. *Studies in the Acts of the Apostles.* Edited by Heinrich Greeven. New York: Scribner's Sons, 1956.

Dodd, C. H. *The Apostolic Preaching and Its Developments.* 2nd ed. London: Hodder & Stoughton, 1944.

———. *Gospel and Law: The Relation of Faith and Ethics in Early Christianity.* Cambridge: Cambridge University Press, 1957.

Donfried, Karl P. "The Imperial Cults of Thessalonica and Political Conflict in 1 Thessalonians." In *Paul and Empire: Religion and Power in Roman Imperial Society,* edited by Richard A. Horsley, 215–23. Harrisburg, PA: Trinity Press International, 1997. Reprinted from "The Cults of Thessalonica and the Thessalonian Correspondence." *New Testament Studies* 31 (1985) 336–56. References are to the 1997 edition.

Drake, H. A., et al., editors. *Violence in Late Antiquity: Perceptions and Practices.* Hampshire, UK: Ashgate, 2006.

Dunn, James D. G. "Altering the Default Setting: Re-envisaging the Early Transmission of the Jesus Tradition." *New Testament Studies* 49 (2003) 139–75.

———. *The Epistle to the Galatians.* Black New Testament Commentaries 9. Peabody, MA: Hendrickson, 1993.

———. *Jesus Remembered.* Vol. 1 of *Christianity in the Making.* Grand Rapids: Eerdmans, 2003.

————. "Jesus Tradition in Paul." In *Studying the Historical Jesus: Evaluation of the State of Current Research*, edited by Bruce D. Chilton and Craig A. Evans, 155–78. Leiden: Brill, 1994.

————. "The Relationship between Paul and Jerusalem according to Galatians 1 and 2." *New Testament Studies* 28 (1982) 461–78.

————. *Romans*. 2 vols. Word Biblical Commentary 38A, 38B. Waco, TX: Word, 1988.

————. *The Theology of Paul the Apostle*. Edinburgh: T. & T. Clark, 1998.

Edson, Charles. "Cults of Thessalonica (Macedonica III)." *Harvard Theological Review* 41 (1948) 153–204.

————. "State Cults in Thessalonica (Macedonica II)." *Harvard Studies in Classical Philology* 51 (1940) 127–36.

Ehrenberg, V., and A. H. M. Jones, editors. *Documents Illustrating the Reigns of Augustus and Tiberius*. 2nd ed. Oxford: Clarendon, 1955.

Ehrensperger, Kathy. *Paul and the Dynamics of Power: Communication and Interaction in the Early Christ-Movement*. London, T. & T. Clark, 2009.

Elliot, Neil. *The Arrogance of Nations: Reading Romans in the Shadow of Empire*. Minneapolis: Fortress, 2008.

————. "Paul and the Politics of Empire: Problems and Prospects." In *Paul and Politics: Ekklesia, Israel, Imperium, Interpretation*, edited by Richard A. Horsley, 17–39. Harrisburg, PA: Trinity Press International, 2000.

Fee, Gordon D. *The First Epistle to the Corinthians*. New International Commentary on the New Testament. Grand Rapids: Eerdmans, 1987.

Fitzgerald, John T., et al., editors. *Early Christianity and Classical Culture: Comparative Studies in Honor of Abraham J. Malherbe*. Supplements to Novum Testamentum 110. Leiden: Brill, 2003.

Fitzmyer, Joseph A. *Romans: A New Translation with Introduction and Commentary*. Anchor Bible 33. New York: Doubleday, 1993.

Fuchs, Harald. *Augustin und der antike Friedensgedanke: Untersuchungen zum neunzehnten Buch der civitas dei*. 2nd ed. Berlin: Weidmann, 1965.

Furnish, Victor Paul. "The Jesus-Paul Debate: From Bauer to Bultmann." *Bulletin of the John Rylands University Library of Manchester* 47 (1964/65) 342–81. Reprinted in *Jesus and Paul: Collected Essays*, edited by A. J. M. Wedderburn, 17–50. Journal for the Study of the New Testament Supplement Series 37. Sheffield, UK: Sheffield Academic, 1989. References are to the 1989 edition.

————. *The Love Command in the New Testament*. Nashville: Abingdon, 1972.

————. *II Corinthians: A New Translation and Commentary*. Anchor Bible 31–32. New Haven: Yale University Press, 1984.

————. *Theology and Ethics in Paul*. Nashville: Abingdon, 1968.

Gager, John G., and E. Leigh Gibson. "Violent Acts and Violent Language in the Apostle Paul." In *Violence in the New Testament*, edited by Shelley Matthews and E. Leigh Gibson, 13–21. London: T. & T. Clark, 2005.

Garnsey, Peter. "The Generosity of Veyne." *Journal of Roman Studies* 81 (1991) 164–68.

Georgi, Dieter. *Theocracy in Paul's Praxis and Theology*. Translated by David E. Green. Minneapolis: Fortress, 1991.

Gerhardsson, Birger. *Memory and Manuscript: Oral Tradition and Written Transmission in Rabbinic Judaism and Early Christianity*. Translated by Eric J. Sharpe. Acta Seminarii Neotestamentici Upsaliensis 22. Uppsala, Sweden: Almquist & Wiksells, 1961.

Bibliography

———. "The Secret Transmission of the Unwritten Jesus Tradition." *New Testament Studies* 51 (2005) 1–18.

Gill, David W. J. "Macedonia." In *The Book of Acts in Its Graeco-Roman Setting*, edited by D. W. J. Gill and C. Gempf, 397–417. Vol. 2 of *The Book of Acts in Its First Century Setting*, edited by Bruce W. Winter. Grand Rapids: Eerdmans, 1994.

Gill, David W. J., and C. Gempf, editors. *The Book of Acts in Its Graeco-Roman Setting*. Vol. 2 of *The Book of Acts in Its First Century Setting*. Edited by Bruce W. Winter. Grand Rapids: Eerdmans, 1994.

Gilliard, Frank. "The Problem of the Anti-Semitic Comma between 1 Thessalonians 2:14 and 15." *New Testament Studies* 35 (1989) 481–502.

Glancy, Jennifer A. "Boasting of Beatings (2 Corinthians 11:23–25)." *Journal of Biblical Literature* 123 (2004) 99–135.

Gorman, Michael J. *Cruciformity: Paul's Narrative Spirituality of the Cross*. Grand Rapids: Eerdmans, 2001.

———. *Inhabiting the Cruciform God: Kenonis, Justification, and Theosis in Paul's Narrative Soteriology*. Grand Rapids: Eerdmans, 2009.

———. *Reading Paul*. Milton Keynes, UK: Paternoster, 2008.

Goulder, Michael D. *Midrash and Lection in Matthew: The Speaker's Lectures in Biblical Studies 1969–1971*. London: SPCK, 1974.

Green, Joel B. "Crucifixion." In *The Cambridge Companion to Jesus*, edited by Markus Bockmuehl, 87–101. Cambridge: Cambridge University Press, 2001.

Hack Polaski, Sandra. *Paul and the Discourse of Power*. London: Continuum: 1999.

Hardin, Justin K. "Decrees and Drachmas at Thessalonica: An Illegal Assembly in Jason's House (Acts 17.1–10a)." *New Testament Studies* 52 (2006) 29–49.

———. *Galatians and the Imperial Cult: A Critical Analysis of the First-Century Social Context of Paul's Letter*. Wissenschaftliche Untersuchungen zum Neuen Testament. Second Series 237. Tübingen, Germany: Mohr Siebeck, 2008.

Hare, Douglas R. A. *The Theme of Jewish Persecution of Christians in the Gospel According to St. Matthew*. Society for New Testament Studies Monograph Series 6. Cambridge: Cambridge University Press, 1967.

Harink, Douglas. *Paul among the Postliberals: Pauline Theology Beyond Christendom and Modernity*. Grand Rapids: Brazos, 2003.

Harrington, Daniel J. "Matthew and Paul." In *Matthew and His Christian Contemporaries*, edited by David C. Sim and Boris Repschinski, 11–26. Library of New Testament Studies. Journal for the Study of the New Testament Supplement 333. London: T. & T. Clark, 2008.

Harrison, J. R. "Paul and the Imperial Gospel at Thessaloniki." *Journal for the Study of the New Testament* 25 (2002) 71–96.

Hauerwas, Stanley. *Matthew*. Brazos Theological Commentary on the Bible. Grand Rapids: Brazos, 2006.

Hays, Richard B. "Christology and Ethics in Galatians: The Law of Christ." *Catholic Biblical Quarterly* 49 (1987) 268–90.

———. "Crucified with Christ: A Synthesis of the Theology of 1 and 2 Thessalonians, Philemon, Philippians, and Galatians." In *Pauline Theology*, vol. 1, *Thessalonians, Philippians, Galatians, Philemon*, edited by Jouette M. Bassler, 227–46. Minneapolis: Fortress, 1991.

———. *Echoes of Scripture in the Letters of Paul*. New Haven: Yale University Press, 1989.

———. *The Faith of Jesus Christ: The Narrative Substructure of Galatians 3:1—4:11.* 2nd ed. Biblical Resource Series. Grand Rapids: Eerdmans, 2002.

———. *The Moral Vision of the New Testament: Community, Cross, New Creation; A Contemporary Introduction to New Testament Ethics.* San Francisco: HarperSanFrancisco, 1996.

———. "Narrate and Embody: A Response to Nigel Biggar, 'Specify and Distinguish.'" *Society for Christian Ethics* 22 (2009) 185–98.

Heilke, Thomas. "On Being Ethical without Moral Sadism: Two Readings of Augustine and the Beginnings of the Anabaptist Revolution." *Political Theory* 24 (1996) 493–517.

Hellerman, Joseph H. *Reconstructing Honor in Roman Philippi: Carmen Christi as Cursus Pudorum.* Society for New Testament Studies Monograph Series 132. Cambridge: Cambridge University Press, 2005.

Hendrix, Holland L. "Archaeology and Eschatology at Thessalonica." In *The Future of Early Christianity: Essays in Honor of Helmut Koester*, edited by Birger A. Pearson et al., 107–18. Minneapolis: Fortress, 1991.

———. "Beyond 'Imperial Cult' and 'Cult of the Magistrates.'" In *SBL 1986: Seminar Papers*, edited by Kent Richards, 301–8. Society of Biblical Literature Seminar Papers 25. Atlanta: Scholars, 1986.

———. "Thessalonicans Honor Romans." ThD thesis, Harvard Divinity School, 1984.

Hengel, Martin. *Crucifixion in the Ancient World and the Folly of the Message of the Cross.* Translated by John Bowden. Philadelphia: Fortress, 1977.

———. "Eye-Witness Memory and the Writing of the Gospels." In *The Written Gospel*, edited by Markus Bockmuehl and Donald A. Hagner, 70–96. Cambridge: Cambridge University Press, 2005.

———. *The Pre-Christian Paul.* Translated by John Bowden. London: SCM, 1991.

———. *Was Jesus a Revolutionist?* Translated by David E. Green. Philadelphia: Augsburg Fortress, 1971. Repr., Eugene, OR: Wipf & Stock, 2003.

Hengel, Martin, and Anna Maria Schwemer. *Paul between Damascus and Antioch: The Unknown Years.* Translated by John Bowden. London: SCM, 1997.

Holtz, Traugott. *Der erste Brief an die Thessalonicher.* Evangelisch-katholischer Kommentar zum Neuen Testament 13. Zurich: Benziger, 1986.

Horrell, David G. *Solidarity and Difference: A Contemporary Reading of Paul's Ethics.* London: T. & T. Clark, 2005.

Horsley, Richard A. "By the Finger of God: Jesus and Imperial Violence." In *Violence in the New Testament*, edited by Shelly Matthews and E. Leigh Gibson, 51–80. Edinburgh: T. & T. Clark, 2005.

———. "Ethics and Exegesis: 'Love Your Enemies' and the Doctrine of Nonviolence." *Journal of the American Academy of Religion* 54 (1986) 3–31. Repr. in *The Love of Enemy and Nonretaliation in the New Testament*, edited by Williard M. Swartley, 72–101. Louisville: John Knox, 1992.

———. *Jesus and the Spiral of Violence: Jewish Resistance in Roman Palestine.* San Francisco: Harper & Row, 1987.

———, editor. *Paul and Empire: Religion and Power in Roman Imperial Society.* Harrisburg, PA: Trinity Press International, 1997.

———, editor. *Paul and Politics: Ekklesia, Israel, Imperium, Interpretation.* Harrisburg, PA: Trinity Press International, 2000.

Bibliography

————, editor. *Paul and the Roman Imperial Order*. Harrisburg, PA: Trinity Press International, 2004.

Hultgren, Arland J. "Paul's Pre-Christian Persecutions of the Church: Their Purpose, Locale, and Nature." *Journal of Biblical Literature* 95 (1976) 97–111.

Jacobs, Alan. Afterword to *Must Christianity Be Violent? Reflections on History, Practice, and Theology*, edited by Kenneth R. Chase and Alan Jacobs, 224–35. Eugene, OR: Wipf & Stock, 2003.

Jewett, Robert. "The Agitators and the Galatian Congregation." *New Testament Studies* 17 (1970–1971) 198–212. Repr. in *The Galatians Debate: Contemporary Issues in Rhetorical and Historical Interpretation*, edited by Mark D. Nanos, 334–47. Peabody, MA: Hendrickson, 2002.

————. *Dating Paul's Life*. London: SCM, 1979.

————. *Romans: A Commentary*. Hermeneia. Minneapolis: Fortress, 2007.

————. *The Thessalonian Correspondence: Pauline Rhetoric and Millenarian Piety*. Philadelphia: Fortress, 1986.

Johnson, Luke Timothy. "The New Testament's Anti-Jewish Slander and the Conventions of Ancient Polemic." *Journal of Biblical Literature* 108 (1989) 419–41.

Judge, E. A. "The Decrees of Caesar at Thessalonica." *Reformed Theological Review* 30 (1971) 1–7.

————. "Did the Churches Compete with Cult Groups?" In *Early Christianity and Classical Culture: Comparative Studies in Honor of Abraham J. Malherbe*, edited by John T. Fitzgerald et al., 501–24. Supplements to Novum Testamentum 110. Leiden: Brill, 2003.

Keesmaat, Sylvia C. "Crucified Lord or Conquering Saviour: Whose Story of Salvation?" *Horizons in Biblical Theology* 26 (2004) 69–93.

————. "If Your Enemy Is Hungry: Love and Subversive Politics in Romans 12–13." In *Character Ethics and the New Testament: Moral Dimensions of Scripture*, edited by Robert L. Brawley, 141–58. Louisville: Westminster John Knox, 2007.

————. *Paul and His Story: (Re)interpreting the Exodus Tradition*. Journal for the Study of the New Testament Supplement Series 181. Sheffield, UK: Sheffield Academic, 1999.

Keppie, Lawrence. "The Army and the Navy." In *The Augustan Empire, 43 B.C.–A.D. 69*, 2nd ed., edited by Alan K. Bowman et al., 371–96. Cambridge Ancient History 10. Cambridge: Cambridge University Press, 1996.

Klassen, William. "Coals of Fire: Sign of Repentance or Revenge?" *New Testament Studies* 9 (1962–63) 337–50.

————. "'Love your Enemies': Some Reflections on the Current Status of Research." In *The Love of Enemy and Nonretaliation in the New Testament*, edited by Williard M. Swartley, 1–31. Louisville: John Knox, 1992.

Koester, Helmut. *Ancient Christian Gospels: Their History and Development*. London, SCM: 1990.

————. "Imperial Ideology and Paul's Eschatology in 1 Thessalonians." In *Paul and Empire: Religion and Power in Roman Imperial Society*, edited by Richard A. Horsley, 158–66. Harrisburg, PA: Trinity Press International, 1997.

Kuhn, Heinz–Wolfgang. "Das Liebesgebot Jesus als Tora und als Evangelium: Zur Feindesliebe und zur christlichen und jüdischen Auslegung der Bergpredigt." In *Vom Urchristentum zu Jesus*, edited by H. Frankemölle and K. Kertelge, 194–230. FS Joachim Gnilka. Freiburg: Herder, 1989.

Lampe, Peter. *From Paul to Valentinus: Christians at Rome in the First Two Centuries.* Translated by Michael Steinhauser. Edited by Marshall D. Johnson. Minneapolis: Fortress, 2003.

Lane Fox, Robin. *Pagans and Christians.* New York: Knopf, 1986.

Lendon, J. E. *Empire of Honour: The Art of Government in the Roman World.* Oxford, Clarendon, 1997.

Levick, Barbara. *The Government of the Roman Empire: A Sourcebook.* 2nd ed. London: Routledge, 2000.

Levine, Amy-Jill. "Anti-Judaism and the Gospel of Matthew." In *Anti-Judaism and the Gospels,* edited by William R. Farmer, 9–36. Harrisburg, PA: Trinity Press International, 1999.

Lightfoot, J. B. *Saint Paul's Epistle to the Galatians: A Revised Text with Introduction, Notes, and Dissertations.* 4th repr. of 10th ed. published 1890. London: Macmillan, 1902.

Lomas, Kathryn, and Tim Cornell, editors. *"Bread and Circuses": Euergetism and Municipal Patronage in Roman Italy.* London: Routledge, 2003.

———. "Introduction: Patronage and Benefaction in Ancient Italy." In *"Bread and Circuses": Euergetism and Municipal Patronage in Roman Italy,* edited by Kathryn Lomas and Tim Cornell, 1–27. London: Routledge, 2003.

Longenecker, Bruce W. "Evil at Odds with Itself (Matthew 12:22–29): Demonising Rhetoric and Deconstructive Potential in the Matthean Narrative." *Biblical Interpretation* 11 (2003) 503–14.

———, editor. *Narrative Dynamics in Paul: A Critical Assessment.* Louisville: Westminster John Knox, 2002.

———. *The Triumph of Abraham's God: The Transformation of Identity in Galatians.* Edinburgh: T. & T. Clark, 1998.

———. "'Until Christ is Formed in You': Suprahuman Forces and Moral Character in Galatians." *Catholic Biblical Quarterly* 61 (1999) 92–108.

Longenecker, Richard N. *Galatians.* Word Biblical Commentary 41. Dallas: Word Books, 1990.

Lopez, Davina C. *Apostle to the Conquered: Reimagining Paul's Mission.* Minneapolis: Fortress, 2008.

Luz, Ulrich. *Matthew: A Commentary.* Translated by James E. Crouch. 3 vols. Hermeneia. Minneapolis: Fortress, 2001—2007.

———. *The Theology of the Gospel of Matthew.* Translated by J. Bradford Robinson. Cambridge: Cambridge University Press, 1995.

Lyons, George. *Pauline Autobiography: Toward a New Understanding.* Society of Biblical Literature Dissertation Series 73. Chico, CA: Scholars, 1986.

Malherbe, Abraham J. *The Letters to the Thessalonians: A New Translation with Introduction and Commentary.* Anchor Bible 32B. New York: Doubleday, 2000.

———. *Paul and the Thessalonians: The Philosophic Tradition of Pastoral Care.* Philadelphia: Fortress, 1987.

Marchal, Joseph A. *Hierarchy, Unity, and Imitation: A Feminist Rhetorical Analysis of Power Dynamics in Paul's Letter to the Philippians.* Atlanta: Society of Biblical Literature, 2006.

Martin, Ralph P. *2 Corinthians.* Word Biblical Commentary 40. Waco, TX: Word, 1985.

Martyn, J. Louis. *Galatians: A New Translation with Introduction and Commentary.* Anchor Bible 33A. New York: Doubleday, 1997.

Matera, Frank J. *II Corinthians: A Commentary.* New Testament Library. Louisville: Westminster John Knox, 2003.

Bibliography

Matthews, Shelly, and E. Leigh Gibson. *Violence in the New Testament*. Edinburgh: T. & T. Clark, 2005.

Meeks, Wayne A. *The First Urban Christians: The Social World of the Apostle Paul*. New Haven: Yale University Press, 1983.

———. *The Origins of Christian Morality: The First Two Centuries*. New Haven: Yale University Press, 1993.

Meier, John P. *A Marginal Jew: Rethinking the Historical Jesus*. Vol. 1, *The Roots of the Problem and the Person*. Anchor Bible Reference Library. New York: Doubleday, 1991.

Menoud, Philippe H. "Le sens du verbe porthein." In *Apophoreta: Festschrift für Ernst Haenchen zu seinem siebzigsten Geburtstag am 10. Dezember 1964 (Berlin: Alfred Töpelmann, 1964)*, 178–86. English translation in Menoud, *Jesus Christ and the Faith*, 47–60. Translated by Eunice M. Paul. Pittsburgh Theological Monograph Series 18. Pittsburgh: Pickwick, 1978.

Metzger, Bruce M. *A Textual Commentary on the Greek New Testament*. 2nd ed. Stuttgart: German Bible Society, 1994.

Michel, Otto. *Der Brief an die Römer*. 5th ed. Kritisch-exegetischer Kommentar über das Neue Testament. Göttingen, Germany: Vandenhoeck & Ruprecht, 1966.

Minear, Paul Sevier. "The Crucified World: The Enigma of Galatians 6,14." In *Theologia Crucis–Signum Crucis. Festschrift für Erich Dinkler zum 70. Geburtstag*, edited by Carl Andresen and Günter Klein, 395–407. Tübingen, Germany: Mohr, 1979.

Mitchell, Stephen. "Imperial Building in the Eastern Roman Provinces." *Harvard Studies in Classical Philology* 91 (1987) 333–65.

———. "Requisitioned Transport in the Roman Empire: A New Inscription from Pisidia." *Journal of Roman Studies* 66 (1976) 106–31.

Mitford, T. B. "A Cypriot Oath of Allegiance to Tiberius." *Journal of Roman Studies* 50 (1960) 74–79.

Moule, C. F. D. *An Idiom Book of New Testament Greek*. 2nd ed. Cambridge: Cambridge University Press, 1959.

Murphy-O'Connor, Jerome. *Paul: A Critical Life*. Oxford: Oxford University Press, 1997.

Nanos, Mark, editor. *The Galatians Debate: Contemporary Issues in Rhetorical and Historical Interpretation*. Peabody, MA: Hendrickson, 2002.

———. *The Irony of Galatians: Paul's Letter in First-Century Context*. Minneapolis: Fortress, 2002.

Neirynck, Frans. "Paul and the Sayings of Jesus." In *L'Apôtre Paul: Personnalité, style et conception du ministère*, edited by A. Vanhoye, 265–321. Bibliotheca Ephemeridum Theologicarum Lovaniensium 73. Leuven: Leuven University Press, 1986.

Neville, David J. "Toward a Teleology of Peace: Contesting Matthew's Violent Eschatology." *Journal for the Study of the New Testament* 30 (2007) 131–61.

Nolland, John. *The Gospel of Matthew: A Commentary on the Greek Text*. New International Greek Testament Commentary. Grand Rapids: Eerdmans, 2005.

Oakes, Peter. *Philippians: From People to Letter*. Society for New Testament Studies Monograph Series 110. Cambridge: Cambridge University Press, 2001.

———. "Re-mapping the Universe: Paul and the Emperor in 1 Thessalonians and Philippians." *Journal for the Study of the New Testament* 27 (2005) 301–22.

Olbricht, Thomas H., and Jerry L. Sumney, editors. *Paul and Pathos*. Atlanta: Society of Biblical Literature, 2001.

O'Neill, J. C. *The Recovery of Paul's Letter to the Galatians*. London: SPCK, 1972.

Pearson, Birger. "1 Thessalonians 2:3–16: A Deutero-Pauline Interpretation." *Harvard Theological Review* 64 (1971) 79–94.

Pearson, Birger A., et al., editors. *The Future of Early Christianity: Essays in Honor of Helmut Koester*. Minneapolis: Fortress, 1991.

Penner, Todd C. "Madness in the Method? The Acts of the Apostles in Current Study." *Currents in Biblical Research* 2 (2004) 223–93.

Pervo, Richard I. *Acts: A Commentary*. Hermeneia. Minneapolis: Fortress, 2009.

Phillips, Thomas E. "The Genre of Acts: Moving Toward a Consensus?" *Currents in Biblical Research* 4 (2006) 365–96.

Plumer, Eric. *Augustine's Commentary on Galatians: Introduction, Text, Translation, and Notes*. Oxford: Oxford University Press, 2006.

Pobee, J. S. *Persecution and Martyrdom in the Theology of Paul*. Journal for the Study of the New Testament Supplement Series 6. Sheffield, UK: Sheffield Academic, 1985.

Price, Robert M. "The Legend of Paul's Conversion: We Have Ways of Making You Talk." No Pages. Online: http://www.robertmprice.mindvendor.com/art_legend_paul_conv.htm.

Price, S. R. F. "Gods and Emperors: The Greek Language of the Roman Imperial Cult." *Journal of Hellenic Studies* 104 (1984) 79–95.

———. "Response." In *Paul and the Roman Imperial Order*, edited by Richard A. Horsley, 175–83. Harrisburg, PA: Trinity Press International, 2004.

———. *Rituals and Power: The Roman Imperial Cult in Asia Minor*. Cambridge: Cambridge University Press, 1984.

Reid, Barbara. "Violent Endings in Matthew's Parables and Christian Nonviolence." *Catholic Biblical Quarterly* 66 (2004) 237–55.

Rich, John, and Graham Shipley, editors. *War and Society in the Roman World*. London: Routledge, 1993.

Richard, Earl. *First and Second Thessalonians*. Sacra Pagina 11. Collegeville, MN: Liturgical, 1995.

Riches, John K. *Galatians Through the Centuries*. Blackwell Bible Comentaries. Oxford: Blackwell, 2008.

Riesner, Rainer. *Paul's Early Period: Chronology, Mission Strategy, Theology*. Translated by Doug Stott. Grand Rapids: Eerdmans, 1998.

Rigaux, Béda. *Saint Paul: Les Épîtres aux Thessaloniciens*. Études bibliques. Paris: Gabalda, 1956.

Robinson, James M. "The Real Jesus of the Sayings "Q" Gospel." No Pages. Online: http://www.religion-online.org/showarticle.asp?title=542.

Robinson, James M., et al., editors. *The Critical Edition of Q*. Hermeneia. Leuven: Peeters, 2000.

Rowe, C. Kavin. *World Upside Down: Reading Acts in the Graeco-Roman Age*. Oxford: Oxford University Press, 2009.

Saller, Richard. "Status and Patronage." In *The High Empire, A.D. 70–192*, 2nd ed., edited by Alan K. Bowman et al., 817–54. Cambridge Ancient History 11. Cambridge: Cambridge University Press, 2000.

Sandt, Huub van de, and Jürgen K. Zangenberg, editors. *Matthew, James and Didache: Three Related Documents in Their Jewish and Christian Settings*. Society of Biblical Literature Symposium Series 45. Atlanta: Society of Biblical Literature, 2008.

Bibliography

Sauer, Jürgen. "Traditionsgeschichtliche Erwägungen zu den synoptischen und paulinischen Aussagen über Feindesliebe und Wiedervergeltungsverzicht." *Zeitschrift für die neutestamentliche Wissenschaft und die Kunde der älteren Kirche* 76 (1985) 1–28.

Scheper-Hughes, Nancy, and Philippe Bourgois. "Making Sense of Violence." Introduction to *Violence in War and Peace*, 1–31. Oxford: Blackwell, 2004.

———, editors. *Violence in War and Peace*. Oxford: Blackwell, 2004.

Schlier, Heinrich. *Der Brief an die Galater*. Kritisch-exegetischer Kommentar über das Neue Testament 7. Göttingen, Germany: Vandenhoeck & Ruprecht, 1965.

Schottroff, Luise, et al., editors. *Essays on the Love Commandment*. Philadelphia: Fortress, 1978.

———. "'Give to Caesar What Belongs to Caesar and to God What Belongs to God': A Theological Response of the Early Christian Church to Its Social and Political Environment." In *The Love of Enemy and Nonretaliation in the New Testament*, edited by Willard M. Swartley, 223–57. Louisville: Westminster John Knox, 1992.

———. "Non-Violence and the Love of One's Enemies." In *Essays on the Love Commandment*, edited by Luise Schottroff et al, 9–39. Philadelphia: Fortress, 1978.

Seland, Torrey. *Establishment Violence in Philo and Luke: A Study of Nonconformity to the Torah and Jewish Vigilante Reactions*. Leiden: Brill, 1995.

———. "(Re)presentations of Violence in Philo." Paper presented at the annual meeting of the SBL, 2003.

———. "Saul of Tarsus and Early Zealotism: Reading Gal 1.13–14 in Light of Philo's Writings." *Biblica* 83 (2002) 449–71.

Shaw, Brent D. "Bandits in the Roman Empire." *Past and Present* 105 (1984) 3–52.

———. "Rebels and Outsiders." In *The High Empire, A.D. 70–192*, 2nd ed., edited by Alan K. Bowman et al., 361–403. Cambridge Ancient History 11. Cambridge: Cambridge University Press, 2000.

Sim, David C. *Apocalyptic Eschatology in the Gospel of Matthew*. Society for New Testament Studies Monograph Series 88. Cambridge: Cambridge University Press, 1996.

———. *The Gospel of Matthew and Christian Judaism: The History and Social Setting of the Matthean Community*. Edinburgh: T. & T. Clark, 1998.

———. "Matthew and Jesus of Nazareth." In *Matthew and His Christian Contemporaries*, edited by David Sim and Boris Repschinski, 155–72. Library of New Testament Studies. Journal for the Study of the New Testament Supplement 333. London: T. & T. Clark, 2008.

———. "Matthew, Paul and the Origin and Nature of the Gentile Mission: The Great Commission in Matthew 28:16–20 as an Anti-Pauline Tradition." *Hervormde teologiese studies* 64 (2008) 377–92.

———. "Matthew's Anti-Paulinism: A Neglected Feature of Matthean Studies." *Hervormde teologiese studies* 58 (2002) 767–83.

———. "Reconstructing the Social and Religious Milieu of Matthew: Methods, Sources, and Possible Results." In *Matthew, James and Didache: Three Related Documents in Their Jewish and Christian Settings*, edited by Huub van de Sandt and Jürgen K. Zangenberg, 13–32. Society of Biblical Literature Symposium Series 45. Atlanta: Society of Biblical Literature, 2008.

Sim, David C., and Boris Repschinski, editors. *Matthew and His Christian Contemporaries*. Library of New Testament Studies. Journal for the Study of the New Testament Supplement 333. London: T. & T. Clark, 2008.

Singer, Irving. *The Nature of Love*. 3 vols. Chicago: University of Chicago Press, 1966.

Smith, Abraham. "Unmasking the Powers: Toward a Postcolonial Analysis of 1 Thessalonians." In *Paul and the Roman Imperial Order*, edited by Richard A. Horsley, 47–66. Harrisburg, PA: Trinity Press International, 2004.

Sokolon, Marlene K. *Political Emotions: Aristotle and the Symphony of Reason and Emotion*. DeKalb, IL: Northern Illinois University Press, 2006.

Stanton, Graham N. *The Gospels and Jesus*. 2nd ed. Oxford: Oxford University Press, 2002.

Stendahl, Krister. "Hate, Non-Retaliation, and Love: 1 QS x, 17–20 and Rom. 12:19–21." *Harvard Theological Review* 55 (1962) 343–55.

Still, Todd D. *Conflict at Thessalonica: A Pauline Church and Its Neighbors*. Journal for the Study of the New Testament: Supplement Series 183. Sheffield, UK: Sheffield Academic, 1999.

———, editor. *Jesus and Paul Reconnected: Fresh Pathways into an Old Debate*. Grand Rapids: Eerdmans, 2007.

Strelan, J. G. "Burden-Bearing and the Law of Christ: A Re-examination of Galatians 6.2." *Journal of Biblical Literature* 94 (1975) 266–76.

Swartley, Willard M. *Covenant of Peace: The Missing Peace in New Testament Theology and Ethics*. Grand Rapids: Eerdmans, 2006.

———, editor. *The Love of Enemy and Nonretaliation in the New Testament*. Louisville: John Knox, 1992.

Tannehill, Robert C. "The 'Focal Instance' as a Form of New Testament Speech: A Study of Matthew 5:39b–42." *Journal of Religion* 50 (1970) 372–85.

Taylor, Nicholas H. "Paul and the Historical Jesus Quest." *Neotestamentica* 37 (2003) 105–26.

Tellbe, Mikael. *Paul between Synagogue and State: Christians, Jews, and Civic Authorities in 1 Thessalonians, Romans, and Philippians*. Coniectanea Biblica New Testament Series 34. Stockholm: Almqvist & Wiksell, 2001.

Theissen, Gerd. *The Gospels in Context: Social and Political History in the Synoptic Tradition*. Translated by Linda M. Maloney. Minneapolis: Fortress, 1991.

Thiselton, Anthony C. *The First Epistle to the Corinthians: A Commentary on the Greek Text*. The New International Greek Testament Commentary. Grand Rapids: Eerdmans, 2000.

Thompson, Michael. *Clothed with Christ: The Example and Teaching of Jesus in Romans 12.1—15.13*. Journal for the Study of the New Testament Supplement Series 59. Sheffield, UK: Sheffield Academic, 1991.

Thurén, Lauri. "'By Means of Hyperbole' (1 Cor 12:31b)." In *Paul and Pathos*, edited by Thomas H. Olbricht and Jerry L. Sumney, 97–113. Atlanta: Society of Biblical Literature, 2001.

Trocmé, André. *Jesus and the Nonviolent Revolution*. Translated by Michael H. Shank and Marlin E. Miller. Scottdale, PA: Herald, 1973. Reprint edited by Charles E. Moore. Maryknoll, NY: Orbis, 2004. References are to the 2004 edition.

Tuckett, Christopher M. "Synoptic Tradition in 1 Thessalonians?" In *The Thessalonian Correspondence*, edited by Raymond F. Collins, 160–82. Bibliotheca Ephemeridum Theologicarum Lovaniensium 87. Leuven: Leuven University Press, 1990.

Vacalopoulos, Apostolos E. *A History of Thessaloniki*. Translated by T. F. Carney. Thessalonica: Institute for Balkan Studies, 1963.

Vanhoye, A., editor. *L'Apôtre Paul: Personnalité, style et conception du ministère*. Bibliotheca Ephemeridum Theologicarum Lovaniensium 73. Leuven: Leuven University Press, 1986.

Veyne, Paul. *Bread and Circuses: Historical Sociology and Political Pluralism.* Translated and abridged by B. Pearce. London: Allen Lane, 1990.

Volf, Miroslav. *Exclusion and Embrace: A Theological Exploration of Identity, Otherness, and Reconciliation.* Nashville, TN: Abingdon, 1996.

Vos, Craig Steven de. *Church and Community Conflicts: The Relationships of the Thessalonian, Corinthian, and Philippian Churches with Their Wider Civic Communities.* Society of Biblical Literature Dissertation Series 168. Atlanta: Scholars, 1999.

Vouga, François. *An die Galater.* Handbuch zum Neuen Testament 10. Tübingen, Germany: Mohr Siebeck, 1998.

Walker, Henry John, translator. *Valerius Maximus, Memorable Deeds and Sayings: One Thousand Tales from Ancient Rome.* Indianapolis: Hackett, 2004.

Wallace, Daniel B. *Greek Grammar Beyond the Basics: An Exegetical Syntax of the New Testament.* Grand Rapids: Zondervan, 1996.

Walsh, Brian J., and Sylvia C. Keesmaat. *Colossians Remixed: Subverting the Empire.* Downers Grove, IL: InterVarsity, 2005.

Walter, Nikolaus. "Paul and the Early Christian Jesus–Tradition." In *Jesus and Paul: Collected Essays*, edited by A. J. M. Wedderburn, 51–80. Journal for the Study of the New Testament Supplement Series 37. Sheffield: Sheffield Academic, 1989.

Wanamaker, C. A. *The Epistles to the Thessalonians: A Commentary on the Greek Text.* The New International Greek Testament Commentary. Grand Rapids: Eerdmans, 1990.

Watson, Francis. "'I Received from the Lord . . .': Paul, Jesus, and the Last Supper." In *Jesus and Paul Reconnected: Fresh Pathways into an Old Debate*, edited by Todd D. Still, 103–24. Grand Rapids: Eerdmans, 2007.

Weatherly, Jon A. "The Authenticity of 1 Thessalonians 2:13–16: Additional Evidence." *Journal for the Study of the New Testament* 42 (1991) 79–98.

Weaver, Dorothy Jean. "Transforming Nonresistance: From Lex Talionis to 'Do Not Resist the Evil One.'" In *The Love of Enemy and Nonretaliation in the New Testament*, edited by Willard M. Swartley, 32–71. Louisville: John Knox, 1992.

Wedderburn, A. J. M., editor. *Jesus and Paul: Collected Essays.* Journal for the Study of the New Testament: Supplement Series 37. Sheffield: Sheffield Academic, 1989.

Wengst, Klaus. *Pax Romana and the Peace of Jesus Christ.* Translated by John Bowden. London: SCM, 1987.

Wenham, David, editor. *The Jesus Tradition Outside the Gospels.* Vol. 5 of *Gospel Perspectives.* Sheffield, UK: Sheffield Academic, 1985.

Wilson, Todd A. *The Curse of the Law and the Crisis in Galatia: Reassessing the Purpose of Galatians.* Wissenschaftliche Untersuchungen zum Neuen Testament. Second Series 225. Tübingen, Germany: Mohr Siebeck, 2007.

Wink, Walter. "Counterresponse to Richard Horsley." In *The Love of Enemy and Nonretaliation in the New Testament*, edited by Willard M. Swartley, 133–36. Louisville: John Knox, 1992.

———. "Neither Passivity nor Violence: Jesus' Third Way (Matt. 5:38–42 par.)." In *The Love of Enemy and Nonretaliation in the New Testament*, edited by Willard M. Swartley, 102–25. Louisville: John Knox, 1992.

Wood, Neal. *Cicero's Social and Political Thought.* Berkeley: University of California Press, 1988.

Woolf, Greg. "Beyond Romans and Natives." *World Archaeology* 28 (1995) 339–50.

———. "Roman Peace." In *War and Society in the Roman World*, edited by John Rich and Graham Shipley, 171–94. London: Routledge, 1993.

Wright, N. T. *Jesus and the Victory of God.* Vol. 2 of *Christian Origins and the Question of God.* Minneapolis: Fortress, 1996.

———. *Paul: Fresh Perspectives.* London: SPCK, 2005.

———. "Paul's Gospel and Caesars Empire." In *Paul and Politics: Ekklesia, Israel, Imperium, Interpretation,* edited by Richard Horsley, 160–83. Harrisburg, PA: Trinity Press International, 2000.

———. *The Resurrection and the Son of God.* Vol. 3 of *Christian Origins and the Question of God.* Philadelphia: Fortress, 2003.

———. *What St. Paul Really Said: Was Paul of Tarsus the Real Founder of Christianity?* Grand Rapids: Eerdmans, 1997.

Yoder, John Howard. *Body Politics: Five Practices of the Christian Community Before the Watching World.* Nashville: Discipleship Resources, 1992. Repr., Scottdale, PA: Herald, 2001.

———. *The Politics of Jesus: Vicit Agnus Noster.* Grand Rapids: Eerdmans, 1994.

Zanker, Paul. *The Power of Images in the Age of Augustus.* Translated by A. Shapiro. Ann Arbor: University of Michigan Press, 1988.

Zerbe, Gordon. *Non-Retaliation in Early Jewish and New Testament Texts: Ethical Themes in Social Contexts.* Journal for the Study of the Pseudepigrapha Supplement Series 13. Sheffield, UK: Sheffield Academic, 1993.

Zimmermann, Martin. "Violence in Late Antiquity Reconsidered." In *Violence in Late Antiquity: Perceptions and Practices,* edited by H. A. Drake et al., 343–57. Hampshire, England: Ashgate, 2006.

Žižek, Slavoj. *Violence.* London: Profile, 2008.

Ancient Document Index

~

New Testament

~

DEAD SEA SCROLLS

~

GRECO-ROMAN WRITINGS

~

EARLY CHRISTIAN WRITINGS

Subject Index